SKI THE WORLD

A TRUE STORY OF LOVE, COURAGE AND DANGER

ARNIE WILSON

BLAKE

Published by Blake Publishing Ltd,
3 Bramber Court, 2 Bramber Road, London W14 9PB,
England.

First published in hardback in Great Britain 1996.
Paperback edition published 1999.

ISBN 1 85782 315X

British Library Cataloguing-in-Publication Data:
A catalogue record for this book is available from
the British Library.

Typeset by BCP

Printed in Finland by WSOY – Book Printing Division

1 3 5 7 9 10 8 6 4 2

© Text copyright Arnie Wilson with William Hall 1996

Inside illustrations reproduced courtesy of
All Action, Alpha, LFI, John Evans and the author.

This is for you, Lucy.
Our love reached even greater heights
than all the mountains we skied together.

"Even as love crowns you
so shall he crucify you."

Kahlil Gibran – *The Prophet*

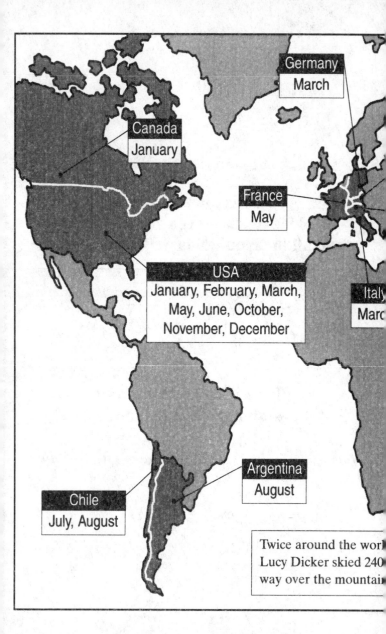

Germany
March

Canada
January

France
May

USA
January, February, March,
May, June, October,
November, December

Italy
March

Argentina
August

Chile
July, August

Twice around the worl
Lucy Dicker skied 240
way over the mountai

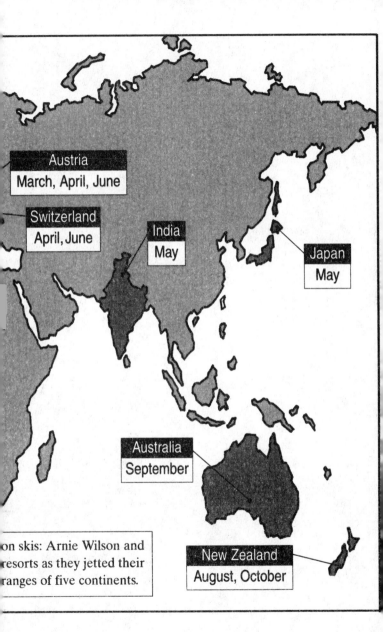

Austria
March, April, June

Switzerland
April, June

India
May

Japan
May

Australia
September

New Zealand
August, October

on skis: Arnie Wilson and
resorts as they jetted their
ranges of five continents.

Contents

Foreword

I was having a quiet lunch in the Seattle Ridge Lodge high up in the Rockies in Sun Valley, one of my favourite ski areas — where I have a home — back in January 1994, when I became aware of a figure standing over me.

He introduced himself, and then his girlfriend, and somewhat intriguingly said they were 'skiing the world'.

That's how I came to meet Arnie Wilson and Lucy Dicker.

Skiing the world? It sounded impossible, even slightly crazy, but I invited them to sit down and tell me about it — and after five minutes I was hooked.

A whole year, skiing every day? And getting round the world by way of a bonus ...

Could they really do it? Arnie had an intensity of purpose that impressed me, while Lucy was a gorgeous French lady, animated and vivacious, who brought out the best — or maybe worst! — of my knowledge of the language when we chatted about their incredible trip.

As a ski-lover myself, I thought: what a challenge! These people are going to explore the slopes that I had never even dreamed existed. I was particularly excited to hear from Arnie about the snows they'd be seeing in South America, because Chile was one place I always wanted to ski.

We shook hands, and I wished them luck.

Much later, I heard what happened to them. How they triumphed in their great quest — and how that triumph turned to unbelievable tragedy of the cruellest kind.

The story of Arnie and Lucy is one I find both heart-warming and heart-rending. I think you will, too.

Clint Eastwood

Preface

Can you imagine skiing every single day for a year? The planning, the dedication, the attention to detail? In some ways, the skiing was the easy part. Although Lucy Dicker and Arnie Wilson had their share of terrible weather on the slopes, it was the relentless driving, flying and writing that was also so energy-sapping. But Lucy's determination and Arnie's enthusiasm made them a strong team. *Tears in the Snow* is a moving, funny and very sad book — and a poignant insight into the emotions of the passionate Frenchwoman whom I know was an enormous inspiration in the punishing day-to-day routine and final completion of their exhilarating odyssey together.

Over the years, I have skied with Arnie on a number of occasions, and once I even persuaded him to come to a race training camp in Copper Mountain, Colorado where we ironed out one or two of his faults. Maybe it helped on his trip — who knows?

But it wasn't until December 1994, when they were almost at the finishing tape of their great adventure, that I met Lucy, the enchanting girl who shared Arnie's life and his dream of skiing for 365 consecutive days, visiting 240 ski resorts and 13 countries on five continents in the process. We all met in Telluride — another Colorado ski area, where I have my

Franz Klammer Lodge and sometimes still race. I remember thinking what a great achievement it was going to be — little realising, of course, that it would end in tragedy so soon afterwards.

Skiing is a wonderful sport, and it has been my life and continues to be so. But like many of life's great challenges, it can occasionally bring tragedy as well as triumph and elation. My own brother, Klaus, a ski racer like me, was badly injured during a race. We all know the risks of pitting yourself against the mountain, but it was very sad that Lucy should have had so little time to relish the success she and Arnie shared. This book is a moving tribute to her.

Franz Klammer
Mooswald, Carinthia, Austria

Prologue

I was planning to write this book with Lucy. Then when I lost her, she became the book. But I knew I could not have written it on my own. It would have been too traumatic without help. I turned to William Hall, at the suggestion of an old skiing friend, Jeffrey Rayner, for a number of reasons. William, too, is an old friend, a skier and a pro. But most of all he has compassion. In the darker days, when I was still traumatised by the accident, William and I spent an entire month in Arundel, Sussex, slaving over a hot tape-recorder in numerous pubs and restaurants. It was difficult to fit in the eating, and even the drinking, as we talked our way through forty hours of my recollections of skiing round the world with my girlfriend, Lucy Dicker.

During this period, William was always acutely aware that there were times when I found talking to him about Lucy's death very difficult. He was always sensitive and supportive on these occasions. Then, when I steeled myself to visit fifty of the ski resorts on both sides of the Atlantic that I had last seen in Lucy's company, William began the monumental task of putting the basic plot of our ski odyssey on paper.

Apart from our taped interviews, William had access to fourteen hours of video, shot by me on the road; hundreds of faxes and letters; a daily account of our adventures started by me and finished by Lucy, recorded on our tiny Palmtop computer; and more than fifty articles from the *Financial Times*. I then spent six weeks fine-tuning the manuscript, and adding a considerable amount of material, much of which William did not know about — even if you visited every pub and restaurant in Arundel (which we came close to doing), you would never recall all the details of 365 days of adventure. Eventually, there was enough material for ten books, but this is the one William and I have written. I shall be eternally grateful to him for his invaluable help and his friendship. I'm sure Lucy would want to thank him, too, for helping to write her story.

A.W., Highgate Village, London

*   *   *

How do I remember Lucy? I remember laughing green eyes. Soft, strawberry-blonde hair carelessly swinging like a curtain of fine silk around her shoulders, hair that would turn into cascades of freshly-blown ringlets after she had washed it. A lilting voice, with its Provençal accent, teasing, cajoling, flirting the way only French women can flirt. Slender wrists, lissom shoulders.

And a smile to melt glaciers.

Tonight, her smile was unusually serene and happy. But

sometimes her eyes gave out other signals. In the Chinese Horoscope which she was so keen that I shared with her, Lucy was a Snake. And occasionally her smile sent out a subtle hint of danger which I learned to pick up — and ignore at my peril.

Now I think of Lucy all the time. She's here, there, somewhere, everywhere, behind the thin veneer of everyday life, waiting for me to join her. Then I look at the vivid scar that extends from my right wrist up my forearm to my elbow, and the nightmare begins all over again.

It is more than four years since the burning ice ripped through the sleeve of my ski-suit and two layers of clothing as I dived across the *couloir* in a desperate attempt to stop her. But the scorch mark once livid, is fading now.

I try to console myself by clinging to the thought: Lucy isn't really dead. She simply went on ahead, that's all.

I talk to her every day. I pray with her first thing in the morning and last thing at night. And sometimes in between, in one of those quiet moments during the day when I find myself standing in a doorway in the rain or waiting for a bus and we can share that snatched moment together.

Sometimes, if I'm alone on a chairlift high in the mountains, I'll imagine she is sitting next to me, and we chat as we did a thousand times that year. Or on a station platform, back in England. I might walk to the far end, where no one is watching, and think of her. That's when the world shuts off into timeless silence, and I see a smile of pure sunshine that I will never, ever forget.

Funny thing. Often I see Lucy — actually see her — when I least expect it. Like I just did a second ago. All I have to do is let my mind drift away from the little everyday things with which I compulsively fill my life now that she's gone. I mean finding things to do to fill the hours. Even if it's washing up dishes — which Lucy never let me do, by the way — twice over, or walking upstairs to fetch something I didn't really need, or cleaning my shoes (three pairs of Chelsea boots) one after the other. And then starting all over again, until I must have the shiniest shoes in London. Little things like that.

But there she is, suddenly out of nowhere, a vision planted in front of me. She is smiling at me through the kitchen window as I stand by the sink staring out at the darkness. It's that special smile which she saved for me when I got back in the evenings.

Somewhere outside, in the black void, lie the sprawling streets of West London. Hammersmith, to be precise: Sinclair Road, a stone's throw from Olympia, Top Flat. I can hear Lucy saying it: '*Top* flat', stressing 'top' rather than 'flat'. A big, roomy penthouse lined with all our books — my ski library, her thrillers, endless rows of them. It broke my heart when I had to sell them, but I just didn't have enough space to keep them all.

The houses are handsome Edwardian buildings, their faded elegance reclaimed with fresh paint and a facelift to make them attractive to high-fliers in the City and newly-weds who can afford the area.

Bed-sit land has been converted into modern flats behind the white balustrades and old London brick. Like their occupants, they remain for the most part anonymous.

Up the road are the rich neighbours in Baron's Court, home of Queen's Club and the annual tennis tournament where the likes of Becker, Sampras and Agassi stroll out to warm up for Wimbledon and stroll off again with a fat cheque in their shorts.

This terraced street which had been our romantic hideaway for so many glorious carefree months seems completely unrelated to the glass and glitz of the new Hammersmith development I can glimpse across the chimneys from Lucy's roof garden. Over the cream walls of the Royal Oak pub rises the shiny brown marble monolith that used to be the old Underground Station, and the extraordinary glass bubble of the Ark, a circular futuristic masterpiece which seems about to set sail up the M4.

Sinclair Road nestles in between like a forgotten

relative. But a lifetime ago I spent the happiest two years of my life there.

*   *   *

The cup from which I have just washed away the dregs of black coffee stands on the draining board, its pale china surface running with fresh rivulets. There are dark brown specks in the sink. I had made the mistake of looking down at it for a moment too long.

When I look up — there is Lucy. Swimming out of the night, the face I loved is framed in the dark square of the glass like one of those photographs you mount on glossy black velvet in an expensive album.

Lucy was always framing things. If the flat had not been so roomy we would have run out of wall space.

'Lucy, we can't frame everything.'

'Why not, baby?'

Baby? Normally I hated that word. But somehow coming from Lucy's lips, and with that accent, '*Bai*-bee!' — it made me feel like the king of all France.

In the kitchen now I turn away from Lucy and look past the alcove into the living room. The sofa is still there, standing solidly in the corner behind untidy piles of cardboard boxes that litter the apartment. What a tip! Lucy would have hated to see her beloved apartment looking like a storage depot.

At that time I didn't want to think about what was in those boxes, and I didn't have the strength to look anyway.

I wanted to remember the good times. How we'd sit and watch TV together — not so much sit, as wallow in the sofa's pale leather, so comfortable that you could drown in its contours.

We were watching *Blind Date*. Lucy enjoyed vapid programmes like that. Strange, I used to think, for a girl who had read Philosophy at University in Aix-en-Provence. But when she switched off from her high-powered job as the

London manager of a French ski travel firm, she switched on to TV banality.

Or *Tee*-vee, as she called it, with the accent on the 'Tee'. Although her English was near-perfect, she had this endearing habit of occasionally stressing the wrong syllable.

'I want to watch this. Please, Arnie. Okay?'

So we watched *Blind Date*.

That night I took my eyes off Cilla to fish behind the sofa where I'd hidden a small package.

'Arnie, what are you doing? Oh — ' She scrunched the wrapping into a ball, and stared wide-eyed at the silver watch mounted on a ring, nestling in a bed of soft tissue.

'Darling, you shouldn't!' Lucy never liked my spendthrift ways, though she herself was very generous. After all, someone had to look after the purse.

'Why not?'

She gave a giggle of pleasure, and kissed me lightly on the lips. '*Because ...*'

Then she snuggled up to admire it more closely.

*   *   *

It was on that sofa that I uttered the words that would change both our lives for ever. It was a spring evening, a warm April night in 1993 almost exactly two years before ...

'Wouldn't it be great to ski the world?'

'What, Arnie?' We were in the flat, sipping chilled Chardonnay as a prelude to dinner.

'I've got a really crazy idea. I'll tell you about it over dinner.'

'What are you talking about?' She was an amused mother listening to the ramblings of a fanciful child.

We drove to Richmond and strolled along the narrow streets, finally settling for a quiet Greek restaurant, the Salamis Taverna in Hill Rise. There, over taramasolata, calamari and a bottle of Domestica, I outlined the Impossible Dream.

It had all started with an article I had written for *Vogue* three years previously. In the morning conference, five floors above Hanover Square, the Travel Editor had been looking for something different. Can you ski in every month of the year? And if so, how and where could it be done? They came to me.

Lucy was intrigued. 'So, Arnie — ?'

'I invented this maiden aunt,' I said, trying to make it sound like a reasonable thing to invent. 'Araminta. She left me a legacy. Very convenient. And I wrote a pretend account of my travels.'

'You didn't actually do it?'

'Well, no. It was fiction. Or rather, faction. Okay, I made some of it up — but I made it work.' I had been to all the resorts, so I had a fair idea of what I was talking about.

As a seasoned ski writer for the *Financial Times* and several magazines for more than a decade, I knew all the fashionable resorts like old friends, and a few others besides. My 'factional' journey had been all too easy.

Lucy shook her head.

'Ski the world!' I said. 'And not only that — but it would be a great excuse to celebrate my half century.' In fact I was still half-joking, but the joke was turning more serious by the second. 'You know I'll be fifty on 14 February. I want to be somewhere ... special.' I paused.

'Yes?'

'And, how about this? Wouldn't it be great to ski every day for that entire year as well!'

She looked at me with those huge green eyes, suddenly alert. The mellow laziness inspired by the wine had dropped from them.

'Brilliant!' she said. 'Arnie, it's wonderful. And I'll come with you. I love the whole crazy idea. I've been looking for something like this all my life.'

I looked into those green eyes, and wasn't sure what I saw in them. Would she really come with me if she thought I was serious?

'Darling,' I said. 'It's just a dream.'

*   *   *

Was it really only three years ago that I had met her?

The company was Touralp. It was based in Knightsbridge, West London, and from the UK they sold ski holidays to the French Alps.

As General Manager, part of Lucy's job was to host get-togethers for the Press, and woo the writers into accepting a trip to the Alps.

I first set eyes on Lucette Madeleine Richaud at one such Press luncheon at the Savoy Hotel. Some thirty of us listened politely while the attractive General Manager outlined her company's plans for the coming season, giving her a generous ripple of applause at the end.

In the throng around the buffet, I found myself face to face with her.

'Hello,' I said. 'I'm Arnie — Arnie Wilson.'

We had spoken on the phone, but we hadn't met. In fact, she had helped me find some photographs of Les Arcs for a book I had written on the world's top ski resorts.

Her green eyes studied me with disconcerting intensity. 'How is the book?'

'I'll send you a copy.'

'I can't wait,' she said. Did I detect a hint of sarcasm? But she smiled to take away the sting.

Delightful, I thought. And bright. Also vivacious, professional and a good image for the company.

Great body, too.

Later, I learned her story. In the space of seven years she had built the company from a staff of one (herself) into a thriving concern employing nine people during the ski season. She was something of a workaholic. Her best friend and former colleague, Sandra Dunne, remembers that it was nothing for Lucy to tear up a presentation she wasn't happy with, rewrite it during the night, and deliver the new version, fresh as a daisy, the following day.

But what did Lucy think of me? These were her first impressions: 'I thought you're a very nice guy, but not too sure where you're going in life, or what you're doing,' she told me, much later. 'You want to do too many things in too little time, and you give yourself a lot of pressure.'

That was in her flat in Sinclair Road. In bed, after the first time we made love there.

Yes, she was perceptive, too.

'Go to sleep,' I said, smiling.

Much later on, I learned that Lucy had said to her mother, Marcelle, about me, 'Maman, this is the good one!'

Later still, I learned about the real Lucy.

At the age of nineteen she had run away from her home in Istres, a market town tucked away in the wooded Provençal countryside some thirty miles from Marseilles. She finished up in London.

'Why run away, Lucy?'

'I just felt I had to get away. I didn't like France very much, especially the South.' I found the atmosphere very claustrophobic and the Mistral used to drive me mad. England, on the other hand, really intrigued me. I admired England and all things English. I even wanted to be English myself. My mother and I were too strong-willed for each other. There was a power struggle. I guess I had to prove to my parents that I could make it on my own in a different world. England was a challenge because I had to learn to speak the language properly. So I just went.'

It ran deeper than that, of course. Her father Lucien, better known as Lulu, was a slim, amiable, distinguished looking teacher. (I noticed, when I finally met him, that he and Lucy had the same domed forehead). Lulu was an advocate of *laissez-faire*. He sank his energies into cycling, tennis and golf, and was disinclined to become involved in family squabbles.

The power struggle was between his wife and his

daughter. It began when Lucy was just two-and-a-half years old. She remembered seeing her mother leave the family home in Istres for the local hospital, with no word of explanation. When she visited Marcelle there later, she was cradling something in her arms. Lucy had a little brother — and never forgave either of them.

It was a question of attention, and who got the most of it. 'Forget about him,' the little girl yelled, pointing at the bundle. 'Leave him there and come home with me!'

There were constant scuffles. Lucy and Maurice would play in the back yard of the family home, but often it ended in tears. When Maurice was seven, he got the worst of one battle and cut his head open.

It was Maurice who would analyse it for me, much later, on the way to the Memorial Service. 'I don't think she ever got over my arrival. I'm sure Lucy felt betrayed. Two-and-a-half is the worst possible age for a child to accept a new baby in the house,' he declared, with the sadness of hindsight.

Even Lucy's father, a peaceful soul, sometimes found himself battling with her. She could be petulant, especially in her teenage years.

Maurice describes a fascinating vignette about her.

One morning, Monsieur Richaud refused to drive her to school — where she was in his maths class — because she was wearing such a short skirt ... and too much make-up.

'You're not coming to school looking like that, Lucette!' he warned her.

'I *am*, papa, I *am*!' she said, stamping her foot.

Lulu strode towards her, but Lucy started to run away. The cycling, tennis-playing maths master was more fleet of foot than his daughter. He caught her.

'Now,' he said with unusual authority, 'go and get something decent on! And be quick about it!'

On this occasion, game, set and match to Richaud senior.

*　　　　*　　　　*

Lucy in London. Trying all kinds of jobs. In the early seventies there was work around, especially for an attractive French teenager with a zest for life. She started on the bottom rung — as a receptionist in a seedy night club.

'What was it like?'

'Dreadful, Arnie. My boss put his hand up my skirt, and when I slapped it away I was fired on the spot!'

And then? 'The easiest jobs were in pubs, as a barmaid, cash paid every evening and no questions asked. But I found a spare room in a convent where the nuns let me stay for several weeks — until they found out what I was doing in the evenings!'

That's when they asked her to leave. It was, they said, inappropriate.

'So you never became a nun?' The idea was a hoot.

'No, Arnie. I did not.'

She found her way into the holiday business via a London company called Travelscene, which specialised in city breaks. After ten years with various companies, she was headhunted by the French ski resort of Les Arcs to sell skiing holidays there. The fact that she spoke Spanish and Italian helped.

Les Arcs is not everyone's idea of the perfect ski resort. Huddled at 6,000 feet up in the Savoie region of the French Alps, it is a friendly informal village constructed of 'warm materials', which means mainly wood. Although cars are excluded from the centre, which keeps the air crystal clear, the purpose-built, high-rise blocks put many skiers off.

It was Lucy's job to change their minds. 'You can get used to anything eventually,' was one of her favourite sayings.

*   *   *

So when did it begin to get serious? Us, I mean. Probably on my first Press trip with her, to preview the French Winter Olympics at Les Arcs and Courchevel 1850, the jewel in the crown of the Trois Vallées, 'planned by skiers for skiers', and, like Les Arcs, 6,000 feet up in the French Alps.

At dinner in La Bergerie, an old shepherd's hut that has been in existence before Courchevel itself, I was sitting next to an old friend, Nigel Lloyd, whose dry wit enlivens any occasion. Maybe it was the wine, but I looked down the table at Lucy, and murmured: 'Stunning!'

'Yes,' he agreed. 'It's a class act.' He paused, then continued, 'She's not happy, you know.'

'What do you mean?' Could this ravishing creature really be a damsel in distress? Could this be a mission for Sir Galahad?

'She's been married twice. Both Englishmen, I gather.'

Her first marriage had only lasted a year or so, and it was she who had broken her husband's heart, she would admit to me later, not the other way around.

His name was Bob Collins, and they ran the bar together at the Coach and Horses pub in trendy Hampstead, North London. When we got on to the subject she summed it up brusquely. 'I was very young in those days, and rather selfish. I think we both knew from the start that our marriage was a mistake.'

Her second marriage — to John Dicker, from whom she now took her name — survived rather longer, some six years, until they called it a day.

Perhaps this beautiful, brilliant, complex woman was not in such distress after all? But by then it was too late. Lucy had entered my life and would never leave it again. Even afterwards.

As for me, my own marriage to Veronica had faltered after sixteen years, but at least it was amicable. My four grown-up daughters stayed close to both of us, which helped. I was a free agent.

So was Lucy.

I'll never forget our first kiss. Berwick Street Market in busy Soho, teeming with noise and movement and the shouts of stallholders.

After that trip to France, I had invited her for lunch. She had accepted. Over cappuccinos and good wine in the Café des Amis du Vin in Charlotte Street, we talked into the long afternoon.

'When I was a little girl,' she said, with a kind of childlike seriousness, 'and I was asked what I wanted to be when I grew up, I usually replied: an astronaut or a trapeze artist. I wanted to fly to the moon. Or at least be agile enough to regale a circus crowd with some gravity-defying stunts. Can you understand that, Arnie?'

I touched her fingers across the tablecloth. It was our first date, and I was proceeding with caution.

'Of course I can.'

Lucy kept both her hands on the table, not attempting to withdraw them. I felt the delicate smoothness of her unpainted nails.

'I guess the ambition to travel far and wide never left me. To discover new worlds. And the need to be noticed — '

Noticed? The whole world has noticed you, Lucy, I thought, but I kept the thought to myself as I linked my arm in hers and we strolled out into the seediness of Soho that had suddenly become touched by magic.

Then a gentle exploratory kiss, suddenly, unexpectedly passionate, blissfully unaware of the teeming market place. I almost fainted. And at the end of it ...

'I'll ring you — ?'

'Yes, please do.'

And she turned, and was gone.

I headed for my bachelor bed-sit in North London and sang all the way home. Only no one else heard.

*   *   *

It was a long way to travel on the strength of a single kiss. Most men would probably have settled for lunch in Knightsbridge, around the corner from where she worked.

I settled for the French Alps.

It was from Cortina di Ampezzo, Italy, that I made the call

back to London, to her home in Sinclair Road. 'It's Arnie. Fancy a spot of lunch?'

'Well, yes — but I'm off to Les Arcs tonight.'

'I know. You told me. That's where I was going to take you. I thought La Gallipette.'

La Gallipette has an open log fire, low armchairs, a guitarist and loads of ambience. The food's good, too.

'Where *are* you, Arnie?'

'In Cortina. I can take the overnight train and meet you there.'

'*Cortina*?' The slightest of pauses. Then, 'That would be really nice. I'm staying at the Golf. I'll be waiting.'

But I got there first.

Before I left Cortina, I confided my inner fears to an old skiing friend, Richard Williams, then editing a Sunday magazine. 'I'll be lucky just to get a cuddle,' I said.

'Don't be stupid,' he replied. 'It's a wonderful thing to travel on a train halfway across Europe just to see someone. It's incredibly romantic. She'll love you for it.'

By train, across the Great Planura through Veneto, Lombardy and Piedmont. The best part of five hundred miles, but in my fevered state I hadn't bothered to check. I may know a thing or two about mountains, but when it comes to the distances between them I'm nursery-slope material. Italy and France are neighbours, right? But it depends from which part of Italy you start out. I started out from the wrong part.

As the train trundled through the night, I could hardly sleep. Would Lucy be pleased to see me?

The train took me with aching slowness down through the Dolomites, along the Po Valley and out of the snow, south to Padua. There I strode up and down a cold platform while I waited for the connection to Milan and Turin. Then across the border to Albertville. Another wait, before the final leg to Bourg St Maurice and the eight-mile bus drive up into the snow line again to Les Arcs.

I checked into the Hotel Golf, a day ahead of her.

Another sleepless night. In the morning, I took three showers, waiting for her.

Finally, she was there, sweeping along the corridor wearing a long coat over a black dress and a brilliant smile.

My heart jumped about six feet.

'Let me take your bag!' And I turned smartly on my heel and headed straight for my room. Not hers. Mine.

Unprotesting, Lucy followed. She propped open the door with her other case. And as she walked through, I quietly edged it aside with my foot. The door swung shut.

Perhaps Richard had been right, after all. Her smile told me he had. Later she would put it into words — how I had underestimated her need for a new chapter in her life.

I was planning to wait until evening, a candle-lit dinner perhaps. Instead, we went straight to bed and stayed there, completely oblivious to a night sky alive with the flash and crackle of a gigantic fireworks display that heralded the end of the Winter Olympics.

We remained there for two wonderful days.

*   *   *

Many people, her two husbands included, had fallen in love with Lucy Dicker. Most men who met her were affected by the Lucy tingle, as I called it. That frisson of interest and unconscious excitement that some women can arouse in complete strangers, an invisible aura they wear around them.

I was no exception. I was hooked. Utterly.

The next time we slept together, only our fingertips touched. As the TGV roared through the night en route to Paris, and the mountains receded into the sunset like departing ghosts, my hand stretched out from the top bunk of the couchette to hers. Slim, cool fingers entwined in mine. I stared across at Lucy as she slept, her face dimly illuminated in the soft blue glow of the tiny night light. She seemed vulnerable, almost childlike. In sleep, she was smiling.

Chapter 1

Preparation

If anyone had told me Arnie would be the man
responsible for the most exciting adventure of
my life, I would have laughed incredulously.
But Arnie re-awakened the dream.

Lucy Dicker, November 1993

mazingly, all it took was one night. At seven o'clock,
with the late spring sunshine of an April evening
flooding through the windows, we started planning
the itinerary of our journey of a lifetime. By midnight, I had
completed a rough draft scribbled on sheets of paper strewn
over the carpet. We were there.

Well, not quite. We had prepared in the usual way — with a
trip down to the corner store for essentials to fortify us for the
long session ahead: Brie, salmon in French bread, rosé wine
and a yoghurt for pudding.

'All right, Arnie.' Lucy sat cross-legged on the floor in
jeans and sweater, barefoot, felt-tip pen poised over a blank
sheet of A4 paper. 'Where do we start? East or west? Shall we
throw a coin?'

'Let's go west,' I said. 'You know how much I love

Jackson Hole. Why don't we start there and finish there, too? The guy who runs the place has already offered to throw a party for us at the finish.' Jackson Hole in Wyoming is my favourite ski area in the whole wide world and I was dying to take Lucy there.

I'd told her many times how I had fallen in love with its desolate beauty the moment I first set eyes on the spectacular valley ten years earlier. The 'hole', in fact, is the flat floor of a valley eighteen miles across and sixty miles long. The skiing is exhilarating. The town itself is a genuine old Wild West community.

And the mountains, the majestic Tetons, are the most awe-inspiring peaks in the Rockies — a spectacular tidal wave of granite frozen by time, rearing up like snow-covered shark's teeth against the Wyoming sun.

'Trust you to love mountains called the Tetons,' Lucy half said and half laughed. She was good at laughing and speaking at the same time. She knew, of course, that 'tetons' was an old French word for breasts. 'They were given that name by a party of lonely French trappers last century because they reminded them of women's breasts.'

I said, 'Actually, you've seen them already.'

'How could I?'

'They were the backdrop for *Shane*.' I knew she'd seen the classic Alan Ladd Western. 'And John Wayne rode his first horse there in *The Big Trail* back in 1930. It's in the town records. They've made scores of Westerns there. You'll love the place, I promise.'

'All right, Arnie, if it's good enough for John Wayne, it's good enough for me. Anyway, you know I'd follow you down any trail you want. So, Jackson Hole it is.'

We had a *Great World Atlas* spread open on the floor. I flicked the pages to the United States. Then I remembered the *White Book*, a marvellously informative manual published in the US which had become my skiing Bible, listing just about every ski resort in North America. I started making notes.

An hour later I realised our first problem.

'Look at this, Lucy. Ideally, we want to ski in a different resort every day for twelve months, right?' She nodded. 'That means starting on the 1st January and finishing on the next New Year's Eve in the same place. Jackson Hole.' She nodded again.

'But — we can't do it.'

She craned over my shoulder as I sat on the carpet, prodding at the map in frustration. 'Why not?'

'It just won't work,' I complained. 'The world's snow just isn't divided evenly between the two hemispheres. We could easily spend all winter in the north, picking any resorts we want to our heart's content. But what happens in the summer? We've got to get down south and there just aren't enough resorts in the southern hemisphere to go round. We can get to Chile, Argentina, Australia, New Zealand ... but then where?'

'So what do you suggest, Arnie?'

'Okay. We'll ski every day, but not always in a different place. Sometimes we'll have to stay in the same resort for two or three days to catch the right connection onwards. But we can get round the world in a year, I promise you!'

I did a spot of fast geography, hoping I could turn rash optimism into reality. At least I had skied most of the resorts, and knew not only the terrain but their accessibility. I could list the nearest airports, how long it would take to reach them by road, and the hazards we could expect to encounter.

On the down — or downhill — side, there were a lot of areas that would be an unknown quantity. I couldn't run away from the fact that the risks were enormous and the odds on our managing to succeed were pretty slim. But at last I sat back, and beamed an encouraging smile at Lucy.

'I reckon that with any luck we can hit around 250 resorts in thirteen countries. That's more than two every three days. Mind you, I haven't gone into the details. That might take a little longer ...

She looked at me pensively, and chewed at her fingertip —

a sign that I would get to know spelled tension, doubt or stress. Or disbelief.

'Well — ' Then her face lightened, and the smile broke through. 'You're mission commander, after all. Like Neil Armstrong going to the moon — '

'Which makes you Buzz Aldrin,' I said. 'But this is a team effort. And actually, I'd rather be Dan Dare. He was my real boyhood hero.'

'That makes me Digby,' Lucy said with one of her Provençal cackles, which eased my doubts. Digby? This exquisite creature was about as far removed from the chubby, comic-strip Lancastrian of *Eagle* fame as one could possibly imagine. But it was a role she seized upon with relish.

She had always said she wanted to be an astronaut. One of our weekend pastimes was to lie in bed together gazing out of the window at the night sky over West London, and listening to recordings I had obtained of the classic 1950s radio series *Journey Into Space*.

'Back in the fifties, people used to listen to this with all the lights out, because it was so spooky,' I told her. 'It's the only way to get the full effect.'

That's what we did, listening to the deep, dark voice of Andrew Faulds as Jet Morgan heading off into hyper-space in those fifteen-minute tapes. I had the complete set, and we played and replayed them three at a time before our eyelids drooped and we joined Captain Morgan in outer darkness.

I also introduced Lucy to one of my favourite movies — *2001: A Space Odyssey*.

'Well,' Lucy said. 'If I can't go to Jupiter, skiing round the world will have to do.'

If I was the commander, then Lucy was the quarter-master, supplies officer, sergeant major, cook and bottle washer rolled into one.

Throughout that seemingly endless summer of 1993 we spent every weekend together at her office or at Sinclair Road. Writing and planning. Rewriting, photocopying. Tearing up one sheet of paper, filling another.

In all, we wrote off more than one thousand letters asking for support. It took us all summer. And this was where Lucy came into her own. I now experienced for the first time the almost obsessive perfectionism which drove Lucy like an automaton. She had tunnel vision, and nothing would deter her from the enormous logistical task that unravelled before us.

*   *   *

Now, in the quiet light of her flat, I marvel at how Lucy, the Human Computer, could constantly release her brain from such responsibilities to allow herself to become the bubbling, dazzling Lucy whom so many people loved? I search through her collection of handbags, trying not to feel the indecency of invading her privacy although I know she won't really mind. She threw nothing away. Lucy's handbags are like a black hole — once something is in there, there is no escape! Old flight tickets, boarding passes, faxes, business cards (other people's), meal receipts, credit card vouchers, bank statements. I never realised how many compartments exist in a woman's handbag. Or what you might find in them. It was as if she had been carrying an entire filing cabinet around the world with us. It certainly felt as heavy!

The one reason I didn't care for her office was that there was a dog howling somewhere outside. Sometimes I would get up and peer out of the rear window into the small alley at the back, trying to identify where the sound came from.

'The owner has obviously gone away.'

That dog howled all summer. But only at weekends.

'Wretched beast,' I growled.

'Wretched owners, you mean.'

The penthouse flat became Command Headquarters, as the files started multiplying.

As we began to see the gaps filling in ('That's January taken care of'), Lucy typed out fresh versions of our year-long itinerary. It became a military exercise, except that the ground ahead was always shifting — ground that was full of minefields that could blow up in our faces.

I tried not to show it, but inwardly I was all too aware that if we missed one flight, or had a puncture when we were running late, or sprained an ankle or the weather closed in at the wrong moment, the whole project would end in humiliating failure. That's if we didn't break a leg first.

As fast as one schedule was cut and dried, we had to change it.

'We can't go there.'

'Why not, Arnie?'

'We'll be too soon for the snow. We'll have to change the programme for that entire week.'

Lucy typed out each sheet meticulously. If she made the tiniest slip, she would spend hours re-typing it. After a time I protested: 'This is crazy, Lucy. We're planning an expedition, not an opus on vellum!'

Her chin tilted. 'I don't care,' she responded stubbornly — Lucy could be very stubborn. 'It's got to be right.'

We started by listing the whole itinerary. When that became too bulky, we divided the itinerary into continents. Then into countries. Finally, into months.

The map became clearer.

Once typed out, Lucy insisted that every document, letter and follow-up missive should be photocopied. 'No one's going to be remotely interested in supporting our trip if we don't make it look professional,' she said briskly.

And we needed support — how we needed it!

                    *   *   *

We approached scores of companies, looking for sponsorship. Every Sunday evening I would trudge down to the post box on the corner with a carrier bag full of letters, which I pushed through with a silent plea: Let this be the one!

For the first weeks the reply to my prayer was a deafening silence. Apart from the dog howling. The replies came back, polite but negative — or else they didn't come back at all. Household names you'd have thought might be falling over themselves to help us totally ignored our call for help.

Undaunted, Lucy kept writing. 'It's in the stars, Arnie,' she assured me. Now *she* was the optimist.

Lucy loved reading her horoscope. She'd come back from the newsagent with a pile of women's magazines each week, leaf through them until she got to the 'Your Stars and You' page, and search through them until she found one that gave her the glad tidings she wanted. Then she would ditch the rest without a further glance!

'God, Lucy, how can you do that?'

'I'm a snake, Arnie, remember? And you're just a monkey. A typical monkey.'

I looked up my simian qualities in a book of Chinese horoscopes, just so I knew the ground I was standing on. I liked what I read. The Monkey is a dedicated traveller, a genius whose brilliance is without equal.

What did she mean, *just* a monkey? I could live with that, particularly the dedicated traveller bit. Then I turned to the Snake's entry to learn that she has a deep understanding of the mysteries of life, that her unchanging gaze never falters as she advances upon her goal.

It was all alarmingly close to the truth. Intrigued, I read on.

The female snake is a dangerous woman whose beauty is hypnotic. Although she may seem to love the easy life, her mind is constantly active. The Snake's taste in clothes and jewellery will be immaculate, with a hint of the classical. You won't find her kitted out in rubbish.

Spot on again! And now for the best bit: in seeking a mate she conforms to the highest standard.

'I told you we were made for each other, darling,' I said. 'And don't forget it was you who got me into this astrology business in the first place.'

Lucy snatched the book, and raced through the Snake chapter until she found what she wanted. She pushed it back at me in triumph. 'Read that!' And so I did: the Snake never forgets and will hold a grudge forever. She could have the patience of a saint and the poisonous bite of a rattlesnake.

'What that's telling you, monkey, is — just watch it!'

Cross-legged on the carpet, she turned back to 'Your Stars and You.'

'Well, I wish you could get the stars to shine on us,' I grunted.

And, eventually, they did.

*   *   *

On 2 June came the first glimmer of light. Snow + Rock, a leading ski and climbing equipment firm in Kensington, gave us the thumbs up. Actually the thumbs belonged to the company boss Mike Browne, an ebullient character I had known for twenty years. He sat in his office above Kensington High Street with a big grin on his face as he studied our letter.

'Just name it,' he said. 'Skis, poles, boots? You've got it!'

'Mike, that's incredible!'

'I'll go one better — if you need fresh supplies of anything, just fax me. We'll deliver them to you anywhere in the world!'

He meant it, too.

The grin spread further. 'You can have some fun with our gadgets as well. We'll throw in altimeter watches, avalanche bleepers and skidometers. And how about some of those Canadian Sorel *après-ski* boots? They'll keep your feet as warm as toast.' He looked at us across the desk.

'It's a crazy idea. But knowing you, Arnie, you might just pull it off.'

Outside, Lucy linked her arm in mine. 'Clever monkey,' she said, and kissed me on the cheek.

Suddenly the stars were smiling on us, and the offers began to trickle in. Hewlett Packard, the computer manufacturers, gave us £10,000. They also provided us with two word processors, one not much bigger than the palm of your hand, that Lucy would use around the world to record our odyssey.

'We'll spend most of the time on the road,' I said, studying yet another map. A well-thumbed airline timetable lay beside it. 'We've just got to get our travel fixed up.'

Initial plan: to spend January, February and part of March skiing the USA and Canada. That would take in more than sixty resorts, from California all the way across nineteen states to the East Coast and New York.

'We'll cross the Banana Belt. That'll be a first for both of us.'

'The Banana Belt? What on earth's that?'

'Down through the Deep South, east of Mississippi' I said. 'Tennessee, Alabama, Georgia — '

'But surely there's no snow down there,' Lucy queried. To her, like most people, the Deep South meant swamps, humidity, a lot of water and mosquitoes.

'Aha,' I said smugly. 'Just you wait and see. They make the snow themselves. And at the right time of year we can ski there. Just trust me.'

'Oh I do, Arnie,' she said doubtfully. 'I do. You're the commander, aren't you?'

Meaning: it's egg on my face if things go wrong.

We would be driving, long and hard, down endless ribbons of highway. The thin red line I traced across the map with my felt tip pen began in Wyoming. Then across the border to Idaho, the Potato State, due west to Oregon, south to California, back to Oregon and up to Washington State. After that, we'd turn our sights north to Canada and British Columbia, on to Alberta and back to the United States again to find Big Mountain in Montana.

'That'll do for now, Lucy.' I drew a deep breath. I was feeling exhausted already. It had been a long night. 'Now we need our Michael Collins.'

'Who's he, baby?'

'The forgotten man. No one remembers him. But he was

the lonely astronaut who stayed at the controls of Apollo 11 drifting around the moon while Armstrong and Aldrin got all the glory for being the first men on it. We need a base, and someone manning it who can monitor the whole crazy trip.'

*   *   *

And we found her. In Maidstone, Kent, to be precise. She was my former secretary at Southern Television, Fran Newitt, who with her undying patience and efficiency would become our patron saint.

She would be the key figure who would chart our progress, relay messages, and respond to any SOS pleas that we would fax or phone her. All she wanted for her troubles were her expenses and a holiday in Jackson Hole at the end of it. It was a lot to ask anybody, but we had to have someone reliable, someone on whom we could utterly depend.

Fran was a brisk, no-nonsense, country girl who, during my seven years as a district reporter at the TV station had often achieved the impossible: being able to find me at any hour of the day or night when no one else could. A quality that had occasionally irritated me at the time, but that would prove vital on our mission. The fact that she didn't ski would not be a problem, although she sometimes got things hilariously wrong because of it, the prime example being when she mispronounced Kitzbühel one day on the phone and came up with a Jewish ski resort: *Kibutzel*!

Fran's timbered lodge, tucked away down a leafy country lane in the heart of Kent, became our nerve centre. In spite of frequent time changes as she followed our progress around the globe, she rarely got it wrong as scores of faxes and phone calls poured in and out. Without her, we would be lost. (Even *with* her, we were occasionally!)

As a child I had been rivetted by the story of Scott of the Antarctic, and his magnificent failure in coming second to reach the South Pole in January 1912, just a month after the

Norwegian explorer Roald Amundsen.

Of rather more practical help was the information I gleaned from accounts of the expedition.

'In particular, Lucy, how to pack.'

'Pack, Arnie?' She looked up from the floor and her notes.

I had come across the address Amundsen gave to the Royal Geographic Society on 15 November 1912. 'Listen to this:

> *Our business was to improve our equipment and*
> *reduce its weight. Of the utmost importance was*
> *the packaging of provisions. Of the 42,000*
> *biscuits that were packed, each and every one*
> *was turned in the hand before the right place for*
> *it was found.*

'Incredible! Now that's what I call packing!'

'Arnie, are you trying to tell me how to pack?'

'No, no! Of course not —' Hurrying away from thin ice, I regaled her with the story of how the President of the Society, in thanking his guest, had injudiciously paid tribute to the great explorer's 'warm and friendly dogs'. This had caused Amundsen great offence, since most of the unfortunate beasts had been eaten for the expedition to survive, and he thought the Society were making a dig at him.

If we were going to be anything remotely approaching the nineties' equivalent of Robert Falcon Scott and that wonderful and equally fanciful venture into the unknown, at least we would survive. We wouldn't starve. And all things being equal, we shouldn't freeze to death in the attempt, even though many of our days — and nights — would be spent below zero.

Because we were going to have to ski at night, too.

'God, Arnie — are you serious?'

'Afraid so, Lucy. There'll be times when we're really up against the clock.' I jabbed my pen at the map. 'Here at Mammoth, for example, and leaving Hintertux for LA. And

11

most definitely before we leave the Himalayas. But if we ski at one minute past midnight, that will give us something like forty-seven hours before we absolutely have to ski again, and we will still have skied every day.'

'What if there's no piste.'

'We'll just have to find a field,' I said. 'With snow on it. By moonlight. Or we can always shine the car headlights ... '

Most important of all, we had the backing of the *Financial Times*. We could hardly have wished for a more powerful ally. I had told Max Wilkinson, the genial but shrewd *Weekend FT* editor, that Lucy and I were going to ski the globe — with or without *FT* backing. He was intrigued. He had also become very fond of Lucy and, to my astonishment, agreed to give me a regular column throughout 1994 to chart our progress. It would be called the *Financial Times* Round the World Ski Expedition. Vitally at that time, the *FT* paid for most of our postage and provided the distinctive-looking pink *FT* stationery.

As the summer wore on, so our finances wore down, on a downward spiral like some small business doomed for bankruptcy. The more I earned, the faster it seemed to be ploughed back into feeding the mission.

Wilkinson took us to lunch at a popular *FT* watering hole, the candle-lit City wine bar called the Boot and Flogger near London Bridge, to catch up with our plans.

'I think you should set yourselves an extra challenge,' he said, with a grin in Lucy's direction. 'How many miles do you think you'll ski in the whole year? Five thousand? Do you think you could do that?'

I did some quick mental arithmetic.

'Five thousand *kilometres* would be more realistic,' I told him. It would be hard enough to accomplish even that.

'Well then, how about a minimum of ten miles a day? It will stop you getting lazy. You won't be able to ski one run and then just have a long lunch. It will also make it more interesting for the readers.'

We explored the possibilities. 'Trying to ski every day is going to be a battle anyway,' I said. 'But we'll set ourselves an average of ten miles, if we can do it. If we get to a resort and only find one mile of snow, we'll try to make it up by skiing twenty miles the next day.'

Max stared directly at Lucy for a long moment as if giving her the chance to change her mind at the eleventh hour. 'Are you really going to do this?'

'Yes, Max,' she told him simply. 'We are.'

And the die was cast.

'All right,' he said. 'I still think you're crazy. But good luck.'

*   *   *

The letters kept coming in, and this time we were getting into overdrive. Each morning we would rush downstairs to search the mail box. We would rip open envelopes to find anything from short impersonal notes saying, 'Sorry, but ...' to cheerful letters wishing us luck, but making it clear that actual funds were out of the question.

But at least in the USA the resorts came up trumps. No problem with hotels, lift passes, hospitality. *Come on over, guys!* We'd have a bed for the night, and a day in the snow. Lucy frantically rescheduled her notes.

John Resor, chief executive of my personal Shangri-la at Jackson Hole, told us he would be laying on the 'party of all parties' for us at his ranch on 1 January 1995 — and we'd better be there!

God bless America!

Lucy negotiated insurance cover for the great 'Round-the-World in 365 Days' trip with the aptly named Fogg Travel Insurance, of which Phileas would no doubt have approved. 'I just hope we don't need them,' I said fervently, scanning the small print.

Distressingly, a week after our meeting in his office, Mike Browne had the most terrible accident in the French Alps. It left him in a wheelchair. The news depressed us a great deal, but his implacable courage and good humour were undaunted, and we received a note from him: 'Of course I'm honouring our pledge — and I'll try and get to you on a ski-bob when you reach the Alps, and ski with you, just as I promised.'

Out of respect and gratitude, I decided that our expedition would try to raise money for Back-up, a charity for skiing paraplegics I knew was dear to Mike's heart, and started by Mike Nemesvary, the former freestyle champion who had broken his back practising on a trampoline nine years previously.

And now, suddenly, light shone at the end of a dark tunnel. Where it counted.

'Look at this, Lucy! Avis will give us cars! And here's a letter from American Airlines, and from Air New Zealand. They'll give us free flights! And Air India will take us to the Himalayas.'

'We're on our way!'

'Clever monkey,' cried Lucy. And hugged me long and hard.

The final letter that clinched our plans came from Summit County, Colorado. The triple ski resorts of Breckenridge, Keystone and Copper Mountain were prepared to throw $25,000 into the kitty, in hard cash, to help us live out our dream — a dream that was now reality. Lucy and I were excited beyond belief.

I had created a rough chart, with coloured pins to mark our route. We would leave the East Coast of the US in March, and locate the high spring snows of Austria, Italy, Germany, Switzerland and finally France. No problem there.

In early May we would fly to India, and then on to Japan. There was a 5.40pm flight from Tokyo on 19 May, which would take us over the International Date Line to arrive soon after dawn on the same day in Seattle.

'Old Phileas Fogg would be proud of us,' I said, triumphantly pressing a blue pin into the Pacific seaboard. 'If you remember, he made use of that extra day in *Around the*

World in 80 Days. So I don't see why we can't!'

On that day we would connect up with Los Angeles and reach the snows of Mammoth Mountain by 6.45pm. It might still be daylight, too.

'Do you realise what this means, Lucy?' I jabbed a finger at the map.

'What's that, Arnie?'

'It means we'll have been round the world in under a month. An around-the-world-trip within our around-the world-trip!'

Put like that, it sounded scary. Could we really do it?. But I shook off the first frisson of unease, and applied myself to the map with renewed vigour. After a few days' pause for breath in California, we would be off again, heading east back to Europe for summer skiing in the Alps where I knew there would be snow on the glaciers.

In mid-June we would venture into the Southern Hemisphere, heading first for wintry Chile and her neighbour Argentina. Then, on 19 August, would come the longest single haul of the whole trip: from Santiago to New Zealand, via Tahiti.

'I wonder what they'll think of us in Tahiti with all our ski gear?' Lucy giggled at the thought.

'Better pack a grass skirt,' I advised. 'Just in case.' A thought struck me. 'I wonder if we could get away with water skiing?'

In October we would leave Australia for the US, and after playing a few more games with the Date Line we would be in Los Angeles the same day we left Sydney. And by 1 January 1995 we would be back where we started.

All things being equal.

*   *   *

I looked at the map of the world, the world we would set out to challenge in a way that no one had ever done before, and shook my head. 1994 was going to be some year. 'Let's go out for dinner and celebrate.'

I gestured at the map. 'To our year of living dangerously!'

We went back to our favourite Greek taverna in Richmond and toasted one another into the early hours. Somehow a milestone had been reached, and passed. At least now we knew where we were going, and — with luck — when.

'You realise of course that sooner or later something's bound to go wrong: a flight delay, or a puncture or we might get stranded halfway up a mountain — '

'Sure, Arnie, but that's half the fun of the trip,' Lucy said.

'And we can expect our normal share of ailments that everybody gets in the course of a year. Coughs and sneezes — '

'Headaches, and my awful migraines.'

'Hangovers, more like. And maybe a touch of earache or toothache — '

'How did those early explorers ever survive?'

'At least we have an advantage over most of them. If we do get like Ranulph Fiennes and Mike Stroud, who ended up hating each other, we can always make up by having a cuddle. Which is more than they could do.'

I remembered that wonderful anecdote when Fiennes rebuked Stroud for being ill one day, saying if it happened again, it might start to jeopardise their mission. Later, he'd apologised, telling Stroud he was an 'absolute brick'. That night, Stroud entered in his diary: 'Ran Fiennes is an absolute *prick*!'

'Oh well, Arnie,' Lucy said, her eyes sparkling with mischief. 'As long as we don't end up hating each other!'

'Do you know, Lucy,' I said, matching her expression. 'I think we'll be lucky if we're still talking to each other after a month!'

'Oh, Arnie!' Then she saw my expression. And threw her napkin in my face.

In bed that night, Lucy said: 'We're really going, Arnie, aren't we?'

'Yes,' I said. 'We are.'

But first, we had to get fit.

*　　　　*　　　　*

The *Lucy Dicker Skiing Conditioning Programme* (yes, it really did say that on the cover in big black letters) was an ominous-looking tome bound in a maroon folder.

It came courtesy of the BiMAL Clinic in Hammersmith, along with its owner, a keep-fit expert named Alan Watson ('physiotherapist to the stars') who promised such delights as: 'Single leg press ... aerobics shuttle test ... Cybex extension and flexion ... bio-mechanical analysis'.

'It sounds like medieval torture,' I muttered darkly, looking at the diagrams that went with it. 'You do it. I'll watch.'

'No, Arnie,' said Lucy firmly. 'You're in it too. This is supposed to be a team effort, remember?'

On our first day in the hi-tech mirrored gymnasium, amid the power press-ups and endless miles of cycling on a stationary bike, I found Will Carling, then the English rugby captain, on a neighbouring machine.

We exchanged brief grunts, but somehow as we sweated it out in our track suits it wasn't the place to discuss the relative merits of dropped goals or giant slalom techniques. Later, we did tell him about our plans, and he wished us luck.

Alan Watson was an energetic figure with dark hair and a black moustache. After our first interview, he wrote us a note.

'You really must make the most of these six weeks. Enjoy!'

Enjoy? 'He must be joking,' I said grimly, easing my aching muscles into a hot bath at home that first night.

Somewhat alarmingly, the Cybex machine's printout indicated that Lucy's left leg was thirty per cent weaker than her right. Apparently, everyone has one leg stronger than the other, but this was unusual.

They also found I was three stone overweight, which accounted for my occasional tetchiness as the deadline rushed up on us.

'I don't believe it,' I growled. 'Three stone?'

'No more cheese for you, Arnie,' Lucy said. 'Not for a month at least.'

We never did finish the course — we simply ran out of time. But we raised a glass to Mr Watson anyway. I was as fit as I would ever be, and so was Lucy.

The evening before we set off, I jotted down a few thoughts, pink prose rather than purple:

> *We shall struggle breathlessly in the mighty Himalayas. Weave our way down the busy slopes of the Japan Alps. Gaze in wonder at the awesome Canadian Rockies. Marvel at the remote wilderness of the Andes. Hear the squawk of Crimson Rosellas in the snow-clad Eucalyptus trees of the Snowy Mountains in New South Wales and ski among the seagulls amidst the maritime peaks of the New Zealand Alps.*

'Oh, Arnie,' said Lucy, nestling in my arms on the last night we would ever see together in her flat. 'Maybe we are both a little crazy after all.'

Chapter 2

Christmas

Arnie, you can be such a pain!

Lucy Dicker, December 1993
And on many other occasions

In the autumn, we had said goodbye to her parents. It was more *au revoir*, really, because, as I pointed out to Madame Richaud, we would be back in Europe in the spring, when Lulu's Chlorodendron and Albesia trees would be in blossom, and wild flowers would be dotting the meadows on either side of the rambling, ranch-style family home — an old barn that Lulu had converted himself.

But Istres is a long way from the snow, so we had made plans to meet them in Verbier, in the Swiss Alps.

'*Au revoir, mes enfants*,' said Lulu, who spoke no English at all.

'Goodbye, *darleeeng*,' said Marcelle, using up half of her entire English vocabulary. The only other English she knew was: '*Cinque* you very much!'

I leant across to kiss her on the cheek, three times, French style. Even in her 70th year, she was still a good-looking woman, blonde and smartly dressed. Like Lucy was now, she

19

had been eye-catchingly attractive in her day.

'We should be in Verbier by mid-April,' Lucy said.

'That's almost half a year away,' Marcelle grumbled in her heavy Provençal accent. Being a schoolteacher, Lulu's French was fairly easy to understand. But in the early days, before my ears became tuned to her accent, I couldn't make out what Marcelle was saying half the time.

But I smiled and nodded encouragingly.

'We'll write,' I said. 'Promise!'

Lucien shook my hand in a firm grip that said: 'Bring her back, won't you!' And with a big grin, he kissed me on both cheeks, as Frenchmen do.

I hope my own grip said: 'Don't worry. I will.'

*   *   *

The flat in Sinclair Road had been rented out for eighteen months with a management agency. We had left our furniture there, but put most of our belongings in store. The rental covered the mortgage payments that Lucy was still paying on the penthouse, with my chipping in occasionally, despite her protests.

'No, Arnie. It's my responsibility.'

'Lucy, please, I want to.'

'And I *don't* want you to!' She had a streak of generosity as wide as the Grand Canyon, matched only by a stubbornness that could be infuriating. But sometimes I managed to slip a cheque in an envelope and send it off to the Halifax then submit myself to her rage (mixed with gratitude) when I confessed to the crime.

Was it just that she wanted to be her own woman? To be totally free and independent? But she gave so much of herself to me, and even more as the days together turned into weeks and the weeks into months, that I had to fight the fierce possessiveness that rose in my own soul for her.

We talked of love, always. And we would talk of marriage — but not yet.

*   *   *

So preoccupied were we with last-minute arrangements that we hardly noticed the arrival of Christmas. I wanted to get to Jackson Hole four days early so that we could get off to a proper start, properly planned, with time to handle any unforeseen hitches.

Our trip to France had coincided with Lucy's final job for her company — organising the British University Ski Championships, with more than a thousand students taking part. She was very good at that sort of thing, which was why she handled the details of our expedition so brilliantly.

The races took place in Tignes, a purpose-built resort set 7,000 feet up in a vast snow bowl that shares the lift systems with the better known Val d'Isère. Towering above the Iseran Valley, and with its great frozen lake a breathtaking vista shimmering 6,000 feet above sea level, it is one of the most spectacular sights you can find anywhere in the Alps.

So I suppose it was appropriate that Lucy and I should choose to have one of our more spectacular rows there — a row that threatened to scupper the expedition just days before it was due to begin. And on Christmas Eve of all times. Whatever happened to the season of goodwill to all men — and women?

Of course, we didn't exactly choose to have it. These things tend to creep up on you and explode without warning. And as often as not they're over something trivial.

In this case, not. The meeting was over, and we were due back in England that night. I reminded her of the date.

'Lucy, it's Christmas Eve!'

Lucy answered defensively, as if she thought I was having a go at her. 'I know, Arnie. But I've had a lot on my mind — '

I knew what she meant. Trying to control a thousand university students in festive mood was not an easy task. She had bitten her fingers raw, and they were patched up with her favourite Mickey Mouse sticking plasters.

We took our leave of Tignes. Lucy had raised a final glass of Kir to her team. Laughter, tears, handshakes, embraces. We trudged out through fresh snow into the car park.

We had to get to Lyon, where we would leave our rental car, and then catch an Air France flight to London.

In the snow-bound village, I had taken advice. Of course you need chains, said the man in charge at *Evolution 2's Bureau des Guides*, when I called in to bid farewell. *Absolument!* And a local guide sitting with him in the overheated office agreed. 'You'd be mad to try to go down the mountain without them,' he declared. 'The police will be checking.'

Point taken, twice over.

Lucy disagreed.

'I don't believe this,' she cried, as I fished around in the boot of our rented Renault to try to find some. 'We don't *need* chains!'

'Lucy,' I said steadily, keeping my head low and my voice likewise. 'We must. Everyone says so. The police are out looking for people without them.'

'We don't *need* the bloody things,' she said petulantly.

There were no chains in the boot. 'We're going to have to buy some.'

'This is crazy, Arnie. We're going to miss our flight.'

'I'd rather miss the plane than go over the edge,' I said, thinking of the hairpin bends ahead.

'Arnie, I've spent the last ten days driving around this resort without them, often in a blizzard. We don't *need* them.'

Lucy drove like a typical Continental, with style and speed, and with safety sometimes coming a poor third.

I looked at her, and said sternly, 'I'm not going down that mountain without chains! And that's that!'

In the end, I won. And in the end, just as Lucy predicted, we missed our flight home. We were, as she put it, doomed to spend Christmas Eve in the bloody airport.

'Have you any money on you?'

'No.' Her chin was tilted firmly in denial.

'Then we'll have to borrow some — to buy the chains.'

'Arnie, this is horrible!'

If there was one thing Lucy couldn't stand, it was borrowing money.

'Then I'll cash a cheque with the Ski School,' I said. 'They know me.'

I could tell she was furious.

With the francs, I bought a set of chains from the garage.

I'm not much good with chains. In fact I would go so far as to say I'm chain illiterate! I can't get them on, and I can't get them off. Fortunately, there was a man to put them on for us. For *me*, perhaps I should say.

Unfortunately, we could hardly take him with us down to Bourg St Maurice to help us take them off again (although we did do something of the kind one desperate day in Chile!)

We started our journey down. By that time, some of the cars coming up were indeed managing without chains.

'You see, Arnie!' Lucy was triumphant. 'I *told* you we didn't need them!'

We drove down in a silence that was as icy as the descending dusk over the valley. Verbal deadlock. The snowline slid away. The pines bowed their snow-clad heads in farewell.

And then we were in the valley where the roads were shiny with rain and slushy with melting snow, and pulling into the forecourt of Bourg St Maurice station.

This time, there was no one to help me get the chains off. I struggled in the snow, eventually having to lie in the melting slush as I battled with those appalling contraptions. Lucy just stood there, snake-eyed, watching me, then:

'Oh, Arnie, I don't believe this! You're getting soaked, you stupid man. And filthy.' She stamped her foot, a petulant habit she had retained from childhood when words failed her. Usually I found it oddly endearing.

In the gathering gloom, I lay on my side in the gutter

wrestling with the chains that gripped the first tyre. Somehow they had become tangled up around the axle. My arms were engulfed in an icy puddle, and growing numb. The rest of me was soaked through from the rain. It took the best part of an hour before they were free.

This drama, I would inform Lucy later, was doubtless the cause of the hacking cough I developed before our trip even began. It did not bode well for twelve months of continuous travel.

Lucy, sensible girl, had walked off to the station buffet. Finally I joined her in the embryonic warmth of the bar, redolent with the smoke of Gitanes. '*Un Pernod, s'il vous plaît,*' I said wearily.

Lucy said, 'We've definitely missed the plane. Happy Christmas!'

*　　　　　*　　　　　*

We'd had other rows before.

Lucy and I could both be volatile characters, and sometimes our personalities clashed like a pair of fighting stags. Horns locked, heads down, neither side giving way. Some of the rows went dangerously beyond the bounds of lovers' tiffs.

Example. During the summer while we were debating what we should take with us, trouble flared like a match tossed into a firework factory, with equally explosive repercussions.

'We'll have to take all the files and letters, and copies of letters,' said Lucy.

'Why take the copies when we've got the originals?' I asked.

'*Because*!' she said, with no further attempt at explanation.

'That's ridiculous,' I said.

'Arnie,' she said, distressed. 'We've got to have duplicates of everything, just in case. Don't give me all this stress. *Please*!'

Lucy was, by her own admission, a 'control freak'. It irritated her that I tried to keep things simple.

'You never seem to worry about anything,' she said. 'I *do*. I worry all the time. I'm stressed!'

'Well, I'm the one who's going to have to lug all this stuff around,' I said.

'That's crap, Arnie, and you know it. I'll be carrying my share of the bags.'

'Lucy, you're being ridiculous.'

She slammed her glass down on the kitchen table.

'I can't believe you're behaving like this! Who the hell do you think you are, Arnie Wilson? Just bugger off! Go on, just leave me alone.'

Bugger off?

Now it was my turn to stare at her in disbelief.

'Arnie, you'd better leave.'

I have my pride, and when people tell me to bugger off, I normally do. I did it when a news editor in Fleet Street made a similar suggestion, and he was most upset when I walked out of the office in mid-shift. Now I found myself doing it again.

Gathering my coat, an overnight bag and what was left of my dignity, I walked out of the flat, and down three flights of stairs to the street — but slowly, keeping half an ear open for the door to open behind me and her voice to call me back. Nothing. No opening door. No voice. I ended up in the darkness of Sinclair Road looking left and right, wondering which way to go.

Bugger off! Had she really said that?

Luckily my mother, Joan, lived in Richmond, ten minutes or so down the road. I drove there in my ancient BMW 728i.

Joan was asleep upstairs. I slept on the sofa. Or tried to. It's all over, I told myself. Before it's even started.

But it wasn't. Hours later the phone shrilled by my ear, and I turned over and almost fell off the sofa to fumble for it.

Lucy's voice: 'Darling, I'm feeling so terrible. Please come back.'

'What — what time is it?'

It was six am.

'I don't know, I don't care. I really hate myself.' Her voice was pleading. 'Please come back.'

And, of course, I did.

I had no idea that this would be a pattern of our year together, repeating itself time and again, once a month at least. We would have one major row a month, a real howitzer, and one minor altercation at least once a week.

But that's love for you.

*   *   *

Christmas Eve, 1993. What are we doing here at the Airport Hotel in Lyon? The restaurant is totally deserted, apart from Lucy and me and one other couple at a table by the far wall under an ornate mirror.

'What are they doing here? It's Christmas, for God's sake!'

'Maybe they missed their flight, too,' I suggest.

Lucy giggles. The giggle grows into a full-throated laugh, an *éclat* — French for thunderclap. It would happen often, that explosive belly laugh, a very earthy Provençal laugh, I would tell her.

We are friends again. The champagne has helped. A waiter had brought it to our room shortly after we arrived, while we were changing for dinner.

Lucy explains. 'It is an old French custom, Arnie. It's traditional. On Christmas Eve, if you are at a hotel anywhere in France, you get half a bottle of champagne. Isn't that nice?'

'I've never heard of it,' I tell her, pleasantly surprised.

'You've never been in France on Christmas Eve, then, *chérie*.'

She has that smile, half loving, half I-could-kill-you, with a twitch of her lips that spells seduction, and I find it irresistible.

We look at each other across the table, and I raise my glass of Bollinger '78.

26

'Friends?'

'Friends, Arnie!'

We made love that night to the sound of Christmas silence. Afterwards Lucy nestled in my arms and stared into my face with her huge green eyes suddenly serious.

'Arnie — '

'Yes — ?' I said drowsily.

'Let's never go to sleep without being friends. If we've had a row, I mean — '

'I know what you mean,' I said gently, caressing the soft strands of her hair. 'It sounds like a very good idea.'

'I always want to go to bed happy and loving.'

'So do I. We'll make it our resolution for the year.'

'Clever monkey,' she said.

We would sometimes break that vow, but tonight we slept in each other's arms, celebrating our very own private Christmas.

Chapter 3

Departure

'I wonder how many miles I've fallen by this time?'
Alice said aloud. 'Let me see: that would be
four thousand miles down, I think. But then I wonder
what Latitude or Longitude I've got to?'

Alice's Adventures in Wonderland
by Lewis Carroll

Equipment check. We had done most of it before we left for France, but we needed a final run-through. What to take with us, what to leave behind.

First, reading. I don't read a lot of fiction, preferring biographies and travel books. But Lucy loves novels. She was always buying the latest Le Carré.

'We've got to travel light, Lucy, and keep the luggage down. Books are heavy.'

'Can we take *Alice*?'

Reluctantly, I shook my head. 'Sorry, we're going to have to leave *Alice* behind. She's a luxury we can't afford.' We were in her flat, going over the final list.

'Oh, Arnie. You know how I adore *Alice* — '

One of the things Lucy loved more than anything was for me to read to her in bed at night. Either before or after making love. Usually after, because *Alice* would often send her off into a deep sleep.

I had an early edition of *Alice's Adventures in Wonderland*, a little book my mother had given to me when I was a small boy, and its battered red cover had somehow stayed in the family for years. Somehow, too, it had found its way into Lucy's bedroom, and when I picked it up and read the first pages the effect on Lucy was extraordinary. Her face lit up like a little girl's. Her smile extended from ear to ear and glowed like a 100-watt light bulb. She would settle back on the pillows, and wait for me to read *Alice* to her as if it was the treat of the week.

Instead of *Alice*, foolishly, I let her take Le Carré's *The Night Manager*, a tome as heavy as the Gideon Bible and three times the weight of little red *Alice*.

Sometimes, while I was wrestling with the schedule for the following day, her voice would surface from the depths of the sofa in our hotel: 'There's a good bit here, darling.'

'Okay, I'll read it later.' But I never did.

Now, after the funeral, I have read every word of *The Night Manager*, and I feel as if I could recite it by heart. There were other books she liked, and I'm gradually working my way through those, too. I feel I owe it to her.

But I still wish we'd taken *Alice*.

Lucy's other favourite book was *To Dance With the White Dog* by Terry Kay. She bought it towards the end of our trip, and found it irresistible. It was a charming story of an old American widower and a mysterious, sometimes invisible (to everyone except him) white dog which befriends him. Lucy found it so enchanting that she sent a copy to Kent Sharp and his wife Beth, our very good friend from Breckenridge, Colorado who first inspired the Ski The Summit resorts to be our main sponsors.

*　　　　*　　　　*

Back in the summer, I had written the word SUPPLIES in large capitals at the top of a blank sheet of A4 paper, then sat back and stared at it for a long time, waiting for inspiration. I could hardly have foreseen how much luggage we would end up with: fourteen bags in all.

I stared at the blank sheet and wrote the word SKIS, two pairs each. Then BOOTS, one pair only. Much as I'd like to have had a back-up pair, boots are far too heavy and cumbersome for excess baggage. And POLES, two sets. Poles are easy to lose, and not hard to replace. Two sets would do.

But it was the ski boots that would become our friends, our comforters, and the one piece of equipment we needed to rely on. So they would have to be moulded to our feet.

At Snow + Rock in Kensington High Street, West London, we put our feet in the hands of the experts. They sat us down side by side on a bench, and poured a kind of plastic into our boots. We had to remain there immobile for several minutes while the stuff hardened.

'It's rather like a dentist taking a mould for a set of false teeth,' I quipped.

'What if we can't get our feet out, Arnie?'

'This must be how Bugsy Siegel felt before they dropped him in the East River,' I said.

'Wasn't he shot in Hollywood?' Sometimes, Lucy could be a real know-all.

For further light relief I got up and clomped around the shop, swatting the air like King Kong pawing at the planes from the Empire State Building.

'Silly monkey!' Lucy gently chided me.

But the boots fitted to perfection. Me, size ten. Lucy, a modest seven.

I was feeling better about our trip by the minute.

We called the bags 'The Good, the Bag and the Ugly'. The 'ugly' bag was a funny-shaped green and red canvas hold-all from Snow + Rock. A French ski company, Dynamic, gave us two huge black and yellow bags, outsize, that squatted like giant wasps on the carpet at Sinclair Road as we started filling them up.

There was also an all-important bag for the computers. The Omnibook 300 lap-top word processor for me and a palm-sized one for Lucy — the 100LX Palmtop — so that she would actually be able to type sitting in the passenger seat beside me while I did most of the driving.

I was rather proud of our hi-tech gear. It included a modem to gain us direct access into the *Financial Times* system.

'Ah, the wonders of modern science!' I shook my head, visualising myself crouched in a shack atop a mountain peak, with a blizzard howling outside, valiantly filing another masterpiece back to base. I had this absurd comic-book scene in my head:

'Wilson coming through, Sir. I think he's in Outer Mongolia!'

'Good man. Never lets us down.'

'Arnie,' said Lucy, interrupting my childish fantasies. 'Have you seen a loose sock lying around?'

Clothes were piled in one corner of the lounge. Skis, boots and poles in another. Hi-tech by the far wall. This bag I packed with particular care. Well, Lucy did!

A video camera nestled in a special pocket, to fulfil our plans to video our entire trip for a possible TV documentary. A BBC tape recorder was in there too, for me to file features for holiday programmes like *Breakaway* from the world's most unusual ski areas.

'That's the bag we dare not lose,' I declared. 'We'll travel naked if we have to, but that bag stays with us.'

'You can travel naked if you want to, Arnie. I prefer to keep my clothes on,' Lucy said.

'Really? I hadn't noticed.' I ducked as the cushion flew across the room.

> *With everything on, we resemble walking ski shops: a tough pair of Sorel boots, for our evening walkabouts; an Ortovox Stratus rucksack and avalanche shovel; Pieps Dual Frequency avalanche transceivers; WRS Sports Med back-supports (corsets to you and me) and Gul knee sleeves, also for support. Then there are Gator*

fleece-lined face masks; a Casio altimeter,
barometer and thermometer watch (for Lucy) and
an Avocet altimeter watch (for me); ski-dometers
to clock speed and mileage; security ski-locks;
and powder traces to prevent our losing skis in
deep powder; Oh, and some skis — Salomon and
Dynamic; and Luhta and Degré 7 ski suits.

Extract from the *Financial Times*,
London, November 1993

Thank you, Mike Browne. Thank you, Snow + Rock.

'We've got enough equipment here for an army,' I muttered, snapping the lock shut on yet another case.

The Ugly Bag was heavy before we'd even put anything in it. 'Do we have to take this one? The bag that dare not speak its name?' I had taken a dislike to it already.

'It's a nice bag,' said Lucy.

We took it.

The green and red brute became the home for our literature. Schedules. Letters. Maps. I was supposed to be writing every week, filing reports as we progressed around the globe, and I needed a portable filing cabinet. The Ugly Bag would be a sort of workhorse.

Lucy, divine creature, knew it all. She knew where everything was located down to the last strip of Elastoplast, and she could put her hands on anything at a moment's notice.

I checked off another list. Six ski outfits. Swimming costumes, for the hot springs. Dozens of sets of underwear. Forty pairs of cheap, unisex socks.

'What about a tie, Arnie? You may have to look smart.'

'When? We'll always be on the road.'

'You never know. Take a tie.'

In the end, I took two. And never wore either of them.

Lucy, now, she was different. Of course there would be times when we were in a nice hotel. And however informal the place or the occasion, she would want to look a million dollars.

I didn't have a million dollars. But I had enough to buy her a blue denim jacket with a red velvet collar (her favourite colour) and gold buttons. It was very Lucy.

'Arnie, it's beautiful!' Three days to go, and she threw the wrapping paper on the floor and raced over to hug me. 'I'll keep it for special occasions.'

'Well, it's Christmas!' It was, too. We had finally flown in from Lyon on Christmas Day, and made it back to her flat as the lights sprang on in the dark back streets around Sinclair Road.

In return, she gave me a beautiful woollen fleece, blue-green, my own favourite colour. She had bought it in Tignes, unknown to me.

But even my Christmas gift was not as precious to her as the present I had given her from Aspen during an earlier trip. It was a small brown bear, only six inches tall, with an appealing face and a shiny snub nose. I spotted him in a gift shop on Aspen's main broadwalk, and remembered something she'd said.

'Do you know, Arnie, I never had a teddy bear in my life.'

I took the bear back to London and presented it to her over a welcome-home dinner in a candle-lit trattoria off Notting Hill.

Her eyes shone.

'Oh, Arnie. He's sweet.' She leaned across the table and kissed me. 'What shall we call him?

'I've already christened him. His name is — ' I paused for dramatic effect. 'The Bear!'

I would leave The Bear in the most unexpected places for her to find.

On the light fittings. In the fridge. Under the loo.

Once, The Bear went for five days before being discovered. Lucy pleaded: 'Arnie, where is he?'

Eventually I heard her piercing giggle, and knew she'd found him. Outside the window in the pouring rain, his brown coat soaking, half buried in the window box.

'Wicked, Arnie! Poor Bear!'

She dried him out, and tucked him up under the sheet next to her pillow.

On our great odyssey The Bear came with us, stayed with us all the way across the world and back, and sometimes kept us sane.

*   *   *

Medical matters. The demands of our insurance company, coupled with common sense, required that we had to have just about every possible innoculation and vaccination known to mankind. Our GP was a Doctor Dua, a handsome Indian sporting a turban whose surgery was close by in Olympia.

In the chair, with the first jab of the needle, I passed out.

'It's all right, Lucy,' I said moments later as I came round. 'I don't know why it happened.' I accepted a cup of tea from Doctor Dua's sympathetic nurse. 'I must be allergic to needles, that's all.'

The great white hunter speaks, from a prone position on the couch, his cheeks still pale.

Lucy had been standing by me when I fainted and looked concerned and a little startled.

'It happened once before,' I said. 'I was having a blood test in Canterbury when I was much younger, and everything went spinning, but I don't think it's the sight of blood...'

My voice trailed away.

'That's all right, darling,' said Lucy, her voice full of compassion, understanding — and perhaps the hint of a suppressed giggle. 'It can happen to anyone.'

*   *   *

Gadget check. 'Hey, Lucy, look at this!' I turned the object over in my hands, examining it minutely. It looked like the kind of spur you find on a cowboy boot, a spinning steel cog with little spikes sticking out. It was part of the package that our friend and loyal supporter Mike Browne had sent over from Snow + Rock.

'What on earth is it?'

'A ski-dometer. Look — ' I spun the cog. 'You stick it on the back of the ski, and the wheel clocks up every mile we travel. And it records our average speed, too.'

Amazing. Scott never had that in his kit bag as he plodded across the Antarctic wastes.

'Whenever you're in contact with the snow, it will keep clocking up the miles.' I was like a schoolboy with a new toy, which in a way it was.

'Fantastic, Arnie.' Lucy was impressed.

Next, I laid out the specialist watches we had been given by Mike, which were equally vital as an official record of our expedition. These would record the vertical feet we would ski down any mountain, the number of runs we made, and how much distance we covered — statistics absolutely vital for the trip. If we had no log, there was little point in even starting.

During our great foray into the unknown, how much time would we be spending on the road? Answer: a lot of time. Perhaps an average of four hours a day. Which meant wheels. A lot of wheels. In all, on our master plan, we would use almost thirty different vehicles, from four-wheel drives to speedy saloons. And all would provide one essential ingredient, apart from reliability: music. The throbbing background to our wordless thoughts, our ambitions, to the half-closed eyes in the passenger seat as the road undulates below our enclosed metallic shell and the scenery speeds past outside breath-misted glass.

We chose a selection of tapes, including 'Enigma'.

What is 'Enigma'?

To this day, I don't really know. Think of an eerie chanting. Think of rock music pulsating behind a confessional curtain. All that mattered was that it was beautiful. And it came to symbolise all that I knew and loved about Lucy, and somehow in its mixture of rock music and monastic chanting it exemplified the levels on which we were approaching our own great Pilgrims' Progress.

That, and our exploration of each other.

Part of Lucy would remain an enigma to me forever, just as

it had done to the five principal lovers she had in her life, including her two husbands. Eventually I would compare notes with all of them. We all agreed there was an area of her, within her, which nobody could quite fathom.

Like, why did she flare up so suddenly, sometimes for no apparent reason? Eventually I came to understand that it was her need to test the man in her life, to see whether he really loved her or not.

Paradoxically, the most dangerous times were when we seemed to be supremely happy together. Suddenly there would be a warning shot across the bows, the yellow-green flash of a tigress' eye, a sharp remark over something completely unexpected.

'Arnie, you don't love me! Why don't you go back to your wife? Or to that ex-girlfriend of yours.' And her lip would curl with a dreadful cold contempt, as my own heart chilled to hear her outburst.

At first I tried to wish the storm away with an understanding smile and a few honeyed words, a method I had employed successfully with other women in my past when they became emotionally over-wrought. I looked on it as smoothing a rumpled bed, while leaving the bumps in the mattress to sort themselves out.

With Lucy, it didn't work. The bed stayed rumpled. In fact, sweet reason only made her more angry. Finally I realised the truth. Lucy wanted me to fight her back. She wanted war. She lit the blue touch paper — and you had to explode! A brief, corrosive flare-up. Harsh, terrible, meaningless accusations.

Then she was in my arms, clinging to me, mouthing incoherent words into my chest in a muffled torrent of anguish and apology. I would feel the bitter tears dampen my shirt as I comforted her.

After that, our love-making always touched fresh heights, as we made it up in the only way we knew how.

'Lucy,' I said to her once. 'Do you realise the emotional gauntlet you make me run?'

'Is that what you call it?' she replied.

So we chose 'Enigma' as our aural sustenance, and to this day I sometimes still cry when I hear it. Because that mesmerising music became our own private litany of adventure — and love. And how do you ever forget anything like that?

*   *   *

So now we are in the final preparations. The countdown begins. Christmas is over, two days to go. In her flat, Lucy is going frantic.

'Arnie, we have to load the bags in exact order.'

At this point she's the boss. Perhaps she was all the time.

'Clothes at the bottom. Files in that case,' she says briskly, bravely keeping mounting hysteria out of her voice. But I can hear it. An endless year stretches ahead. Our whole life will be contained in those fourteen bags. Our survival kit.

She tells me: we cannot afford to miss out on a single misplaced letter of introduction to a ski resort that will be hosting us for a day, or a week.

She goes on packing, referring to the Master List we had compiled so painstakingly on the computer.

'No handkerchiefs, Arnie. They take up space. Take tissues — they're disposable.' Inarguable logic, though I would have preferred hankies.

'I shall call you Quarter Mistress,' I declared, bestowing an invisible medal on a humble, worthy recipient.

'Arnie, what are you talking about?' she inquired. 'You're in charge of the stores,' I told her.

The Quarter Mistress wrote out the final supply list and at last we were ready to go.

'Any famous last words?' I said, as I prepared to close the front door.

'Where's The Bear?' asked Lucy. He was safely packed.

The door slammed shut.

'We're on our way!' I said.

Chapter 4

New Year

*I learned to ski in a cabbage patch when I was thirteen
with the postman's son — the dashing Aimé
of the cornflower-blue eyes. I loved the towering, jagged
mountains, the deep-blue skies, the wine and the laughter,
as well as the aches and pains.*

Lucy Dicker, January 1994

tanley and Livingstone. Scott and Amundsen. Burton and Speake ... ' I sank back in the seat of the airliner that was taking us on the short hop to Jackson Hole from Salt Lake City, sniffling miserably into a tissue. '*Arnie and Lucy*. I wonder if they all felt like death on their first day?'

It was that cursed puddle outside Bourg St Maurice Station. I knew it. Now I was full of antibiotics, care of Lucy's ministering, as well as all the bacteria that had caused my embarrassing fadeout back in Dr Dua's surgery in West London.

30 December 1993. Two days to lift-off. We would spend the intervening time checking and rechecking our gear, giving interviews to local radio and TV stations and generally preparing ourselves for whatever fate had in store during the twelve months to come.

I stared down out of the window at white, craggy peaks,

those notorious 'shark's teeth' baring their fearsome fangs along the huge valley floor of Jackson Hole.

'Those early French pioneers,' I grumbled. 'They could have christened them *Aiguilles du Ciel* — "Needles in the Sky". That would have been nice. Or something dramatic like *Tour Infernale* — "Towering Inferno". But what do they call them? "Tits". Typical!'

'Typical of what?' said Lucy quickly.

I recognised early-warning signs. Was I about to insult the French? Although Lucy had deserted her homeland and was strongly pro-British, she could be quite defensive about her native France.

'Er — pioneers,' I said, retreating.'Typical of pioneers.' Not Frenchmen, certainly not, oh no, not in a million years. I felt too weak for battle. My throat was sore, and I had all the symptoms of bronchitis. What a way to start the trip.

Instead of sparring, I watched the small airfield slide up out of the mist blanketing some of the greatest skiing terrain on this earth.

Only the captain himself is permitted to land a jet at Jackson Hole. In fog, the runway at that airport is unnervingly on the short side, and those white-capped breasts loom far too close for comfort.

But we touched down with the briefest of thuds, and I turned and took Lucy's hand. 'Here we go,' I croaked hoarsely. 'Next stop, the *Guinness Book of Records*!'

'Why not?' she said. And meant it.

*   *   *

We arrived at the spectacular ski resort of Jackson Hole, Wyoming on a magical day, with champagne glasses at the ready. The vast valley floor was blindingly bright with fierce December sunshine glinting off fresh snow straight back into a cold blue sky. We will not be tempting fate on our first day by risking Jackson Hole's more intimidating runs. We gaze in awe for a few seconds at the vast valley floor. It's almost 1994. Our skiing odyssey is about to begin.

Financial Times

With fourteen items of luggage and two pairs of skis apiece trundling out of the carousel, we grabbed bag after bag, slinging them on to trolleys as fast as they came off the moving caterpillar. I wondered whether anyone thought we were stealing them all.

I was sweating already, and we hadn't left the Arrivals Hall. 'God, Lucy, we must have more stuff than the rest of the passengers put together.'

It had been a long flight from London via Dallas, all day chasing the sun, with a brief stopover at Salt Lake City before the one-hour hop to Jackson, and now I was aching all over. I couldn't wait to get to bed, with or without Lucy. Preferably with.

'Let's find the car.'

Avis had done us proud, though from Day One we had no idea what kind of rental car they would provide for us. The first of a whole fleet of vehicles we would use was sitting outside on the hard-packed snow. A Chevrolet Corsica saloon, brand new, gleaming as white as the peaks of the Tetons.

'Look!' Lucy gestured at the number plate. 'Registered in Idaho.'

Idaho, the Potato State. 'In that case,' I said, 'we'll call her Spud.'

And Spud she became, for the next 6,000 miles. Spud wasn't as spacious as we would have liked. We would have preferred a Jeep. But beggars, even nomadic ones, can't be choosers, so we filled every available inch of space with our fourteen bags. Lucy took control: first the boot, then the interior. She knew which bags would be in most demand, and placed them nearer the access point. Me, I was merely the camel.

'Where do you want this one?' I hefted the Ugly Bag her way.

'In there. Down by the spare wheel.' It fitted to perfection. I did a swift recount. Every bag in place.

'Darling, you are *formidable*!'

She turned and blew me a kiss.

We headed for the Teton Village Inn, just below the ski slopes. No guide or map necessary — I knew every snowy street and corner like a second home.

'Everyone has a spiritual home, Lucy, if they can only find it.' Jackson Hole was, and remains, mine.

The sun was settling over the Tetons in the west, painting the jagged peaks a glorious pink.

'Arnie, it's beautiful here,' said Lucy.

It could have been a film set. Driving through the colourful old Western streets towards the edge of town, I said, 'Wyoming is America's least-populated state.' I remembered hearing Alistair Cooke on the radio confirm it once. 'He suggested that the reason the crime rate is so low here is that there aren't enough people to form a gang!'

I got us to the hotel. And, for the first time, stumbled on a curious pattern that would dog us throughout the months ahead: why, oh why, did our rooms have to be the furthest away from the lifts, right at the end of the corridors and the hardest to locate? It became a familiar saga, then a joke.

'You go first, Lucy.'

And off she went, obediently lugging the first bags over the hard, crusty snow between the car and the foyer of the Teton Village Inn. I trailed behind. Then we went back again and again for all fourteen bags, four sets of skis, poles — and boots. By the time the last case was stacked in the foyer it looked as if a coach party had descended on the place, and I was out on my feet.

We checked in. We slept. In fact we fell into the king-size bed like zombies and slept the clock round.

'Arnie, it's ten o'clock!'

I stirred. And mumbled: 'Morning or evening?'

'Morning. We've been asleep for fourteen hours!' She shook me reproachfully. 'And you know — you never even said "Welcome to America".'

I was feeling marginally better.

'I think we can do something about that,' I said, reaching out to her from under the sheets.

Afterwards, I stroked her cheek, and smiled down at her.

'Frisky monkey,' she smiled back.

'Welcome to America!'

I realised with a jolt that tomorrow night would be New Year's Eve. For us, it was the eve of a year unlike any we had experienced before, or probably would ever experience again. There was so much at stake. So much we had planned for and dreamed about. So many imponderables that could wreck our plans without warning at any moment of the day or night. For the first time, I felt a shiver of apprehension.

Staring down at Lucy's hauntingly lovely face, in that moment I sensed that deep in her bones she felt the same frisson of unease. Perhaps it would lurk like a shadow within both of us all year — if we lasted the year. What had we got ourselves into?

Quite deliberately, I had pushed all thoughts of failure to the recesses of my mind. And kept them there.

'Jackson Hole,' said Lucy, lying back on her pillow. 'Tell me about it.'

There are so many stories.

I lie beside Lucy, our fingers entwined, and regale her with the story of how I met Bill Briggs, a living legend of the slopes, the first man to ski the noblest Teton of them all — the Grand.

*   *   *

On my first trip to Jackson Hole, Bill had limped up to me in the bar of the Stagecoach Inn at the nearby hamlet of Wilson (population: 201), where he sang with a rock band every

Sunday night, and ordered both of us a beer.

Bill Briggs, a prominent ski guide, had been born with a congenital hip problem. Later, doctors warned him that he would need a hip replacement and that he could say goodbye to his skiing career.

I couldn't help noticing his walk: he was in a slightly crouched position, his lower limbs curved in the bow-legged gait of an old Western gunfighter, as though he were riding an invisible horse.

Bill elaborated. 'The doctors told me that once they had set my new hips I would never be able to crouch in the skiing position again. Holy cow, I said to myself. Then I thought for a moment, and I had an idea. I told them: "Why can't you set my hips in a skiing crouch, instead of standing me up straight?" And that's just what they did.'

His decision was to write him into local folklore. One summer's day in 1971, Bill and two friends battled their way up the fearsome Grand Teton, which soars all of 13,770 feet, carrying their skis. Half-way up, the other two decided they had had enough.

'You go on down,' Bill told them. 'I want to get to the top.' It had become a personal challenge.

The others started climbing down. Briggs continued the climb solo, his skis on his shoulders, staggering through the snow to make it to the summit of the Grand Peak, the Everest of that entire great range. At the top, he struggled to put his boots into his skis. 'As fast as I managed to get one ski on, the other would start to slip away on its own,' he told me, over another beer. But finally he got them both on, and started his awe-inspiring descent. It took him four hours.

The way Bill tells it, he cartwheeled into ravines, lost a ski here and another one there, retrieved them, and lost them again when he spun into a *couloir*, a potentially lethal chute carved out of solid rock, one of the challenges extreme skiers enjoy.

Finally, breathless and almost fainting with fatigue, he made it down to the safety zone. The first man ever to ski the

Grand Teton.

Near the base, a couple walking their dog strolled by as Bill leaned on his poles, panting for breath.

'Been skiing?' the husband inquired.

'Sure have,' responded Bill.

'Where did ya go?'

'The Grand,' volunteered Bill, gulping in air.

'How high did ya get?'

'The top.'

'Yeah? How many times did ya ski it?'

'Just the once.'

'Oh,' said the visitors. 'Too bad!'

Yes, I wanted Lucy to meet Bill Briggs, Jackson Hole's favourite son, crouched slightly in a permanent ski posture. Later she would, and hear the story all over again.

'The way I see it, Arnie, it's not just the skiing. It's who we meet and how we meet them that's going to make this trip memorable.'

People like Bill.

'You know, Lucy, we should get a diary to record all the people we meet and keep our skiing statistics.'

'No, Arnie, we don't need one. We've got enough to carry.' This had all the hallmarks of another chains row.

'Lucy, I really think we should buy a proper diary. Next time you go to the shops, please will you try to get one.'

A strangled, exasperated cry from Lucy. Later that day, she came back into the room with bulging shopping bags.

Something heavy and black came hurtling across the room, just missing my head. 'There, Arnie. There's your bloody diary! Don't say I don't do what you want me to.'

But her scorn for the diary did not last long. As our adventures began to unfold, the much-maligned black tome became one of our most treasured possessions. And having begged her to buy it, I was eventually only allowed to 'borrow' it on pain of death if, God forbid, I mislaid it. Typical Lucy. Typical snake.

*　　　　*　　　　*

New Year's Eve. Midnight would soon strike and our great adventure would begin. Officially. We never heard it because we were sound asleep. We had retired early, though not through choice.

And, worse, not even for romantic reasons. It was that bad.

'God, Lucy, I feel terrible.'

My bronchitis had closed in again, my throat was on fire, and we had actually gone to bed at ten o'clock.

'What a way to start!' I let out a mock groan of anguish. 'Do you realise this is the first time in my adult life that I haven't seen the New Year in?'

'Darling Arnie,' she said, reaching for the throat lozenges. 'Me, too. But don't worry. It can only get better. Now go to sleep.'

'All right,' I said. 'See you next year.'

'Night, baby.'

My final thought as the lights went out in my head and in the valley was: 'I love this woman.'

Marvellous to relate, something happened between dusk and dawn that had me on my feet next morning like a spring robin, chirruping in the New Year with zest.

I walked around the room, slapping my naked midriff with flat hands. Slap-slap-slap!

'Arnie, stop that!' Lucy said from the pillow. 'I'm trying to sleep!'

'No time for that,' I said heartily.

Then I remembered how she, too, had been fading the night before, and so I sat down beside her and ran my fingers through the long red-gold hair, caressing her neck where the little golden curls nestled in tiny circles. I bent to kiss her ear, nibbled the lobe. She stirred in pleasure.

'Happy New Year, darling,' I said softly.

'You, too, beauty.'

She turned her head at last, and looked up at me with those

intense sea-green eyes. 'When do they want us?'

'Soon,' I said.

Lucy was short-sighted, though she strove to conceal it. She was also too vain to buy glasses, and refused to have anything to do with contact lenses. 'They might fall out in the snow, Arnie, and then where would I be?'

'Or in the red wine,' I said unhelpfully.

Then, as she glared at me: 'Just joking — '

Me, I was the other way. Far-sighted, old hawk-eyes himself — but I needed spectacles to read.

'And to drive, Arnie,' Lucy would say anxiously, more than once, which tended to irritate me. 'Please be careful.'

'I am careful,' I would reply testily. 'I need glasses to see the dashboard, not the bloody road.'

But she was never totally at ease.

'Anyway,' I added as an afterthought. 'How can you drive if you can't see twenty feet ahead of you?'

But somehow she could, even if she drove like every other Frenchman — and woman — I've known. Like a bat out of hell, in other words. But they call it style, and maybe they're right.

Oddly enough, Lucy would sometimes take the lead when we were in what I privately regarded as my domain — skiing in bad weather, struggling down a mist-shrouded slope in appalling conditions, or in heavy sleet. She could see the immediate terrain two or three yards in front of her, whereas I could not.

'We're due on the slopes in half an hour. For our first interview,' I told her now.

Over coffee and croissants in our room, I had a sudden thought. 'Tell me again where you first learnt to ski. They're bound to ask us that.' Lucy loved telling the story.

'My first experience on skis was in a cabbage patch in the French Basses Alpes.' Her eyes were laughing. 'I was thirteen, and I was taught to snow-plough by the postman's son. He was called Aimé — the dashing Aimé of the

47

cornflower-blue eyes.'

*   *   *

Our first big day turned out to be a *baptême de neige*. I couldn't shake off an irritating cough, which boded ill for any TV or radio interviews. Lucy looked as pale as goat's cheese, despite an intake of anti-biotics that should have sent every germ in the State scuttling for cover.

Our target was Rendezvous Mountain, a famous peak which boasts America's highest continuous vertical drop — the distance travelled by skiers descending from top to bottom of a run, in this case more than 4,000 feet. 4,139 feet to be precise.

We took the brightly painted cable car, its polished sides as cheery and cherry-red as the morning sun, packed with early enthusiasts, to head for the aptly-named Rendezvous mountain where we would meet our hosts and the waiting media. I put my arm around Lucy's shoulders, and kissed her.

'First day, Lucy.'

'First day, Arnie!'

'Let's make it a good one.'

Our woes fell behind us like dead leaves as another awe-inspiring view loomed into sight. The tree line fell away. In its place an uninterrupted vista stretched across the vast 600-square-mile valley to a mountain shrouded in white under the crystal clear blue sky. Resembling ... what?

'You tell me, Arnie.'

'Can you see it? A pot-bellied Indian Chief in full head-dress lying on his back.' Lucy squinted out of the window. 'They call it the Sleeping Indian. And the whole area is known as the Gros Ventre.'

In other words: 'Fat Stomach'. Amazing, isn't it, what one's imagination can conjure up! And you don't have to be a pioneering French trapper, either.

'Over here, Arnie. Look!'

Lucy had rubbed her gloved fingers to clear a look-out hole in the iced-up window. I peered through. She was pointing into the jaws of one of the more terrifying aberrations that nature has invented. If you intend to ski it, that is.

'Ah,' I said. I kept forgetting it was her first visit to the regal Tetons of Jackson Hole. 'You're looking at Corbet's Couloir.'

Lucy shivered. 'It looks impossible!'

From the warm safety of the cable car we stared out at a sight that has caused more skiers to turn and trudge away, shaking their heads, than any other drop I know in twenty years of pursuing this crazy, wonderful sport.

There are others. But Corbet's Couloir is special. Designed by a quirk of nature for skiers to risk their necks in search of the ultimate thrill.

Imagine an enormous whale's mouth, a great hollow carved out of solid rock by storm, tempest, wind and ice. To ski Corbet's, you simply leap into the void — starting with a jump of at least twelve feet, and up to twenty feet if you choose the alternative point of entry. Plummeting into deep snow, hopefully with nerve and limbs intact, you must turn immediately to avoid slamming into the bare rock face before hurtling off down a slope of forty degrees, some of it even steeper.

Yes, strictly for extreme skiers.

Or people like me, with more bravado than sense.

'That's one you won't be skiing today,' I said firmly, and for once Lucy didn't attempt to argue. 'Maybe when we come back next year. Don't let's tempt fate.'

The lift-operator's voice broke in, stilling the hubbub in the crowded cable car.

'If I could have your attention for a moment, please.' He was a young man with long hair under a blue woolly hat. An ex-college kid perhaps, on a winter job before going back to a dreary office. It wouldn't earn him a lot of money. But fresh air, fun and free skiing draws them like a magnet to the slopes, and most of them get hooked for life.

'All runs down from the top of the tram are for expert skiers only. Visibility is good. There may be unmarked obstacles, so ski with caution at all times. For anyone who does not want to ski down, there will be a tram leaving every fifteen minutes. Thank you, and enjoy the skiing.'

'I wonder how many people take one look at that,' Lucy nodded through the window again, 'and say, "No thanks, I'm going home!"'

'You mean chicken out? A few. I don't blame them. But there are easier runs from the top.'

Corbet's had haunted me for years. On every trip I made to Jackson Hole I had ridden that same bright red cable car, emerged at the top, and skied gingerly up to the single rope that was stretched across the rim of the ravine. Then I would duck under the frozen cord and stand on the very lip of the drop that yawned beneath me before daring even to look down into it. That's when you feel your heart stop.

For five successive winters I tried to respond to nature's challenge. But I had never picked up the gauntlet.

What is so beguiling about Corbet's is that it is possible for any good skier, but only just. Unlike the lethal S & S Couloir which lurks just around the corner, with a thirty-foot initial leap that renders it out of reach for all recreational skiers, Corbet beckons, flirts, mocks and dares.

Four years earlier, on my forty-sixth birthday, I had finally faced the grinning demon, and dived off into the abyss. The rest of my plunge down this precipice remains a blur to this day. The jolting thud of my skis landing in the snow, burying themselves out of sight in deep powder. The rock face roaring up at me. Instinct taking over, as I threw myself to the right, away from the faces pressed to the window of the cable car above.

On I went, tumbling all the way down, until I finally slithered to a halt, covered in snow from head to toe like a circus clown after a flour fight. My relief was tangible. Relief that I had survived. Relief that I had finally, although not very elegantly, jumped into Corbet's. Now I would have to climb all the way up again to ski it properly.

But at least I had conquered a demon that had haunted me for five long years.

Except that now, there is another demon ...

*   *   *

God, Lucy's falling. She's going! Stop her, someone! STOP HER!

*   *   *

'No, Lucy, I don't think we'll try Corbet's today.' The cable car swung into its moorings and clattered to a halt.

'Arnie, Lucy — hi! I'm Dave. From Radio Jackson.' In the small snack bar, a young, fresh-faced fellow rose from a table.

'Happy New Year! Over here. We're all set up.' He led the way to a side room, where a portable tape recorder and two plastic chairs awaited us. Three or four other men made themselves known, led by John Resor, the resort's chief executive, and including a photographer from the *Jackson Hole Daily*.

'Lucy,' I said. 'We are about to become famous.'

Famous, that is, if you count fame as a few thousand listeners. I imagined them glued to their sets across the valley before old Fat Stomach, the Sleeping Indian belly up, promptly cuts off the radio waves like an invisible portcullis coming down. Sorry, fellers, end of show.

Meantime, Dave had switched on the machine. 'So, hi, Arnie. Hi, Lucy. You two guys are skiing the world?'

'That's the plan,' I said cautiously.

'Wow. Isn't that something? And are you going to get married on the way?'

Silence. A long one.

In radio terms, it's called 'dead air', when something

should be happening and someone should be saying something — and isn't.

'Er — '

Lucy and I looked at each other. We had discussed it, of course. But not often. When we had, we had both become curiously defensive. Finally we had come to an agreement (unwritten) that at this stage of our lives neither of us thought that marriage would enhance our relationship. Or our progress round the world. Between us, we had been married three times already, and we were both aware that marriage can sometimes be the kiss of death for — 'Well, for romance, Lucy.'

She agreed, sort of. But although we both went along with it, in my heart I knew that I was going to marry this girl some day, somehow. When all this was over, and we could get our heads together and think straight. Because right now I could only think about what our crazy, wonderful love affair and this whole eccentric, wonderful Mission Impossible was all about: romance.

Could we risk ruining it? Dave was looking inquiringly at us, his finger poised above the Pause button. The silence reverberated all the way down the valley to the comfortable curves of Fat Stomach, and all the way back again. No doubt Dave would edit it out.

Aloud I said: 'We'll let you know when we're here again,' I smiled at him. 'This time next year.'

'Well, good luck.' Dave's own smile radiated encouragement. 'You folks have a good time. By the way — '

'Yes?'

'How much is this trip costin' you?'

COST? MARRIAGE? These were both questions we would get asked, inevitably, again and again. But this first time I wasn't ready for it, and answered without thinking.

'I don't know exactly. But around $400,000, at a guess.' I'd plucked the figure out of thin air.

Actually, if we'd paid for everything, it was probably even more.

At last, interviews over, we skied. First we cruised a little, gently, down one of Jackson's signature runs, Rendezvous Trail. Then, against our better judgement, we began to speed up. With a powerful skier like John Resor, you don't hang about. The chill early morning air whistled into our faces as we started hurtling down the slopes, floating, diving, jetting and snaking our way across the glistening white arena, tiny flecks of snow tingling in our lungs, the vast valley floor shimmering below us in the wintry Wyoming sunshine. This was skiing at its most exhilarating and effervescent. This was why we were here.

Let me tell you about powder.

There is nothing like it. Skiing fresh powder is an extraordinary sensation, which I can only liken to floating through a soft sea of white foam. The powder rushes up at you, exploding in little whispering spindrifts over your legs and body. First, ankles disappear into the feathery snow. Then the feathers envelop you up to your knees. If you're lucky and it's really deep, the powder sometimes creeps up to your waist ... under your elbows ... and all the way up to your armpits! Get your rhythm and your balance right, which is not easy, and you actually find yourself skiing in slow motion. The deeper the powder, the more it slows you down. And you're floating, an astronaut doing a space walk.

Sometimes that seductive white blanket even covers your face — and when that happens, it's a supreme moment! And you turn, and turn again, deep and steep, carving your own special signature through the snow, in a surreal world of your own.

But for all our joy, on paper, it wasn't a very good day. Our diary shows that we only skied four runs: just 6.8 miles on our ski-dometers. Vertical feet: a rather disappointing 6,770. But then we were feeling pretty groggy. And it was a start.

That night, I made a confession.

'Lucy, I have to tell you something.'

'What?' Her face on the pillow, suddenly anxious.

I reached over and cupped her chin in my hands. 'I always imagined that if ever I did this, I would be doing it alone. My skiing Odyssey. My personal Pilgrim's Progress. And then a beautiful French woman called Lucy Dicker came into my life, and the whole idea seemed even more remote.'

'Why, Arnie?'

'Well. She was ten years younger than me, a career girl with her life mapped out, or so I thought. And leaving her behind, I mean — a whole year away ... ' My voice trailed off.

She nestled more firmly in my arms, and nibbled gently at my ear.

'Aren't you glad you didn't leave her behind?'

'Yes,' I said. 'I'm very glad. In fact, I'm deliriously happy that she's here!'

> *Swooshing down a mountain near Santiago, Chile and then jetting off to the slopes of New Zealand may sound like an exotic vacation, but for one long-time skier, it's just a way to suffer through mid-life. 'I want to tell the world that Arnie Wilson is not too old at 50 to do active things,' said Wilson, who, in Jackson Hole, Wyoming yesterday kicked off a 365 day skiing expedition around the world. 'It's probably a mid-life crisis.' Wilson and his travelling companion, Lucy Dicker will span 5 continents, 13 countries and 18 time zones during their year-long adventure. 'I suppose I'm a ski fanatic,' Wilson said. 'Whether I'll still be at the end of the year, I don't know.'*

> The *Jackson Hole Daily*
> Sunday 2 January 1994

*   *   *

'Next stop, Pebble Creek, Lucy!' Unlike Jackson, and Sun Valley where we were due to arrive on Day 4, neither of us had ever heard of Pebble Creek, or its neighbour Pomerelle, until we had virtually picked them out with a pin from the White Book.

As we left Jackson, gales were sweeping snow across the highway. One hour out of town, we were lost.

'I said we should have turned left,' said Lucy from the passenger seat. It was the first of many, many arguments among the pilot and co-pilot on the flight deck.

I peered grimly through the windscreen, past the wipers swishing the swirling snow away, and on down the highway that should be taking us into Idaho.

The steep and daunting Teton Pass was behind us. We had made it across in a virtual blizzard, and finally hit a T-junction. And turned east instead of west.

'I don't believe this,' Lucy's head was bent over the road map.

At least she wasn't smug about it.

'I wish I knew where the damn sun was,' I muttered. 'At least we'd know if we were going the right way.'

*   *   *

We had skied that morning, bright and early, in crisp cold sunlight on crisp cold snow. Only four runs, but enough to justify our personal pledge that we wouldn't cheat, and it also notched up a few more thousand vertical feet.

We had lugged our fourteen cases (and the rest) along endless corridors and out to Spud in the car park, which eventually coughed into life.

Leaving Jackson Hole that morning had been like fleeing a warm, familiar nest. Lucy turned and watched the last wooden shack slide past out of sight. My own thoughts turned to Alan Ladd, hunched in the saddle, trotting his horse out of town and into screen legend.

'They say he was shot, and probably dying,' I said.

'Who, Arnie?'

'*Shane*,' I said. 'They filmed it here, remember? There was always a mystery about that ending. Had he been shot, or not?'

'What do you think, Arnie?'

'He'd been shot,' I said. 'That's what it was all about.'

Lucy always maintained she had an excellent sense of direction. '*C'est épatant*, Arnie!'

I looked the word up. *Épatant*: perfect, splendid, capital, staggering. Super, in fact. Well — she would say that, wouldn't she?

Throughout the ensuing months we would have numerous spirited discussions on the subject, usually when we were stuck at a crossroads, or on a remote mountain pass as dusk descended, arguing over a map.

For two supposedly seasoned travellers, it is painful to admit how hopeless we could be.

Thus, at the cross-roads into the Potato State, I had sent Spud hurtling in the wrong direction.

'Pebble Creek is *here*!' Lucy jabbed an irate navigator's finger at the map. 'And we are *here*!' A sign had just flashed by. 'Arnie, we are sixty miles off course, going the wrong way — and there are three television crews waiting for us!'

I was aware of it.

'Lucy, you're supposed to be the bloody navigator, for Christ's sake!'

'There's no need to swear, Arnie.'

A swift U-turn took care of the compass, and we were heading back down the road to Pebble Creek. For the next two hours, we didn't speak. By the time we were in Pebble Creek, daylight was fading, and the TV crews were packing up to go home.

'Sorry, fellers. There was a snowstorm back there — '

'That's okay.' Americans are refreshingly breezy and laid back about this sort of thing. The crews, in lumberjack shirts and leather jackets, posed us against the mountain background, pointing their shoulder cameras.

We were dog-tired, the lifts were closing, and it was almost too late to ski. We did one descent for the cameras.

'Ready to roll? Right, let's do it.'

At the bottom, I went hurtling into some netting — an undignified end to the day captured on video and duly screened throughout Idaho that night. Lucy chuckled. She, too, had fallen, but the cameras missed it.

*   *   *

Pebble Creek turns out to be run by a former psychiatric nurse and her husband, a psychiatrist. We are booked into the Riverside Inn. Dogs are welcome in this hotel. There is a notice in the lobby:

> *We never had a dog that smoked in bed and set*
> *fire to the blankets. We never had a dog that*
> *stole our towels, played the TV too loud or had*
> *a noisy fight with his travelling companion. We*
> *never had a dog that got drunk and broke up the*
> *furniture. So if your dog can vouch for you,*
> *you're welcome too.*

'Are we guests, or patients?' Lucy mutters, as they hand us the key over the counter.

'Do you reckon they've got a lamp-post for a loo?'

And we laugh all the way to our kennel.

Next morning, in the breakfast room, I feel light-hearted. Eggs over-easy, crisp bacon, toast, coffee. No sign of a dog biscuit.

We check out and take our loyal, over-laden Spud to Pomerelle, one of America's least-known resorts, and Sun Valley, one of its most famous.

'Let's make this our New Year's Eve!' I said.

We stood together in the snow, hand in hand, outside the

floodlit Sun Valley Opera House. Huge snowflakes drifted lazily out of the night sky, lit by myriad fairy lights that turned them into soft white feathers.

Lucy tilted her face up in child-like wonder, allowing the flakes to settle on her.

'Snow Goose!' I said teasingly, and kissed a feather from her forehead.

'Come on, Lucy, let's meet Glenn Miller!'

The sounds of *Chatanooga Choo-Choo* filtered out from the Opera House. Inside, I knew, they were screening for the zillionth time the 1941 black-and-white musical *Sun Valley Serenade* to a scattered audience. It was as regular as your old Saturday morning children's matinées, the timeless golden oldie that put the resort on the world map and made an international name for the blonde Norwegian ice skater Sonja Henie.

'Fifty years on, and they still play it,' I said, as we took our seats inside the old building. There must have been all of ten people with us. 'The locals are very proud of it, and regard it as important for tourism. I think they look on it as their film.'

'How many times have you seen it?'

'About a million. Could be two. It was nominated for two Academy Awards. One for that song, one for the photography.'

Lucy hadn't even heard of the film, let alone seen it. But she was much taken by the simple story of a band manager affording sanctuary to a glamorous, if naïve, Norwegian ice star. 'Well, they deserve it.'

Afterwards we strolled by the ice rink which features in the film. Children wrapped up in woolly hats and scarves twirled and pirouetted like small dolls to the sounds of Glenn Miller. 'Pardon me, boy ... is that the Chattanooga Choo-Choo?'

'Magic,' I said. 'Now you're going to meet some more celebrities.'

In the piano bar of the Sun Valley Lodge, I introduced her to Clark Gable, Gary Cooper, Marilyn Monroe, Judy Garland

and a host of old friends.

'Well, they feel like old friends,' I told her as she surveyed the incredible display on the pine walls of America's Grand Dame of ski resort hotels. The faces of the famous, and occasionally infamous, stared down at us from their silver frames, lining the bar and the long museum-like corridors.

An hour before, we had arrived from Pomerelle after an incident-free drive, having taken the usual precaution of an early-morning ski before breakfast. Just in case. You never knew if a pass would be blocked, if Spud would be in a bad mood and refuse to start, or, worst of all, if we came off the road and couldn't get back on the highway. At least we'd have our skis with us, I reasoned. So if one of us were injured, the other could go for help.

We had located the condominium where we were staying for two nights and ducked through the snow to check in. Our room shrank visibly as we piled our fourteen bags in it, leaving pathways through the stacked impedimenta like a jungle trail.

The manager, a willing young man who had escorted us to the second floor — furthest as ever from the elevator — handed us the key, and grinned.

'Moving house, folks?'

I slumped back on the bed, and spoke to his departing back.

'No, we're just bag ladies!'

Now we were looking forward to a romantic dinner. 'How about the main restaurant here in the Lodge, Lucy?' I suggested.

'No, Arnie, let's not. I don't feel like getting dressed up. I'm tired.'

A quick shower, and we had changed into casual *après-ski* gear, sweaters and slacks, just right for an evening in a ski resort, unless you aim to spend that particular evening in the historic Sun Valley Lodge.

This was the place that made its name in the thirties as the super-plush magnet for Hollywood stars, big-time producers, millionaires, moguls, politicians, the odd gangster or two, and assorted celebrities and café society hangers-on when they wanted somewhere to unwind.

They came and went by train, and it must have been one great party. The hotel, secreted away from prying eyes amid rambling lawns and pines, became a national shrine to wealth and glamour, and eventually a national monument to past glories.

And it still looks that way today.

We looked around at the ornate chandeliers, thick pile carpet and polished finery of this most elegant of all the places we would set foot in during the whole of our travels.

I felt as out of place as a rusty hub cap on a Rolls Royce.

Worse, I knew Lucy felt the same.

'That's okay, Arnie — ' She squeezed my hand. 'Don't worry. But I wouldn't mind a peek into the restaurant. We don't have to eat there.'

'Do you know,' I had remembered something else, 'they even refused Robert Kennedy entry into the dining-room, when he turned up in a polo neck? Even though he was wearing a jacket — and he was Attorney General!'

'When was that?'

'Twenty years ago.'

'Maybe times have changed — '

'I doubt it.' I finished my beer. 'All right, let's take a quick look.'

From the doorway, we peered into the restaurant. Soft candle-light washed over a scene from another era. A live six-piece band was playing *I've Got You Under My Skin*. Couples moved sedately on the dance floor under the gleaming chandeliers. Outside the windows, snow was still falling as if it would never stop. Nostalgia reigned, and the ghosts of the past were there too, looking on with benign approval. I could feel them.

Through the candle light, the dinner-jacketed figure of the

Maître d' approached.

'*Bonsoir M'sieur, Madame* — '

Lucy took over. '*Bonsoir*,' she said brightly. Then added a few choice words in French.

Three minutes later we were seated at the best table in the room, close to the dance floor.

'How did you do that?' I managed to stutter, as the Maître d', after personally ushering Lucy into her seat, snapped his fingers at a passing waiter, and called for champagne. For us. Lucy had ordered it.

The Maître d' was back, waving two large and impressive (and expensive-looking) menus.

'I'm afraid we haven't changed for dinner — ' I began. He waved my apologies away.

'Please,' he said.'It is not every day ... ' casting a fond fellow-countryman's look at Lucy, 'that we can welcome someone from Marseilles! My home town. My name is Claude Giguon — and the champagne is on the house!'

'What on earth — ?' I began again, as he waltzed off to attend to the needs of another table.

'Ssh!' Lucy lifted a finger to her lips. 'I told him it was our special New Year's Eve. Well — it is, isn't it?'

And, as if by telepathy, the band struck up *What Are You Doing on New Year's Eve?*

'I know what I'm doing,' Lucy declared. 'I'm spending the best evening of my life!'

She nudged my arm. 'Look, Arnie!'

I reluctantly took my eyes away from the menu, and temptations like duck á l'orange and the local rainbow trout. Lucy was gesturing at the dance floor.

'Aren't they wonderful?'

Up to that point, I hadn't looked closely. Now I did, and saw an elderly couple swaying together as if they were one person, making the dance floor their own private palace where, for a few supreme, delicious moments, they were king and queen. They must have been in their seventies, but they danced like youngsters. He was in black tie, she was in a flowing pink cocktail dress. His lined face under a healthy thatch of white hair was lost in his own private dreams, reflecting her seraphic smile as they swirled past our table.

Lucy breathed: 'Oh, Arnie, isn't that wonderful? They're so in love.' Her eyes shone in the candle light.

Later, Claude would confide: 'They come every year — to dance, not to ski. For this same week, every year, as long as I have been here. I like to think maybe they are lovers ... ' He glided away.

'Why not?' I said, and raised my glass. 'Happy New Year, Lucy!'

'Happy New Year, Arnie!'

Chapter 5

January

Arnie, if we ever part, will you go on loving me?

Lucy Dicker, February 1994

I had rather shamelessly driven Spud into the small town of Ketchum, not far from Sun Valley, and one-time home of Ernest Hemingway. I knew that Clint Eastwood liked skiing, liked this whole area, and particularly liked the Pioneer Inn. It was his favourite watering-hole.

Everyone in Ketchum knows the Pioneer, and we only had to ask one person to find it. The Inn turned out to be a bungalow built in Western style, its flat roof thick with fresh snow, set back off the road with a wagon wheel outside and a great log fire crackling away inside. There was a barbecue glowing red behind the counter, an intimate atmosphere, and an aroma of burning fish that instantly activated my taste buds.

'Trout and salmon from the lakes and rivers,' I said, studying the menu. 'House speciality.'

To the waitress who had handed us the menus, I inquired: 'Any sign of Mr Eastwood?'

'You mean Clint? He hasn't been in yet this week.' She looked over at the far corner. 'That's his table, but we ain't seen him. Heard he's around, though.'

Well, that was encouraging.

'Heard Arnie's comin' into town, though,' she added.

'Arnie?' I sat up.

Could the advance publicity have preceded us?

'Arnie Schwarzenegger,' said the waitress deflatingly. She pulled out her pad. 'Care to order? Trout's special tonight, barbied with almonds.'

Next morning, bright and early, we met up again with Claude Giguon, our new-found friend last seen bowing us out from the chandelier-hung restaurant at The Lodge, to the strains of *My Way*.

Claude had booked us in for the personal guided tour of his latest restaurant — the man seemed to have a finger in every important pie in the entire valley.

'But this one is *very* special. My pride and joy.'

This one turned to be the Seattle Ridge Lodge, a brand new restaurant perched by the mid-station with a commanding vista of shining peaks and snow-shrouded forest slopes.

I paused on the threshold to look at the view. 'Now that is something!'

'That's why I'm here, Arnie. I used to ski regularly back home — but here, I never have!'

'You've never skied in Sun Valley?' Lucy shared my incredulity. We were both in our purple Degré 7 suits, ready for the slopes. I noticed for the first time that under his dark green anorak Claude was in a sweater and slacks. And fur-lined moon boots.

'On my first day, fourteen years ago, I took my skis up the mountain with every intention of skiing. But when I got to the mountain restaurant ... ' He gestured up to the high slopes a further 2,000 feet above us — 'they needed help, because there were many visitors. I stayed the rest of the day. Late in the afternoon, as I was putting on my skis to descend, they said: "Why don't you ride the chair down with us? It's such a wonderful view." I did, and it was beautiful. And ever since then, I've gone down the mountain on the lift, and that is how I get my happiness.'

He shrugged his Gallic shoulders. 'That was fourteen years ago, and I've never skied since!'

Lucy and I looked at one another, then out across the valley.

'Claude,' I said, 'I see what you mean.'

He pushed open the heavy wooden doors for us. 'There's a table waiting,' he said. 'I'll see you later. Have fun.'

Inside, noise. A lot of it. Clattering dishes. Shouts from the kitchen that would swell and fade in waves of sound as the swing doors flew open and shut. The scrape of trays. And always the heavy clumping of ski boots as everyone behaved like Neil Armstrong on his first day on the moon, robotically lumbering between the tables, clutching drinks.

We were shown to our table. I ordered two Bloody Marys, and picked up the menu.

Lucy hadn't moved. In fact, she was sitting unnaturally still. I followed her gaze, which was frozen like a startled rabbit caught in headlights. And, at the next table, became aware of steely blue eyes boring into me. Clint Eastwood's steely blue eyes. I looked away. Then back. Yes, it was. He was in a light blue ski outfit, sitting with another man who would turn out to be the owner of a local restaurant.

Two Bloody Marys later, I said abruptly, 'I've got to say hello to him.' I stood up.

'No, Arnie. You can't — !' Lucy grabbed at my sleeve, but missed. Her cheeks were reddening in a rare blush.

I stepped across the chasm that separated us, and stood by his table. The remains of a large T-Bone steak littered his plate.

'Mr Eastwood,' I said, and paused. I mean, what do you say to a movie star that he hasn't heard a million times already?

I thought of it. 'We're skiing the world, my girlfriend and myself — ' I gestured back without looking at Lucy's chair, where I hoped she was still sitting and hadn't slumped off on to the floor. 'I just wanted to say hello to you.'

'Skiing the world?' The familiar lazy drawl. 'Now that sounds exciting. Tell me about it.'

I beckoned Lucy over, and she joined us with an embarrassed smile, pinker than usual.

The big man bestowed a craggy smile on her. 'You too?'

I could almost see Lucy's heart thumping under her sweater. But in seconds she had recovered her composure, and answered him in that voice that I had never known any man to resist. And when it came to Lucy's accent, Clint Eastwood was no different from ordinary mortals.

'You're from France?'

'From Provence.'

'*Ah, bon*!' God, the man was talking her language. He let loose with an impressive stream of French dialogue, not a word of which I understood.

He then apologised. 'I'm sorry. That's the only French I know!'

And he grinned like a sheepish schoolboy caught cheating at the back of the class.

Later, I said: 'God, Lucy, what was all that about? You looked slightly shocked.'

'That, Arnie, I would call "Foreign Legion French".'

'You mean rude?'

'Pretty rude, Arnie. But it didn't bother me.'

In Anglais, we told Clint Eastwood about our great odyssey. He listened intently, then wanted to know all about South America.

'I've heard the skiing's good down there. I've always wanted to ski in Chile. Can you recommend it?'

We said we'd let him know!

Our steaks arrived far too soon.

Before he left, he signed our lift pass. To Arnie and Lucy. And wished us luck.

Later, through the window, we watched his tall, rangy frame ski elegantly off into the sunset.

'That man skis like he rides a horse,' I said. 'With style.'

Lucy turned on me. 'Arnie, I don't know how you could just go up to him like that!' But secretly, I knew, Clint had made her day.

*   *   *

The town of Ashland, Oregon is celebrated for its Shakespearian festivals.

The local book store has an entire department specialising in the works of the Bard, and the town's three Elizabethan theatres are busy in rehearsal when we arrive.

'Look, Arnie — the names of the ski runs. They're nearly all from Shakespeare's plays!'

They were, too!

Well, Lucy does have A-level English. She knows her Shakespeare.

'To ski or not to ski?' I said.

'No question,' said Lucy. 'We have to!'

So we ski runs like Romeo, its neighbour Juliet, and even an off-piste area called Ado!

'Can you find Hamlet?' I search my pocket map of the area.

'If skiing be the food of love, Lucy — ski on!'

And I *did* fall in love in Ashland.

Not, of course, with another woman, but with a mountain.

We suddenly saw it, a breathtaking, towering solitary cone of a peak, which seemed to be bathed in mystique, and looked enormously powerful even on the distant horizon, perhaps a hundred miles away.

'My God, Lucy. Just look at that!'

'It's amazing, Arnie. Where is it?'

'Looks like it must be across the border into California.'

We asked its name.

It was Shasta. *Mount* Shasta.

'Lucy, we've just *got* to ski there.'

'It's not on the schedule, Baby.'

'*It is now.*'

*   *   *

We invented the Body Count Game. It was a way of passing the time on the innumerable chair-lifts we took to transport us to the higher peaks during our relentless trek across North America.

Lucy liked it not one bit.

'Arnie, it's so cruel!'

'Well, it is a bit unkind,' I acknowledged.

But great fun, all the same.

The Game went like this: there are always a lot of beginners at any resort, particularly on the nursery slopes, and from our vantage point we could watch them falling around like ninepins. Then came the joys of seeing a show-off or merely an enthusiast who had jumped one mogul too many, and paid the price.

So ... we climb into the quad lift at the base area, and lay bets on how many skiers we would spot measuring their length in the snow before we reached the top station.

'I reckon fourteen, Lucy.'

'Just because you don't fall as much as they do! It's very arrogant of you, Arnie.' She squints through her dark glasses at the icy slopes. 'All right, I'll say nine.'

And as another yell drifts up from below our moving feet, followed by an explosive puff of snow, I would triumphantly count it off. 'Hey, there goes another one!'

'I hope he's all right,' Lucy, anxious, craning her neck to look back.

Usually I tended to exaggerate the numbers, while my caring companion was always on the conservative side. Make of that what you will, but an analyst could probably write a thesis on it.

One resort where the Body Count proved particularly useful as an antidote to boredom was Mount Bachelor, in

Oregon. Like Shasta, it is an extinct volcano whose cone-shaped peak normally permits a complete 360-degrees of challenging skiing. There are four high-speed quad chair-lifts that cut down the waiting time and, mercifully, the time you are exposed to the high winds that can whip around this tempestuous mountain.

There is also the Rainbow Chair. Old Faithful was the original two-seater chair-lift, the most reliable in the entire State. It was also the slowest, and regarded as something of an ancient monument to impatient modern skiers. The ski school director Ken Klecker described it as 'a lift forgotten by time'. But the Rainbow had its uses, and one of them was as a moving office for Mr Klecker. 'It's so slow I take my paperwork up the mountain,' he told us, handing us our ski passes for the day. 'By the time I get to the top I've finished all the book-keeping, and I can go skiing.'

That day fierce winds had closed the top mountain area, and that meant the quads too. So Old Faithful it was. It was slow, but we persisted.

'Arnie, we did 18,260 vertical feet today!' Lucy sat on the bed, bent over the diary.

Next door, soaking in the tub, I called back: 'Not bad for such a grim day!'

Above the soothing suds of a bubble bath, I could see her reflection in the mirror, studiously scribbling. You couldn't fault the meticulous way she went about it. Two columns, one giving the day's figures, the other the grand total, growing by the hour.

'And how many miles did we do?'

'Almost seventeen!'

Seventeen was good. Well, not bad. It was better than the minimum ten miles we had set ourselves, but less than I would have liked. Ten minimum. Our personal target was twenty. It was vital to have a mileage piggy-bank to make up for lost days when we might only cram in one obligatory run of maybe a few hundred yards in order to make the next resort

— or continent — on time.

Ski the World!

We're trying, we're trying.

The black diary included Miles Driven, Number of Resorts Skied, Number of Runs. Also the names of people we'd met, and TV and radio interviews we'd given. Even a daily Gary Larson 'Far Side' cartoon.

And Falls. Lucy had pulled a face. 'I'll have far more than you, Arnie. You're a much better skier. That's probably why you're doing it!'

Maybe some little imp was at work.

'No, honestly, it's not that,' I assured her. 'I just think it'll be fun to look back on afterwards, that's all.'

'Well — all right, then,' she said. 'But I'm still not happy about it.'

'So, what constitutes a fall?'

'You tell me, Arnie.'

Being a compulsive statistician, I analysed it.

'If you lose your balance and touch the snow with your hands, is it a fall?'

She shrugged.

'Look, that's all right. It's not a fall. I don't want to be a referee. But if you *do* fall and I don't see it, will you tell me?'

'I will, Arnie.'

On the second day, her zip broke. It was the orange one-piece suit, and neither of us had really liked the colour anyway. It was supposed to be *FT* Pink, but it looked more bilious orange, and her squeal: 'Oh God, Arnie — my zip!' halfway down the piste clinched it. Lucy had to hold it together with one hand to preserve her modesty and prevent the draught. Gratefully, we ditched the suit.

She grew happier by the minute as the weeks went by. In fact, Lucy's skiing had improved dramatically, every day, in a way neither of us could have foreseen. Though I suppose it was inevitable that if you ski every day, often all day, you have to improve. It meant she fell less — at first. Then, as her

70

confidence improved and she began to take chances, the falls increased — but it didn't matter. Her streak of adventure started showing through the original veneer of caution like rock you glimpse under melting ice.

Lucy had been bitten by the skiing bug, and from now on it would become a growing obsession. Starting with small signs. 'Come on, Arnie. We're running late. We should be out on the slopes by now!'

'Lucy, you're insatiable. Just let me finish my breakfast, will you?'

*   *   *

Mount Shasta started flirting with us when we were still 100 miles away — her massive white cone surged up unexpectedly in the distance, beckoning through valleys, disappearing for long periods of time and suddenly looming up through forests of pine.

Like a huge, white, beached whale, she dominated the skyline as we approached. Although this magnificent volcano is now dormant, it still emanates a powerful and irresistable attraction.

Even the names of nearby roads and mountains seemed to contribute to Shasta's mystique.

'Look, Arnie, we're at Dead Horse Summit!'

The name obviously amused her.

The view from here was stunning. And from Sheep Dream Road, even more so.

'Do you think sheep count humans when they're trying to get to sleep, Lucy?'

'Silly monkey!'

It was a very Larson-esque thought.

Mount Shasta Ski Park turned out not to be on the mountain at all. An earlier version of the ski area was on the lower flanks of the ancient volcano, but it closed in 1978 when a huge avalanche destroyed the lifts. The present ski area was built in 1984.

For a moment or two we felt disappointment at not being able to reach Shasta's shimmering slopes. On reflection, it might have spoiled the mysticism to have succeeded in skiing on this untouchable mountain.

As it is, Shasta provides an amazing backdrop to the ski area.

The avalanche which swept away the old lifts may have been the vengeance of the gods — the mountain, one of the world's seven sacred peaks, is steeped in legend and myth.

I read to Lucy from a book I'd bought about the mountain's fascinating history.

'Look, Lucy, Shasta's supposed to be inhabited by a race of Von Daniken-type creatures eight feet tall with a single eye planted in the middle of their foreheads!'

'Very nice!' said Lucy, fixing me with her own big green eye, flashing ridicule in my general direction.

'And listen to this — one of the locals here, a guy from Weed, the town we just drove through, claimed he was abducted by these creatures and given a tour of the inside of the mountain.'

'Hah!' said Lucy. 'Maybe they'd give us a tour of the ski area.'

'It might be worth it, Lucy. This guy claims to have seen vast quantities of gold and other priceless treasures hidden in the mountain.'

Shasta is big — 14,162 feet. No wonder we could see it from such a distance.

*   *   *

We had pet names for each other.

She called me — wait for it — Beauty. Yes, Beauty. Why? God knows, I certainly don't. But all the things I hated about my body, Lucy seemed to love.

'You're the beauty around here,' I told her, and I wasn't fishing for compliments. 'My legs are like tree trunks — '

Top left: No wonder she grew up to be an aggressive driver!

Above: At fifteen, Lucy in a sultry mood.

Middle left: Friends for a change: Lucy and her brother Maurice.

Bottom left: In the making – my 'lovely big legs' that Lucy admired so much.

Top left: Lucy with her first husband, Bob Collins.

Top right: Femme fatale.

Middle right: Lucy's love affair with the camera continued.

Bottom left: At 19, Lucy became a dizzy blonde but soon reverted to her favourite auburn hair.

Bottom right: Me as a young footballer! Half-time for the captain of the team at Friends' School, Saffron Walden. (Lucy was nine when this was taken).

Top left: Lucy loved cats. Her favourite was called Lucky.

Top right: The Richaud family: Maurice, Lulu, Marcelle, and, behind them, Lucy.

Bottom: The boss of Touralp shows Frank Bough around her Knightsbride HQ.

Top: Lucy looking coquettishly French during a blissful holiday together in Barbados in 1992.

Bottom: My favourite picture of us, taken with an automatic exposure in Barbados.

Top: Will Carling and I work out at the Bimal Clinic in West London.

Bottom: Christmas 1993: Excitement in the air... the day before departure.

Top: Lucy and I in Colorado during a stunning twenty-mile walk from Crested Butte across a mountain pass to Aspen in the summer of '93.

Bottom left: Lucy takes pity on an injured calf en route for glacier skiing at Neustift, Austria.

Bottom right: The only passenger in Mammoth Mountain Ski resort's executive jet (I took this shot from the co-pilot's seat) as Randy McCoy gives us a lift across the High Sierras to catch their flight from Los Angeles to Munich.

Top: Lucy in a flamboyant mood over dinner in Villaricca-Pucon, Chile.

Bottom: Cold tub – a make-believe bath after a day's skiing at Porter Heights, New Zealand.

Robert Redford, who welcomed our record-breaking ski attempt to his resort at Sundance, Utah as we neared the end of our round-the-world odyssey.

They were too, but mighty useful for skiing. Those tree trunks had been ready for a gruelling ski session that day in the snowy wilds of Lake Louise where we were spending a couple of nights during our foray into Canada. We had struck lucky. The tourist office had generously booked us into the Château Lake Louise, one of the country's truly grand hotels. Our suite dated back to 1913, and was as big as a barn. There was even a huge whirlpool at the end of our sumptuous bed, and Lucy was quick to immerse herself under the bubbles.

Outside, it got ever better. A magnificent view of the frozen lake, five huge glaciers at one end, the skating rink at the other, and impressive ice sculptures dotted like white sentinels around the grounds. There was even a carved frozen replica of the hotel itself. Ice topiary — that was a new one!

Lake Louise is owned by an unlikely character called Charlie Locke, a former mountain guide who one day hit one of life's rich veins. In the bad old days, so the legend goes, Charlie had been so poor that he would sit on a bench in nearby Banff chewing on a couple of slices of dry bread, and trying to imagine he had something tasty between them. Then he had an unexpected windfall. He did well out of some stocks and shares, cattle and oil, and with some wise investing he became a millionaire. Charlie called his company Locke, Stock and Barrel, which shows he had kept his sense of humour — and left his mark on the summit of Fortress Mountain (which he also owns) by spelling out his name there in small rocks.

But enough of history.

Lucy was leaning across the bed, feeling for my thighs under the white towelling robe.

'No, they're beautiful legs. Big legs.' She rolled her eyes heavenwards in mock adulation, and pursed her lips, 'And just f-e-e-l those muscles!'

'I'm putting on weight — '

'You're not fat, darling. You're just ... strong.'

'And I snore. I know I snore. You've told me.'

'No darling, you don't snore. You just — purr a little. '

Sometimes Lucy could be irresistible. Most times, actually.

I reached out for her.

Rather churlishly, I sometimes called her 'Mooron'. I suspect this was a combination of silly moo (which, I have to admit, I had occasionally called my beloved) and moron, though this was never made explicit by the radio programme that dreamed up the whole absurdity in the first place. We had heard it in Jackson Hole. A radio phone-in in which listeners were invited to guess the answers to various questions. If they got it wrong, a metallic voice would grind out: 'You are a Mooron!'

So a Mooron, Lucy became. In return she called me a Bull-ron, the male equivalent.

But there were times when the insults were less childish, and therefore potentially dangerous. Without warning, the emotional barometer would swing from Equatorial to Arctic, and a screaming match would start from nowhere, a blizzard of wounding barbs — before the hot tears of making up and exhausted reconciliation.

The one that was about to be sparked off came, aptly enough, when I was searching for a battery for our video camera. In our motel in Mount Hood Meadows in Oregon, I turned out the bag, then turned on her in frustration.

'The last time I saw it was when you put it in here — '

That did it. Spark, fuse, gunpowder — boom! And all in a single millisecond. She screamed at me. Shouted at me. Used words that were part-French, part-English, part-Provençal fishwife. A fleeting thought came to me as I was engulfed under the onslaught: I hope to God she never gets upset near deep snow, or we'll all be buried by an avalanche!

I never did find that battery, but I found another layer under Lucy's emotional skin that was equally illuminating. She liked a good, quick, clean scrap, and I knew by now that she would have been disappointed — worse, resentful — if I hadn't risen to the bait.

It was a small price to pay, set against the greater scheme of things. Her most endearing qualities (I wrote them down) were: Generous, Loving, Witty, Amusing, Compassionate. Oh, and Sexy.

I showed her the list.

'Oh, Arnie, that's nice.' The last squall was over. We were back on the bed together, but on top of it. It didn't take long to burrow beneath the blankets.

In my arms that night, her voice was a whisper.

'Arnie?'

'Yes?'

Hesitant now. 'I can't believe you're so easily hurt. Don't you realise you're the only person in the world I can explode at when I'm stressed? If I can't relieve my tensions with you, who *can* I do it with?'

I remembered then how often I had tried to coax her anger out of her. 'Why, Lucy, why?'

But all she could reply was: 'Because ... *because* ... '

So I never knew.

Now I touch her damp hair, red-gold hair soaked with the sweat of anger and passion.

Her eyes still pin me, huge and serious.

'Arnie, if we ever part, will you go on loving me?'

'I share Jane Birkins view on that,' I said, citing the actress who remained so close to Serge Gainsbourg after they split up.

'Do you know what she said? "But I never *unlove* anyone!" I'll go along with that.'

Typical Lucy. Her eyes flared. With a contemptuous 'Pfutt!' she swung her hand in the air in a dismissive upward sabre swipe. So much for Serge and Jane. That's my peasant girl. Provençal to her roots!

*   *   *

Get a grip, Lucy. Dig in! Dig in! Oh, God! Catch her, somebody ...

*   *   *

At Bluewood, a small but very friendly ski area in Washington State, we finally got to meet Cricket. Cricket Rogg Lodmell (try saying that without your teeth) had been one of our chief sources of inspiration during the long summer of 1993 when Lucy and I had been preparing for our adventure. In fact Bluewood had been one of the earliest ski areas to reply to our request for a brief visit. And it had been Cricket who sent us a welcoming fax.

To our amused dismay, Blackie, my mother's cat, had got to the fax before we had, and for some reason had started to eat it. We managed to salvage it, albeit in tatters, and from that moment on, the prospect of meeting Cricket became one of the *leitmotifs* of our trips. Having been fond of the cartoon character of Jimmy Cricket as children, we imagined Cricket to be a short, bouncy, middle-aged man. So we were slightly disarmed when, walking into Cricket's office, we found ourselves looking into the blue eyes of a most attractive 30-year-old girl. "Great to meet you at last" she said. "Why Cricket?" we asked, over a coffee. "Well my real name is Stephany." she said with a smile. "But when I was a baby, I apparently used to make strange chirping noises, a bit like a cricket. So my dad nicknamed me Cricket. It kind of stuck!"

Soon we'll be in Whitefish, Montana. 'Now here's another funny story about a ski-lift, Lucy.'

'What?'

In the car, our own small metallic Universe, with all we possess in the world on board. Including each other. We are travelling down an endless six-lane ribbon of highway, heading out through Oregon, on the good old Chisholm Trail. No four-wheel wagons this time, because that's a century behind us, only a four-wheel drive.

Listening to 'Enigma'.

Some idiot has pasted an extra sticker on our side. 'Don't Californicate Oregon!'

'Arnie,' she reminds me, listening to my chuckles. 'We're on our way to California. Don't you think we should perhaps remove it?'

'Okay.'

I pull into a lay-by, and with some reluctance I scrape the offending sticker off with our plastic ice-scraper.

'What was that story? The ski-lift — ?'

Ah, yes.

It happened on 20 December 1947. Big day — the historic opening of their first ski-lift. More than one thousand people from Flathead Valley wrapped up snugly against the cold, made their way to the slopes of The Big Mountain here to witness the Great Event.

Two gentlemen named Ed Schenck and George Prentice, the principal investors in the Hell Roaring Ski Corporation, which was named after a nearby mountain, had spent the whole night getting the lift ready.

Schenck told it this way: 'We sat down with the book of instructions, and tried to puzzle out how to adjust the T-bars. The directions said: "Turn the retracting springs eleven times." Working by candlelight, we managed it. Next morning, the motor roared into life, and the first skiers took off on the T-bars. But — Oh no! Instead of riding up the slope with the bar supporting them under their hips, these first riders were suddenly whipped off their feet and found themselves hanging ten feet in the air, spinning round and around like yo-yos. It was like a Bob Hope movie!'

What had happened was that the retracting spring had evidently been wound up to full stretch at the factory. But since most of the skiers had never seen a T-bar lift, they didn't realise anything was wrong. And upwards of two hundred skiers took off up the mountain and went up that way dangling like socks on a clothes-line before Messrs Schenck and Prentice got it right.

'If only I'd been there with a camera,' I said.

They still talk about it in Whitefish.

*   *   *

On the road. But where are we, exactly? Lost again, in a blizzard, somewhere between Oregon and California, with four hundred miles on the clock.

A flickering light off the highway beckons, just outside a place called Vale. We are dog tired, travel soiled. High Plains drifters, looking for a place to rest our weary heads. Lucy spots a faint light, away to our right, which turns out to be the welcoming glow of a small, dark inn.

'There, Arnie.'

I turn Spud into the forecourt, and we both see the sign.

'The Bates Motel'.

No thank you. I slam my foot hard on the pedal, and we accelerate away into the night. In my mind's eye, I see the spectre of Anthony Perkins gibbering at us from the window. In his mother's wig.

Let's get out of here!

*   *   *

In Snowshoe Sam's, we rode shotgun. That is to say, we drank shotgun. In our helter-skelter ride backwards and forwards across America and Canada, we seemed to stumble on places like Snowshoe Sam's and people like John Mooney. And initiation ceremonies like the great Gunbarrel Coffee experience.

'Are you the guys who are going to ski for ever and ever?'

Lucy was used to being called a guy by now, though originally her French femininity had been faintly outraged.

But we were the guys, and we had just arrived in the resort of Big White from its neighbour Silver Star. Tomorrow would be our last day in British Columbia before heading across the border to Alberta.

We had been accosted by a stranger in the snow-packed street and asked the familiar question.

For ever and ever?

'It seems like it,' I replied.

We shook hands. 'John Mooney,' he said. 'I run Snowshoe Sam's. Come on over for dinner tonight. I've got a surprise for you.'

'Oh? Well — thanks. Thanks a lot.' We had no plans, other than to get in a quick run before the lifts closed down for the night. It was dusk already.

'Eight o'clock, then.'

In our small motel room (made even more claustrophobic by our private mountain of baggage) Lucy filled in the Black Diary while I shaved and showered. We could be in for a good night.

'I'm looking forward to this one, Lucy!'

I heard her laughing, and put my head round the door. 'What is it?'

'A funny *Far Side* for tonight, Arnie. Come and see.'

Back in London we had also invested in the marvellously surreal *Far Side* calender for 1994 by Gary Larson. A little light relief, Lucy. We may need it! We would cut out and stick one into a fresh page, every day.

'Fine with me, Arnie. You're probably right.'

I was, as it turned out. And at least we could always be assured of going to bed with a chuckle.

'Do you know, Arnie, we did 8,280 vertical feet at Silver Star? That brings our total to ... 238,870 feet since we set out!'

'Amazing,' I said.

We had also notched up 4,247 miles on workhorse Spud's clock, and skied in twenty-one resorts.

One thing about Silver Star — it's friendly. Exceedingly friendly. I mean, how many resorts do you know where the lift attendants actually give you a hug before you scramble on to the chair?

The previous year, Silver Star had opened up her slopes at Putnam Creek, and like a snowy Cinderella at the ball, had transformed a pleasant enough family ski hill into a challenging beauty with international potential. No longer could any smug skier complain it was 'just too easy'. Not with twenty-three new runs on wonderfully varied terrain aimed specifically at intermediate and advanced skiers.

The lift, now, that's another matter. Cupid lift, aimed strictly for romantics.

Why, I wondered, was Tom jostling his way to the side of the queue like this? Tom Campbell, along with his wife Betty, was our host for the day to show us around the various runs. A retired engineer, with a twinkle in his eye and a laid-back sense of humour.

I looked at Lucy as Tom pushed and squeezed, and raised an eyebrow. No, she didn't know either. What had got into the fellow? Tom, it transpired, was making sure he would be standing next to one of the attractive lift girls who would assist him on to the quad. As he approached the turnstile, the nearest girl in her bright red outfit and matching peaked cap suddenly grabbed him in an affectionate bear-hug. To which Tom enthusiastically responded.

On the four-seater, bound for the heights of Aberdeen with a rug over our knees, I looked at the others. 'You know that girl, Tom?'

'Not really.'

And he went on to explain.

'Ten years ago we had a liftie — that's what we call the girls — named Mary-Jane Rutherford. She was a real little ball of fire, very outgoing. One real cold day she started putting her arms round the skiers and giving them a big warming hug, before they climbed aboard. And the habit just caught on. Soon other girls were doing it. Now they'll all hug you to order! It's kind of a tradition here. You've just got to make sure you're standing in the right spot to get a hug. What d'you think of that, Arnie?'

I thought: only in North America ... Aloud I said: 'It'll never catch on on the London Underground.'

At the end of the day, we headed for Snowshoe Sam's.

Inside, a crackling log fire, a convivial table, and introductions. Ken Sinclair, from the resort; Jason Monteleone, 'communications'; Jim Loyd, head of the ski school; Blair Ireland, from the ski shop, who had kindly agreed to give our long-suffering skis a much-needed overhaul; and another Blair — Blair Baldwin, the resort's vice-president.

Steak and lobster, baked potato, huge salads, followed by Pecan Pie. After all, a man's got to eat. Washed down with several bottles of full-bodied Californian burgundy, because a man's got to drink, too. And so has a woman!

Then, with due solemnity we were ushered into the saloon area, hung with cowboy hats, rifles, the antlered head of a giant elk that hadn't moved fast enough, and dog-eared sepia pictures of hoary old-timers staring out fixedly from their silver frames. John Mooney flicked a switch — and the unlikely sounds of Pachelbel's *Canon and Fugue*, redolent of marble palaces, bewigged courtiers and eighteenth-century romance, flowed out from the bar in pastel shades of sound. We would play it later, at Lucy's memorial service.

What is all this? I thought. Mooney was taking a shotgun down from the wall.

'I hope that thing's not loaded,' I said, a mite nervously.

'No, it isn't,' he said. 'But you soon will be.'

Mooney warmed some tumblers, mixed brandy and fresh-ground coffee into them, then topped it with whipped cream. Then he heated the gun barrel over a flame. And finally, with a flourish, he poured flaming Grand Marnier down the barrel.

'Now that,' I said, as the first of several slugs churned a path of volcanic lava down my throat, 'is what I call an itchy trigger finger!'

'Ski the world, guys,' said jovial John, three hours later, raising his glass with the rest of us. 'And come back and see us some time, the both of you, you hear?'

We heard. And we promised. But we never did make it.

*   *   *

There is another Gunbarrel. In a place called Heavenly, a ski resort spreadeagled across the border between California and Nevada.

We had arrived in style, with Spud labouring loyally on to get us there. To find an enormous red and white banner proclaiming: 'A HEAVENLY WELCOME TO ARNIE WILSON AND LUCY DICKER, THE ROUND-THE-WORLD SKI TEAM' emblazoned on the slopes.

Highly flattering, even though we learned that twenty-four hours earlier the banner, created by a local sign-writer named James Bond, had read 'NANCY DICKER'.

We had our picture taken, smiling. My arm around her shoulders.

'Listen, I must tell you about Gunbarrel, Lucy. It's a really tough run.'

Gunbarrel lives up to its name — a long, steep and treacherously bumpy ride where she would face her first Waterloo of courage and determination. The moguls, giant dome-shaped mounds of snow, are created by skiers constantly turning and re-turning around them, sculpting them into blocks as hard as marble.

'It's not exactly dangerous, Lucy, but very punishing. I mean it.'

'Don't worry, Arnie.' She flashed that famous, all-encompassing smile that said everything would be all right, always. 'I'll get down.'

And off she dived, head low, body curved and balanced, in her gold and grey ski suit, brimful of confidence in her new-found ability to tilt at windmills. Or at moguls. She never would listen.

What could I do, but follow? And I did, hurtling after her down the icy sheen of Gunbarrel, keeping my sights fixed on the tiny fleeing figure ahead of me, a colourful doll whipping up the snow in exhilarating puffs as she dug her skis and sticks into the hostile mountain.

But Lucy made it that day, on that un-heavenly run. And at the bottom I caught up with her, and doffed my woollen ski hat to her in a courtly bow of tribute.

'Well done, darling. I'm so proud of you.'

'Proud monkey?' Her cheeks were aflame with triumph. 'That's nice! Thank you, Arnie.'

From that moment, I sensed it was more important to her than ever that we were a team.

*   *   *

Two days later, she said: 'Arnie, I think I'm pregnant.'

Chapter 6

February

Arnie, if you want a baby with me, go for it!

Lucy Dicker, Summer 1993

'Jesus Christ, Lucy! I can't believe it!'

'Arnie, I don't *know*. Maybe it's all the tension. All I know is that I've missed my period. By two weeks. It may be a false alarm ... '

Her voice trailed into uncertainty. She looked suddenly forlorn, the exact opposite of the glow an expectant mother should radiate.

'You know, Arnie — the stress of always having to be, well, somewhere. We can never relax — '

'I know,' I said, as gently as I could.

But inside, my brain was scrambled. Where exactly are we? Suddenly, I've lost my bearings, and with them all sense of time and place.

I stare through the window. Outside the frosted glass, pine trees shrouded in fresh snow stand motionless like a white-cloaked praetorian guard. Beyond them, the jagged teeth of distant snow-covered peaks against the far horizon. And above, a brilliant blue sky with scurrying cirrus clouds high in the atmosphere, fleecy messengers announcing to all the world that it's going to be another glorious sunny day out there on the slopes. But which slopes?

God, we could be anywhere. I lie back on the pillow, trying to remember.

Lucy always got out of bed first, and she had done so this morning, with no hint of the bombshell about to be dropped. She loved being in bed, so it was an extra effort. But we had established the pattern, and it had become a discipline she followed religiously. 'Okay, Arnie,' a sigh. 'I've got to get up now — ' and then she'd start counting up to ten, slowing down as she reached the moment of truth.

Sometimes, with a grin of mock encouragement, I'd follow the litany from my warm cocoon, counting her out of the bed on my fingers like a referee counts out a boxer. Then she would scamper off nude into the bathroom, take a leisurely shower, and emerge clean and sparkling to tell me: 'The bathroom's all yours, darling!'

But not today. Today she had seated herself carefully down beside me in her towel robe, and stared at me with huge, serious eyes. Still half-asleep, I hadn't taken too much notice. Until she spoke. Then I took notice all right.

Lucy was right, of course. For the past few weeks, life had been one relentless conveyor belt of grey road unwinding before us, frequently hazardous with snow and slush, and mountain slopes that varied from modest to potentially lethal. While indoors had meant another moving escalator of bedrooms, bathrooms and bars. Maybe it had been a crazy idea, after all.

I stare out of the window, seeking a focal point. Something secure, a sanctuary, a polar star. There isn't one.

Above all, I need to hear a message of comfort. It's okay, Arnie. You've got your rock-solid base. Anyway, who needs a physical place to call home? Bricks and mortar are transient things, after all, and they can crumble into dust any time. Home is where the heart is, Arnie. And your heart is with

Lucy. And you may be about to become the father of her child. How's that for secure? A baby? I didn't know whether to laugh or cry.

End of expedition. End of the impossible dream. End of all you had been praying and hoping for these past months, finding layers of courage and adventure within the two of you that you never knew existed. In short, end of the line. And at this time, for God's sake, when it could have happened at any time over the past two years!

I couldn't take it in, but suddenly I wanted to laugh. The fickle finger of fate had played the joker's card, all right.

Well, what the hell! We'd have the baby! Suddenly the baby seems more important than the trip. But maybe, just maybe, we could have both.

'What was that, Arnie? What did you say?'

Panic attack over. And I was back in the real world.

Lucy slides across the bed and into my arms. And looks up at me with those eyes that can melt any heart, especially mine.

'Arnie, I love you more than you will ever know.'

I stroke her hair, and utter the only words that matter. 'Whatever happens, Lucy, it's going to be fine.'

The green eyes brim over with sudden, unexpected tears.

'Do you mean that, Arnie? Really mean it?'

'You know I do.'

The father-to-be holds her tight, and cries softly with her.

But Lucy is forty, and had never given any real hint of wanting to slow down, meaning settle down, and raise a family. We had even toyed with a sequel to our trip.

'Lucy,' — this at our Greek taverna back in London. 'After we get back, let's go and explore the world's most unlikely skiing areas — '

'Such as —?'

'Well, China for a start. Then Korea, South Africa, Morocco, Iran, the Lebanon ... '

Over the last glass of Metaxa brandy Lucy had become intrigued.

'Yes, baby! Why not?'

Of course we had talked babies. Two years together, and you show me a couple who haven't. Except that in all probability the would-be parents are not planning to plunge off on a crazy excursion around the world, searching out snow-blanketed hills where they can descend at speed on two fragile planks just to say they did it!

To be honest, I didn't particularly want any more children. I had already helped bring four lovely daughters into the world, and at no time had their mother been expected to rise from her bed of labour and head for the nearest ski slope. I felt no special need for any more — even with Lucy.

But I also was aware that if she didn't have a baby soon, she never would.

In the first flush of our love affair, whenever the subject cropped up she would shake her head and assure me: 'No, Arnie. That's all right. I don't want a baby. I don't need a baby.'

And then one day after one such speech came the crunch, as she looked at me — and the hitherto unspoken message came through loud and clear as she added: 'But if you want a baby with me, go for it!' Now, in the wilds of the Rockies, it looked as if, however unintentionally, I had gone for it. We even agreed on a wonderful name for our child: Shasta, the awe-inspiring mountain we had fallen in love with in California. We thought it would be a brilliant name for a boy or girl. And a wonderful way of celebrating our odyssey.

*   *   *

By sheer, wondrous, stupid chance we lost our way again that same morning — and ended up having champagne for breakfast. And caviar.

I'd recovered enough to make my way to the bathroom and get myself ready to face the day. *Que sera, sera*. The cursed song came into my head, and wouldn't leave it for a week. Thank you, Doris Day. You can be godmother!

But as Lucy and I made our way hand in hand along the corridors (furthest from the lift as usual) for breakfast, we managed one of our regular directional errors. It took us into the wrong dining-room, and by the time I realised our mistake it was too late.

'Champagne, sir? Ma'am?' The waitress was trim and prim, and I didn't feel like owning up that we had strayed off the beaten path. She sat us down, plopped the menus on to our table mats, and retreated.

I stared at what was on offer. 'Lucy — I've just realised something. It's Sunday.' Sunday in that place meant a sumptuous brunch of champagne, gravadlax, king prawns, cream cheese pancakes, more champagne, eggs benedict, crème brûlée. Oh, and more champagne. And all for $35 for the two of us.

'There's one thing missing,' I said suddenly. 'And I know where to get it.'

Leaving my companion open-mouthed, I ran through the lobby and out to the car.

Spud sat patiently under a fresh white overcoat, but at least the snow was keeping her warm. No problem with frozen door locks today.

This time I knew where to look. After all, I'd been the one to pack it, back in Jackson Hole. I fished around under the spare wheel.

Fresh from the Caspian Sea, there it was. A jar of real caviar. It had been a Christmas gift to Lucy that we had promised ourselves we'd open at the right moment. If a baby isn't a right moment, tell me what is.

'Oh, Arnie! Brilliant!' Lucy's face lit up as I returned to the table with my trophy.

'What better time?' I said grandly. 'And it's nicely chilled after being left in the Spud freezer all these weeks.'

I studied the label. Sevruga. Excellent.

'Did you know, Lucy, that there are still some twenty varieties of sturgeon worldwide, but that ninety per cent of the world's caviar comes from just three? Beluga, Oscietra — '

I gestured at the jar, and the steely-grey eggs packed inside.

'And Sevruga. Furthermore, Beluga, which produces the largest eggs, can weigh up to one thousand kilos and measure four metres in length. That is some fish. But we're settling for Sevruga, which measures only one metre in length and is the smallest of the Caspian sturgeon — '

'How come you know all this?'

'It says so here!' I peered at the label, which was proving highly informative.

I was getting the tiniest bit drunk. With the general shock of impending fatherhood, coupled with champagne and the altitude who could blame me? So we ordered melba toast, and ate the whole jar. It must have inspired me.

'We'll get a nanny!' I declared.

'What?'

'We'll get a nanny. To accompany us. So that you can ski while she looks after the baby.'

'Arnie, wait a minute — '

But I was up and running. We'd hire a nanny, an au pair who would be prepared to travel with us, and look after the new arrival while we completed our mission.

'Listen darling, as long as one of us keeps skiing, we can do it. We won't be cheating. I mean, we don't need to let a baby get in the way. Do we?'

Lucy just didn't know what to say. I put Nanny on the back-burner, for now at any rate.

*   *   *

We are heading for Squaw Valley, and by luck the Emerald Bay route along the lake is open. Its centrepiece, Lake Tahoe, second only to Lake Titicaca as the highest alpine lake in the world, is one of the scenic gems in the bejewelled crown of California, and like the sculpture of Helen of Troy, beautiful from every angle. Like Titicaca, which straddles the border between Bolivia and Peru, Tahoe laps at the shores of both California and Nevada. But Emerald Bay just takes your breath away.

Normally the route across the high Sierras is closed in the winter. But that season there had been a marked lack of snow. Which meant that we could take Spud up the road that climbs high and steep above the bay, almost separated from the main lake by a narrow inlet through which the Tahoe Queen paddle steamer makes regular calls.

Passengers gasp at the scenery, and with reason. You can hear the cameras clicking like a tap dance chorus in double time.

This glorious day, the lake stretches below us with a gunmetal sheen, as if God had poured quicksilver across the land.

'There's a ghost story about this place, Lucy!'

Intrigued, she switches off the radio.

'What sort of ghost?'

I told her.

Emerald Bay was once the haunt of an old British sea dog, Captain Dick Barter, who retired and set up home there in the 1860s. He was given a job as caretaker at an isolated house on the shore, and used to row himself over in his boat to visit various saloons of dubious repute across the lake.

In the event of bad weather, Cap'n Dick would lash himself to the mast to prevent himself falling into the dark and freezing waters. Lake Tahoe also happens to be very deep.

On one sortie, rendered somewhat comatose by drink, the old seafarer had allowed himself to get so cold during a storm that he developed frostbite on two of his toes. So he amputated them with a knife, and kept them pickled in a jar on his sideboard to show visitors. Despite this devil-may-care reaction to his brush with death, the experience apparently chastened our nautical hero, and he selected a plot of land on the island below us for his future grave.

Sadly, the brave Captain never made use of it. On a

subsequent saloon crawl, he fell overboard from his rowing boat. His body was never recovered, thereby creating a local legend that to this day Dick Barter's ghost haunts Emerald Bay. Especially on moonlit nights.

'And tonight's the — ' But I was stopped in mid-sentence by a muffled explosion. It came from somewhere in the car behind us, ruining my punch-line.

'Arnie! Did you hear that bang?'

I'd heard something. 'I think Spud just blew a fuse.'

'Arnie, please. It's in the back.'

It was, too. Or to be more accurate, in the boot. I pulled into a lay-by, and scrunched out into the snow to investigate.

'Oh, Lord!' I looked down into something vaguely resembling an abbatoir. The whole of the inside was sprayed red, our luggage, boots, the Ugly Bag, the lot. Soaked.

Then I remembered. Back in Jackson Hole they had given us a parting gift of a bottle of special Californian red wine, Château bottled, from the Napa Valley. I had tucked it away in the side of the boot, out of sight and, alas, out of mind. After surviving varying degrees of temperature, mainly below zero, across two thousand miles and several States, the bottle had finally rebelled and exploded.

The wine permeated our bags, and just about everything else. Later, at the next motel, I couldn't believe how many of our belongings were stained pink. The trouble was, they stayed pink for the rest of the year. And it wasn't even *FT* pink!'

*   *   *

February 14, my 50th birthday, at Breckenridge, started before dawn with an endless round of TV (some live), radio and newspaper interviews – mainly on the slopes, since, of course, we had to ski — organised by the indefatigable Beth Sharp, the girl behind our main sponsorship deal. Among the journalists, to my joy, was the small coterie of ski-writing colleagues from England who were among our closest friends, some of whom, sadly would never see Lucy again. When the interviews were all over, we repaired to a local restaurant. Here, I am reliably informed, I was so exhausted that I fell asleep with my head almost in my splendid birthday cake, designed in the shape of a mountain, complete with skiers. To be fair, it had been a tiring though exciting day. And I wasn't getting any younger!

*   *   *

Pretzels. They became a way of life. The salty biscuits that Americans worship evolved into our staple diet during the long driving hours. Pretzels, plus American hard-gums for me to chew on, and soft gooey apples for Lucy. Personally, I hated those apples. Give me a crisp Grannie Smith any time.

But the pretzels were Lucy's idea. And now — surprise, surprise — I was eating more of them than she was.

'Pretzels are ideal for you, Arnie, because there's no fat in them. Doctor Dua will be pleased!'

I recalled the turbaned and urbane Dr Dua, and his warning before we set out. 'Watch your diet, Mr Wilson. You are still somewhat overweight. Only one egg a week.'

That was a laugh. Just try it in a country where your average breakfast contains at least three eggs, and often more. But no mention of pretzels. So while we drove, I munched on everything my lady handed me. Stringy ones, crisp ones, even large crunchy ones as big as the famed Idaho potatoes.

Lucy, sweet girl, was always concerned about my diet. She hated it when I ate the crispy skin of a chicken, or tucked into fatty meat. Or, worse, when I ate hers — reaching across to spear it when I thought she wasn't looking.

But she would spot my probing fork.

'Arnie!' a yell of displeasure, loud enough to make heads turn at other tables. 'Don't eat that! It's disgusting!'

Too late. It had already gone down the hatch.

'Sorry, darling. I really fancied that.'

'Arnie, listen to your body! If you're not hungry, don't eat!'

I tried listening, but didn't hear anything. In point of fact, I have to admit that Lucy's concern for my welfare was not merely offered on a nine-to-five basis. She really cared. Her dedication throughout our months together to ensuring that I suffered as little pain and discomfort as possible was above and wondrously beyond the call of duty. 'I hate it when you're ill, darling,' she'd say.

Lucy herself was very fussy about her own intake. She liked good organic nutrition, and hated junk food with a deep loathing. She had once had a major dietary problem when she was a teenager. She even put herself in the hands of a Harley Street specialist to sort out her problems. Now she was as slender as a model.

The end result was that I would pay the price for her constant fear of becoming overweight.

On the road, we established a curious ritual. She would leave a token amount of food on her plate, and never actually finish anything. She left that to me. But only the lean bits. And she had to choose the left-overs, which I was allowed to dip into, a vulture waiting for scraps.

But she still insisted on having lunch every day, even if it was only a bowl of soup at a snack bar on the mountain. 'We must have regular meals, baby,' she'd say.

*　　　　*　　　　*

More than once, Lucy developed an intense dislike for our accommodation – sometimes even before we had actually stayed in it – and we would flee into the night! Fair enough. During such an exhausting schedule, it was important to have somewhere clean and comfortable to recuperate. But sometimes her criteria for what was clean and comfortable were rather more critical than mine. On one famous occasion at Cascade Mountain, Wisconsin, we abandoned two hotels in one night. And when I criticised Lucy in my daily diary, she demanded the right of reply! Here is my version followed by hers:

"The first motel we tried she took an instant dislike to, convinced it would be dirty before we even opened the door. Triumphantly she found a few specks of dirt. You would think that Mr Bates himself had been lurking behind the shower curtain! The next motel seemed OK until Lucy felt the mattress, which wobbled and quivered like a huge jelly fish. It turned out to be a water-bed. "I'm not sleeping on this" she half-screamed, as if confronted by a roomful of mice. The more I wallowed on the bed, the more her provençal pique prevailed. "There's no way we're staying here" she said. "If we do, I shall sleep on the floor." Needless to say, we left.

Lucy's version begins: "The first motel was dingy to say the least. It was dimly lit, and had litter outside as well as old oil barrels and rags scattered around. I had a sinking feeling about the state of cleanliness of the room. It had a brown, threadbare carpet, with unidentified bits that looked like gravel next to the bed. The bathroom was small and the loo was suspect. The smell in the room was stale. I couldn't bring myself to stay. I would have been happy to stay at the next motel, but the bed had a strange look to it. When I felt it, it moved like a living mass. I was seized by a nauseous sensation and backed off as if in danger of being engulfed by a warm sea of jelly. We drove off into the night in search of more comfortable bedding."

*   *   *

There were some things that even Florence Nightingale, as I sometimes called Lucy when she was being especially caring, could not handle. The spectre of illness, and I mean serious illness, had always lurked behind our shoulders — though we seldom, if ever, tempted fate by discussing it.

We were just over eight weeks into the trip when

something happened that I wouldn't wish on my worst enemy. We had reached the small, unremarkable town of Bedford, Indiana. Aspen it wasn't.

At the hotel, in the bathroom, the pains began.

Time for a spot of medical history. When I was eight years old, I almost died from peritonitis. My appendix burst, and the doctors nearly lost me during the emergency operation in a London clinic. As a result of this I had a long history of what I can most decently describe as bladder problems. Scar tissue had built up and caused a partial blockage in the urethra.

I had treatment for years. But at the age of thirty I thought: what the heck! And gave it up. From then on, in layman's terms, it simply meant that it took me five minutes instead of two minutes to have a pee. No big deal. You can get used to anything.

But in the bathroom that night, sudden panic. I couldn't pass water at all! After a ten-minute struggle, feeling the dreadful pressure building up somewhere inside my abdomen, I finally forced it out. That's it, I thought.

'Are you all right, Arnie?' Lucy, anxiously, from the bed.

'Fine now,' I said.

But I wasn't fine. Next afternoon, we were to drive to a small resort called Ski World.

Half-way there, I doubled up in agony. Shooting pains in the general area of my waterworks took me unawares, and I actually cried out with the pain.

'I'll drive, Arnie! I'm getting you to a hospital.'

Lucy was always brilliant in an emergency. She turned Spud on its axis, and hurtled back to Bedford.

Gathering thunderclouds were darkening the evening sky on the far horizon, and from my foetal position in the passenger seat I watched the first drops of rain spatter down on the windscreen. This was not going to be the best day of my life.

We followed the red cross street signs to the hospital. Lucy helped me out, and hanging on to her arm I hobbled into the lobby.

Five minutes later I was lying on a couch in a side room with a young doctor named Greg Walker trying to ease the blockage. It was not an experience I would recommend.

'You'll be okay,' he assured me. 'Try and relax. This'll ease it.'

And it did. I paid by credit card, obtained a receipt for the insurance claim, and took Lucy's arm again.

'Darling, you're wonderful! Now, we've still got to get our day's skiing in.' Or night, because now it was 10pm, and Cinderella Hour was fast approaching.

This time we headed for the floodlit slopes of Ski World's neighbour, Paoli Peaks. The rain had showed no inclination to turn to snow, but this was Indiana where they make just about every snowflake artificially. We were going to get very wet, but that wasn't unusual.

We left our car with all our gear aboard in a quiet corner of the car park, snapped on our skis, and duly completed one run and all of 295 vertical feet.

But I was in agony once more.

'Oh no, Arnie. Not again!'

But this was worse, far worse, than anything I'd felt before. The other pain by comparison had been merely a rehearsal before the main performance. Excruciating spasms ripped through me like shards of broken glass. I couldn't help it. I groaned out loud, and kept groaning.

Lucy was at the wheel once more, her face set as she battled back through another cloudburst to the now familiar frontage of Bedford Hospital. It was twenty-six miles, and I heard myself crying out in agony during every one of them. Lucy drove like the wind, and this was one occasion when I was grateful for her Le Mans-style driving skills.

Twice we stopped at garages when I thought I'd be able to relieve the situation. Twice I tried. And twice I had to come stumbling back to the car, bleating like a lost sheep.

At last the comforting lights of the hospital appeared out of the night. Lucy ran ahead of me as I limped after her, bowed like an old man. For no reason the picture of Bill Briggs, locked into his own permanent crouch back in Jackson Hole, came into my mind. What a fitting pair we'd make!

Through the torrential rain, I saw Lucy shaking the glass doors. Then banging on them with clenched fists. The foyer inside was lit, but there was no one to be seen.

'Is there a bell?' I could hardly speak. 'There must be a bell somewhere.'

No bell, at least not one that we could see.

'Round the back,' Lucy shouted.'We've got to get you in! There must be someone on duty.'

And thank God — behind the building was an emergency entrance.

Inside, Lucy spotted a startled night duty nurse. She tried to keep her voice calm. 'I think my boyfriend is in big trouble, he needs to see Dr Walker again.'

Dr Walker had given us his mobile number — just in case. He was at a party. Lucy could hear the sounds of merriment in the background.

'Put me over to the nurse,' and the doctor rapped instructions down the phone.

Seconds later, the hospital sprang into action like a scene from *Casualty*. I was whisked into a private room, helped into a cotton night-shirt, and became the focal point of a lot of people in white coats.

'We're going to operate,' Dr Walker told me cheerfully on his return. 'You won't feel a thing!'

Someone slid a needle into my arm. The pain in my lower regions receded, and the room started to darken. The last thing I saw was Lucy's face, anxious and loving.

Then the lights went out.

Dr Walker operated at 2am.

At dawn, I opened my eyes — and the first sight I had was the one I most wanted to see in all the world. Lucy, fast asleep, curled up on a couch next to the bed. Within touching distance. The early-morning sun played on her hair.

She awoke at once, and took my hand in hers.

'Oh, Arnie. How do you feel?'

'Surprisingly well,' I said. 'All things considered. What have they done to me?' I didn't like to look.

Lucy had pressed a bell. A nurse appeared, brisk and smiling.

'How are we today, Arnie?' They're very friendly, the American medical services. It's all Christian names and bonhomie, as long as you've signed the insurance forms.

'I'm hoping you can tell me — '

'Dr Walker will be here to see you at around nine o'clock. Meantime, you're not to move.'

On the dot, the door opened and my saviour walked in. 'How's things, Arnie? That was quite a night!'

'A lot better, thanks.'

'Great. As you've probably discovered, we've given you a catheter, just for a few days. Until everything gets itself back to normal. '

I felt down below. Sure enough, I had a tube emerging from me, linked to a bag strapped to my thigh. Oh well, at least the pain had disappeared.

'Doctor, I'm supposed to be skiing today.' He knew all about our great journey. 'I've got to — I can't give up now.'

'Well ... ' The doctor looked dubious. 'I suppose if you're very careful, you should get away with it. We certainly don't need to keep you in. Just be very cautious!'

'Don't worry, I will!'

'Let's be grateful it happened here and not in some godforsaken place with no medical facilities,' said Lucy.

'You should be okay,' said Dr Walker. 'But just in case, I'm going to give you a spare catheter to take away with you.'

I was thinking: This is Indiana. It could have been India. I hastily put the thought out of my head as I proceeded, gingerly, to the slopes.

For the next day or so I skied one gentle nursery run a day, complete with catheter, at Paoli Peaks, notching up an unimpressive average of a quarter mile each time in the process. We were going to have a lot of catching up to do.

Looking back, I realise that those few days were the longest Lucy and I went throughout the year without making love ...

But least it proved unequivocally that we weren't interested in cheating. We could have done just that, any time. But, as I said more than once to Lucy, and to anyone else who asked: 'We'd have had to live with ourselves afterwards.'

If anything, the experience brought us closer together. Later, I would tell her, 'Lucy, you got me to the hospital. You stayed the night with me. You heard my screams. You consoled and comforted me. You're wonderful and I adore you!'

'Yes, Arnie, and I'm keeping the catheter in my hand luggage. You'll only lose it!'

God, I loved that girl.

The catheter stayed with us for the whole of the year. It was never required again, not even in India.

*   *   *

'The rocks, Lucy! You're going to hit the rocks. Watch out! WATCH OUT!'

*   *   *

Lucy was also suffering from her own medical problems — a recurring migraine. It would surface from nowhere, give her hell for several unspeakable hours, then retreat back into dark limbo.

The first time it struck during the trip was during an all-night drive through the Rockies between The Big Mountain and Bridger Bowl.

Lucy had this Napoleonic ability to cat-nap. In fact she would often be talking to me, stop in mid-sentence and nod off.

'Arnie, give me a second or two,' she'd say in the middle of taking notes on the Palmtop. And she'd be gone, head lolling on her shoulder, slumped against the window. Fifteen seconds later, she'd be back. 'What was I saying — ?'

But on this night, beside me in the passenger seat, staring out at moonlit snowfields scudding past during our 410-mile drive she suddenly flinched, and held her head in both hands.

'Lucy! What is it?'

'This bloody migraine.'

A whisper of pain passed her lips. Lucy never wanted to show any suffering because she knew how it would worry me.

I pulled in to the side of a snow bank, and hurriedly cleared a space in the rear. 'Here, come back and lie down.'

For once she did as she was told without question — a sure sign that she was really unwell. She dozed fitfully through the long night. I thought of playing the 'Enigma' tape softly to try to soothe her into sleep, but thought better of it. With her kind of migraine, I knew the slightest sound could be torture.

Five weary hours later we reached Bridger Bowl. Her migraine was back with a vengeance. I persuaded her to report straight to the sick bay.

'Arnie, my head hurts.'

I massaged her temples gently, feeling utterly helpless.

'Make it go away.'

We both knew I couldn't.

'Stay here, darling.' I lowered the Venetian blinds, cutting out the dazzling early morning sun. Cool shade flooded the room. 'I've got to go up the mountain. But you don't have to. As long as one of us does it ... '

Fortunately, the ski station had been waiting to greet the two world explorers, and we were given VIP treatment. Free lift passes. Meals. And, best of all in the circumstances, a sympathetic Medical Surgery, with a warm and understanding nurse in attendance.

'No, Arnie, I want to ski.' Lucy's mouth tightened in mutiny.

If she put even one foot on the floor, she'd probably fall

down in a dizzy spell.

'Please darling, stay where you are. I'll be back — just as soon as I've done the Ridge.'

Skiing the notorious Ridge at Bridger Bowl had been a life's ambition, and I had been building up to this moment for weeks. I planted a firm no-arguments kiss on Lucy's forehead, and left the Medical Room with as much authority and sympathy as I could muster.

My guide — and I was going to need one for what lay ahead — was Doug Wales. The marketing director was a keen-as-mustard skier and black run specialist. I sensed I was in safe company at the top of the chair-lift when he told me to put on my avalanche transceiver, and showed me how to attach my skis to a special back-pack for the steep climb on foot that lay ahead.

I tried to put Lucy out of my mind and concentrate on the job in hand. The Ridge requires complete focus of thought, and complete commitment. It would brook no distractions.

The climb itself took twenty minutes. A rope tow had been set up for the Ski Patrol to use to haul themselves to the top, but we had to climb up without it. Even at this altitude — around 8,000 feet — my heart was pumping like a trip-hammer before I was even half-way up.

The Ridge has to be one of the Montana's most celebrated off-piste areas. It is not a place for recreational skiers, and the customary warning on my lift-pass seemed suddenly to take on extra significance:

> *The purchaser-user of this ticket agrees and understands that skiing is dangerous, and includes risk of injury from: changing weather conditions, avalanches, bare spots, variations in snow, ice and terrain, bumps, moguls, stumps, forest growth, rocks, debris, lift towers and other structures, and collisions with other skiers.*
>
> *The purchaser-user acknowledges that skiing*

may result in serious injury or death from these
risks and accepts such risks.
If you do not wish to assume such risks return
this ticket before its use.

It's a bit late for that, this particular purchaser-user thought, peering over the rim as we breasted the final rise and standing, stunned, by the vista that unrolled below me.

It was like being on the roof of the world! Massive mountain ranges were stacked up in every direction, and seemed to go marching off into the far distance as if they would never stop.

'Incredible,' I said.

My voice faded into an awed silence. I've seen some views in my life, but this one was going to be hard to beat. 'You can see for more than seventy miles everywhere you look, Arnie.' Doug never tired of the view.

Over to the north was the Bridger Range, surrounding the legendary valley, a snow-Mecca to skiers who would make the pilgrimage from all over America just to taste the experience. The range is named after Tim Bridger, a pioneer who discovered a new route into the valley for the settlers of old when the local Indians were sending up unfriendly smoke signals.

I squinted into the sun.

'What's that one?' An isolated, pure white range with no visible marks or tracks.

'The Crazy Mountains! Named after some poor woman who was the sole survivor of an Indian attack. That's where she took shelter — and went mad. That's what they say.'

Doug pointed out Sawtooth, and the Bangtails, 'So called because the wild horses that roamed the mountains would get their tails all knotted up with snow and ice. You could hear them banging against their thighs.' It was hard to tear myself away from the scenic splendour, but it was time to ski.

'Snow's good today,' said Doug. 'Somewhere between breakable crust and heaven!' His voice grew serious. 'One thing. If you lose it on that first bend,' he gestured with his ski pole at the narrow path leading into the Apron, the chute we were about to ski. It undulated like a roller-coaster.

'You'll see a tree immediately to your right. Just grab it and hang on. Otherwise you'll go over the drop.'

As he dug in his poles and skied off, he called back over his shoulder.

'They call it Desperation Pine!'

And we were away, swooping like gulls, whooping like school kids, down that almost sheer plunge into the white abyss, our skis leaving trails criss-crossing the virgin snow behind us.

There's a word to describe that run on that crisp, clear, cold, brilliant afternoon. Outrageous! One of the most outrageous runs of my life. And I am happy to report that I made it, with only one fall, and without the help of Desperation Pine.

To my astonishment and delight, Lucy was waiting for us at the bottom on skis, her face a delectable picture of triumph.

'Did you really think I was going to let you have all the glory, Arnie?'

We hugged each other. She'd been skiing the lower slopes.

'Lucy, I'm so proud of you — '

'Best of all, darling, my headache's gone. It's so cold it seems to have driven the pain away. Now I can be human again.'

*   *   *

Next day, Spud died on us.

We'd had a few early warnings. Spud had been sluggish on the cold starts, with the battery fighting a losing battle against the elements. Sometimes I had to jump-start her with a pair of leads and an obliging fellow motorist to give a hand.

Other times I put my shoulder to the rear, and with boots scrabbling on the ice I'd push Spud down a slope while Lucy would crash the gears and manage to get Old Faithful back on the road.

But as we set off from Bridger in a state close to euphoria

— I'd skied the Ridge, Lucy's migraine had miraculously vanished — Spud was sending out distress signals. And after a few brave wheezes and coughs, our willing steed finally gave up the ghost. We stood by the roadside, staring sadly at our inert friend.

At least Avis came up trumps. Within an hour of our emergency call for help, a low-loader rumbled out of the horizon to locate us on the hard shoulder. On board, a spanking new version of Spud, only in cheery blue instead of white.

The mechanic checked Spud's battery. There was the dust of seven States on its body, and 5,910 miles on the clock.

'Dead as a rock,' he pronounced.

I started to apologise about Spud's condition, but he cut me short.

'No problem. In Montana we never worry about clean!'

With that, he winched Spud up on to the loader and drove off. Lucy and I raised our woolly hats in salute to an old friend who had done us proud.

*   *   *

We woke early, to find ourselves in the local paper. The headline in the *Hungry Horse News* read, 'SULTAN OF THE SLOPES WITH $400,000 AND 365 DAYS TO SKI THE WORLD!'

God, it was all over Page One! Together with a huge picture of us across four columns, with me grinning like a fat cat into the camera.

A happy millionaire swanning off across the world's exotic skiing grounds.

'I said we'd be famous, Lucy.' I shook my head, stunned, as we spread out the paper over breakfast. 'Now they'll all think we're carrying half a million dollars around with us, and we'll be mugged for sure! Sultan! My God ...'

'Does that make me your Sultana?' Lucy's infectious giggles broke the tension.

*   *   *

That night, as I was drifting off to sleep, Lucy came out of the bathroom and slipped under the duvet beside me, I felt her cool fingertip on my lips.

'Arnie, don't say anything.'

'Hmmm?

'The baby — it was a false alarm. It's not going to happen. I was just ... very late, that's all. I think I'm relieved.'

I wasn't sure, either.

'Now go to sleep, baby. You're the only baby I need. I love you.'

I felt at once relieved — and very, very sad. There was to be no baby Shasta after all...

Chapter 7

March

Mon cher amour, je t'aime de tout mon coeur, et j'ai si peur de te perdre. Je voudrais porter ton enfant. Je voudrais t'épouser et je voudrais vivre avec toi le reste de ma vie entière. Reviens vite et dis moi que tu m'aimes.
I miss you terribly, and more terribly at night.

> Fax from Lucy Dicker in London, Summer 1993,
> to Arnie Wilson on assignment in Barbados

Arnie, you're bloody selfish, self-righteous, hard as rock, emotionally dishonest, ruthless, bloody infantile, really stupid, self-indulgent.

> Verbal message to Arnie Wilson, Spring 1994,
> skiing round the world, Gargellen, Austria.

From Canada and Montana, we took the southern route all the way down south.

And I mean the Deep South.

Like the States of Tennessee, Alabama, Kentucky, North Carolina, the Virginias and all the way to glory.

You didn't know they had snow east of the Mississippi? Neither did I. In the deep south, except for the occasional freak snowstorm, they make every flake themselves. They use snub-nosed guns, compressed air with water that spits out icy snow. The only proviso: the thermometer has to be around zero.

The great mass of the Appalachian Mountain range covers eleven States from Birmingham, Alabama, in the south all the way up to New York State in the north. The ski resorts have names like Cloudmont (Alabama), Wisp (Maryland) and Cataloochee (North Carolina).

Between us we meticulously kept the Black Diary going, filling in vignettes to treasure, and to recall during the trip when the going got really tough — and we still had to keep going.

Such as this extract from the Captain's Log:

> I did most of the driving, as usual, which continued to displease Lucy, although there were times when she was grateful for the opportunity to sleep. Or daydream.
>
> She would often observe, 'It's really strange, Arnie. When I look out of the window I sometimes go into a dream-world. It's almost as if I'm in a trance.'
>
> One night, faced with a long drive from Virginia to Maryland, my cherished navigator prepared the route and left me to it. It wasn't exactly auto-pilot, but with her instructions it should have been close. One of the most tiring elements of our trip was not only choosing the wrong direction, but the wrong sort of road.
>
> The quicker we got to a resort, the more time we had to rest and ski. But in the mountains, finding a good, direct road wasn't always easy. Tonight Lucy said, 'This should be a good route, darling. There are no mountain passes.' And with that, she fell into a deep sleep. But as the night unfolded, I encountered a mountain pass, and grinned affectionately towards her

*slumbering form, still cosseted in her Degré 7
ski-suit.*

'*So what do you call this, Lucy — a
motorway?*' *I was tempted to ask, as I went into
a series of hairpin bends. But I didn't want to
disturb her slumber. The second mountain pass
was soon upon us. And then a third. By now I
was not feeling quite so benevolent or good-
humoured towards my travelling companion,
who was still sleeping peacefully by my side.*

*By the time we had reached Maryland, I
had counted no fewer than seven mountain
passes. So much for Lucy's map reading. Finally,
utterly exhausted, we faced a meteorological*
coup de grace *high on the final pass. Fog. Thick
fog. So thick that I just had to stop the car and
get off the road. Humiliatingly, (and
dangerously, if we'd stayed dithering on the
road), the occasional truck came hurtling out of
the fog before disappearing into the chilled
gazpacho atmosphere a few yards later.*

*Trucks do that in America. Just when you
think conditions are utterly impossible, one roars
by as if it's a bright spring morning. And then we
hit the highway from hell. We were on Interstate
84, in the bleakest of Pennsylvanian winters.
This was not a good place to be*

*Our car was slithering all over the road,
its radiator grille encrusted in six inches of ice
like a fishing trawler tossing in the Arctic.*

*It had got worse and worse as we had
moved through some of the strange-sounding
towns that dot the bleak Pennsylvanian
countryside. Sagamore, in the words of the Simon
and Garfunkel song, really does* '*seem like a
dream to me now ...* ' *And on through Accident*

*(who on earth would want to live there?),
Mechanicsville, Krumsville and even Ambridge.*

*At Windham, up in New York State, we
discover that all the runs begin with the letter
'W', and include such gems as Why Not,
Wolverine, and Wheelchair.*

*'That's not very nice,' said Lucy. 'Let's
avoid that one.'*

*Perhaps if our mission were successful,
they'd name one of their trails 'Wilson'. Oh, the
vanity of the man!*

*   *   *

It was from Windham that we almost missed our flight home.
By home, I mean Europe.

As always, we left things late. Sunday 13 March, we got in
our obligatory run bright and early. We were enjoying
ourselves so much we lingered too long. And the day started
to go wrong.

'Arnie, you've lost us again!'

Our flight was at 4.00pm, a domestic hop from La Guardia
down to Chicago, arriving at 5.24pm in time to catch the
6.05pm to Munich, which would get us to Germany at
10.00am the following day.

In fact we would see a lot of the Windy City during the
year, mainly because Chicago is the home base of American
Airlines, the sponsors doing their bit to get us around the
Western Hemisphere. This time around, we would check our
bags through from New York, all the way to Munich, and
have forty minutes to transfer at Chicago. Time enough. Or
should have been.

That's if we ever got to La Guardia.

We had left Windham at noon, on a bright, sparkling blue-
sky day. Quite suddenly, in the bleak snow-bound wilds of
upstate New York, we started seeing towns that we shouldn't

be seeing. What's more, the petrol needle was flickering towards empty at an alarming rate.

'Arnie, where are we?'

I gritted my teeth. If I knew, I would have told her. It was almost three o'clock, we had fourteen pieces of baggage and four sets of skis to unload, and I had no idea if we were going north, south, east or west.

But finally we found ourselves on the Interstate into New York — and ended up lost again, in the Bronx.

'Arnie, I don't like the look of this area.'

'Don't worry. We'll be out of it soon.'

I tried to keep my gaze averted from the neglected buildings, the boarded-up shops with steel shutters instead of windows, the peeling paint, the graffiti sprayed everywhere. And from the gangs of youths clustered on the corners, watching us pass with empty, sullen eyes. Great place to run out of petrol.

But just then, mercifully, another sign: La Guardia Airport. Even an arrow, pointing the way. We made it with minutes to spare.

I didn't even have time to check the car back to its rightful owners. We screeched up to the American Airlines entrance, grabbed trolleys, piled on our luggage and skis — don't ask me how, but somehow we stacked them — and ran for the check-in desk.

Before we raced off, I threw the keys at a startled Sky Captain, shouting: 'Please give these to Avis!' and zig-zagged my unwieldy trolley in Lucy's wake without waiting for a reply. We caught the flight to Chicago by the skin of our teeth.

A few hours later, after changing planes, the skyscrapers of Chicago dropped away in the gathering gloom, and we relaxed at last in our Business Class seats, bound for Europe.

Lucy opened her Palmtop and I leafed through our precious Black Diary.

'Do you know, Lucy, in North America we gave fourteen TV interviews and appeared on eight radio stations. And that's not counting all the newspapers and magazines.'

In ten weeks, not bad.

Not bad at all.

We wanted to keep our sponsors happy.

On that first leg, we had driven 10,959 miles across nineteen States in North America and Canada. We had skied 746,740 vertical feet, or 140.26 vertical miles — more than twenty-five times the height of Everest. In all, we had actually skied 649.27 miles. And we hadn't missed a day.

The stewardess poured champagne, and we clinked glasses.

'To us, Lucy.'

'To us, Arnie.'

Roll on, Europe!

*   *   *

How strange to be back! Stranger still for me to be heading for a part of Austria that I had not skied for years.

My spirits lifted as I gunned the VW Passat along the smooth highway, heading for Kitzbühel. The weather was bright and breezy, the sun was out, and there was spring in the air.

Lucy caught my mood as we passed through green fields with cows dotted around like cardboard cut-outs, grazing peacefully. The hollow sound of their bells carried in a cheerful chorus across the broad valley.

'Welcome home,' I said.

She smiled, and squeezed my leg.

'Yes, it does feel like home.'

It was good to be back in Europe. You cannot beat the wide open spaces and the incredible snow plains of America for wonderful vistas and beautifully manicured runs. But when it comes to dramatic scenery — the jagged peaks, towering cliffs and plummeting gorges of the Alps have the edge.

Nature has taken different sized bites of the apple, with breathtaking results.

So far, so good. The long Atlantic crossing was behind us.

With no undue headwinds to delay us, we had arrived spot on time, 10.00am.

It didn't take us long to have our first European row of the trip. As we often did during a long flight, we were wondering what to call our book. *This* book, which should have been partly written by Lucy, but instead is about her.

I came up with the jokey *Abroad with a Broad on Our Boards*. Lucy hit the roof. We were waiting at Munich Airport to collect our luggage.

'That's the stupidest idea you've had so far,' she said, letting rip. 'I hate it. What does that make me sound like — '*a broad*' — some kind of tart?'

'It just means "woman", Lucy,' I said. 'And you are one, right?'

'Yes, but it means a brazen, cheap sort of woman! Is that what you think of me, Arnie?'

Later, it did become a joke, but for now I had to promise that the title was not a candidate. Lucy calmed down like a tempest that suddenly fades.

*　　　　*　　　　*

At Munich Airport we had picked up the most sensible car that had yet been offered us. A roomy Estate that felt as solid as a tank and drove as smoothly as a Rolls, even when packed to the rafters with fourteen bulging bags, the Goods, the Bags and the Ugly. Our skis stayed on the roof rack.

We called our latest vehicle Wolfgang.

During the next fifty-one days, we would attempt to ski a daunting seventy-two resorts. All of them were expecting us, thanks to Lucy's military precision planning.

'Amazing,' I said. 'Yesterday, America. Today Europe. And tomorrow ...' I put on my thickest guttural accent ' ... tomorrow, ze vorld!'

'Silly monkey,' said Lucy.

Then I suddenly woke up to the fact that there was

something missing. Austria was looking extremely green.

'Where's the snow, Lucy?'

We knew that the Tyrol had been enjoying temperatures higher than those in Turkey, but we hadn't been expecting the sun to be melting the snow off the lower slopes with such a vengeance.

We had twenty-four hours to get to the higher slopes, which should be time enough. All things being equal.

The trouble is, all things seldom are.

Meantime, I drove Wolfgang through springtime in Austria with increasing speed and increasing unease, heading for the first pit stop.

At Worgl, we turned left off the dual carriageway — and glimpsed our first uplifting sight of snow on the high peaks as we drove through Söll, then Brixen, Kirchberg and on to our final goal — the old walled town of Kitzbühel.

I hardly had time for more than a passing glance at the colourful Tyrolean buildings, their painted walls dating back to the thirteenth century. Or even the outline of the Schloss Kapps, an old castle hotel towering behind the pines to our right as we skirted the town centre, heading for the slopes past shirt-sleeved tourists strolling in the sun.

'It's like summer, Arnie,' Lucy's voice was filled with dismay.

'That's the trouble with spring snow,' I said grimly. 'It tends to melt.'

'But where are we going to find it now, today?'

'Up there!' I pointed in the direction of the Hahnenkamm, normally an over-populated ski area with a huge variety of runs filtering down to half a dozen villages in the valley. And, of course, the most feared downhill in the world.

A cable car should be running to take us up to 5,400 feet, and other lifts could get us as high as 6,383 feet. There'd be snow up there, for sure. But I had to admit that from where we sat the snow cover appeared pretty thin, even on the upper slopes.

'Come on!' We parked Wolfgang by the rail station. Off with

our skis, on with our boots. And grab the first ski bus that comes along! That was a mistake — as we found when the bus headed off to the wrong area, directly away from the Hahnenkamm.

The first glow of sunset was starting to fill the sky in the west above the mountains, painting the high snows glorious pink.

I clumped down the bus like Godzilla.

'Where are we going?'

'Bichalmalp!' The driver said shortly, keeping his eyes (quite rightly) on the road.

I knew the place. A small ski area, mainly for beginners, that you reach from the neighbouring village of Aurach. First, a chair-lift to 5,400 feet. Then two drag-lifts up the Stuckkogel to a height of 6,100 feet.

'What time do they close the lifts?'

'This is the final bus!'

The irony is that half an hour ago we had driven through Aurach to get to Kitzbühel, thereby wasting a good forty-five minutes. The snow line looked further away than ever.

'Are we going to make it, Arnie?'

'We've got to, even if we have to walk up.'

The single chairs took us over green fields speckled with yellow spring flowers, darkening as the light faded fast. I stared anxiously up to the half-way station. Would there be enough snow?

At the top, the mountain was as silent as the Marie Celeste, its stolid face speckled with a few patches of white. The T-Bars hung static and silent. There was no sign of human life until the door of a small wooden hut opened abruptly, and an elderly figure in a faded jacket and flat cap appeared.

'*Ein fahrt und das ist alles!*' he shouted. Only one run before we close!

And the T-bar cranked into movement.

One run was all we had, but it was enough. Ten minutes later we were notching up the hairiest mile of the month to score our obligatory day's tally. Five minutes after that we were back in the chair lift, dangling over those same green pastures and yellow flowers in the gathering gloom.

At the bottom, I found a small inn. We ordered Gluhwein, and drank to our arrival.

'That was close, Arnie.'

'Too close,' I said.

I needed that drink. We both did.

*   *   *

One of the many incidents we'd still be chuckling about months later involved a wonderful old rascal called Andler. (I've found out since that it should be spelt Anderl, but why spoil the story?) Charly, our guide in Mayrhofen, had been keen to show us a "great schnapps hut" but was disappointed to discover that the piste which led to it was closed that day.

"It's a shame" he said. "Shall we do it anyway?" he asked, temptingly. Lucy, always keen on a little adventure — and a little schnapps — didn't need to be asked twice. In a trice we were at the door of Andler's dilapidated hut, which looked like something out of a Hansel and Gretel movie. The toothless incumbent, not unlike a Tyrolean version of Mr Punch, fixed Lucy with a sparkling eye and planted a wet kiss on her cheek. To our surprise, a makeshift bed sprawled in the corner of the room where the old man made his schnapps and his cheese. He promptly suggested that Lucy must be very tired from skiing round the world, and might like to curl up after her drink. Lucy chuckled explosively with delight at this chat-up line, but declined. This did not prevent his hands wandering as we left, giving her a farewell kiss in the process.

"He may have been 82, but he was certainly not dead to the world!" grinned Lucy later. "Andler is a pretty appropriate name!"

As we lay in bed that night, we had been locking horns in an animated, if inconclusive, discussion about what irritated us. As in How Did Arnie Bug Lucy? And How Did Lucy Rile Arnie?

We had gone through the familiar list of my shortcomings. Arrogant, selfish, boastful, etc etc. The usual qualities, or lack of them, that I knew off by heart.

Now it was my turn. There are times when things have to be aired. This seemed as good a time as any, and better than most.

This particular time was in bed, after dinner but before making love. Dinner had been a warm and cosy affair, a quiet celebration of another glorious day on the slopes. These particular slopes being around Gargellen, which is one of Austria's finest small ski resorts, nestling at the end of a sunny valley.

Statistically, it had been an average day: 10.17 miles, and 11,695 vertical feet, which allowed us to feel relaxed enough to repair to the candlelit glow of the Montafoner Stube cellar bar with its traditional stone oven and centuries-old wooden panelling.

Now, three hours later, we were back in our small pension. And she was nibbling her fingers again.

'Lucy, you must stop this dreadful habit of chewing your fingers. And another thing. You're always locking everything. It's a compulsion, an obsession. It's — unhealthy.'

'Give me a break, Arnie. What's unhealthy about it? And by the way, I don't like that word.'

'What word — ?'

'Obsession.'

But it was.

'For a start, you always lock the bedroom door, even though we could be roasted in our beds if there's a fire. Look, the key's in the lock. I can see it!' I pointed to the door.

'Security,' said Lucy, chin dangerously high. 'You can't be too careful.'

'And the car. You lock and double-check every door when we park, even for just a moment.'

She did, too, with a crisp: 'Keys please, darling!' within a second of my putting a foot out on to the ground. Her reflex action of pocketing the ignition key had become so automatic that sometimes she forgot she'd even done it.

'You never gave them to me. I haven't got them. Where are they, Arnie?'

'Look in your bag,' I'd say wearily.

And after a lot of scuffling and muttering, there were the keys.

But Lucy was such an efficient organiser, her brain darting this way and that, doing most of the thinking for both of us, so who was I to complain? Too late, I *had* complained. And this time it wasn't just a squib that went off — it was the entire firework display: rockets, catherine wheels, bangers, the lot.

'That's really stupid,' she shrieked. 'You're so bloody self-righteous and bloody infantile.' The exocets kept coming. 'How can you be so bloody selfish? So self-indulgent? You're as hard as a rock! Ruthless! And emotionally dishonest!'

Nothing serious, then. What had I done to deserve this show of affection, I wondered? I sat silently, calmly writing down the names she was calling me in rough capitals on a paper napkin.

'BLOODY SELFISH, SELF-RIGHTEOUS, HARD AS A ROCK, EMOTIONALLY DISHONEST, RUTHLESS, BLOODY INFANTILE, REALLY STUPID, SELF-INDULGENT.'

Qui? *Moi*? A long pause. What happened, I wondered, to those supremely magical things she'd said to me in her love-fax to Barbados when I'd had to leave her in London during an assignment a year earlier? Like:

> *I love you*
> *I want to marry you and have your baby.*
> *I'm frightened of losing you.*
> *Hurry home and tell me you love me.*

I looked again at her hate letter. Well, the words I'd noted from her torrent of abuse.

'I wonder which of these would be appropriate for you?' I said finally. I ticked off 'bloody infantile'. No problem there. And I was tempted by 'stupid'. But I couldn't really accuse her of the rest. 'But I do have another one, just for you, Lucy.'

'What's that, then?' she said, her eyes glinting dangerously.

'Potty!' I said. 'You're bloody potty.'

'Well,' she said, 'at least we know where we stand.'

And then, thank God, we both started laughing.

Chapter 8

April

I was quite proud of my skiing progress
until I saw a video of myself. To my horror,
I looked just like a grasshopper. It was my green outfit
and the skipping technique as I transferred my weight
from one leg to the other that did it!

Lucy Dicker, April 1994

'*R*emember what the guide said, Lucy? "Don't fall
here. Whatever you do — DON'T FALL HERE!" '

*　　　*　　　*

The spring of 1994 had been phenomenally warm. I knew that
snow starts to disappear in Austria before it vanishes in other
Alpine countries, and had worked out our itinerary
accordingly. But with the sun burning off the lower snow-
cover so dramatically, it was time for a reshuffle, or we'd be
skiing on grass, which wasn't in the game plan.

I got out the *Audi Ski Map* again.

'Austria, Italy, Germany, Switzerland, France, Italy. And,
in May, back to France. That should do us.'

'And then?' Lucy sat across the room, sipping an early
evening whisky and drawing on a small cigar. She liked the

121

occasional cheroot, as indeed did I, but never, for either of us, a cigarette.

For the hundredth time, I examined the schedule. 'It gets tricky in May, doesn't it? We'll be in India.'

God alone knew what was in store for us there. It had never been our idea to go to the Himalayas, largely because we had visions of being stranded by delays and cancellations miles from the nearest mountains.

Then it would be Japan, and on to California, before returning to Europe.

'And we'll have been right around the world in less than a month!' Lucy said with a touch of amazement in her voice.

But first, we had to get through Europe.

Out of Austria, into Italy. Selva ... Cortina. Back to Austria, into Germany. Garmisch-Partenkirchen.

Sixteen Swiss resorts, among them Klosters, St Moritz, Andermatt, Verbier, Villars and Zermatt. France would include La Plagne, Val d'Isère, the famous Three Valleys of Courchevel, Meribel and Val Thorens.

Finally I got it right, and Lucy got on the phone to fine tune our plans.

At first Lucy didn't know quite what to make of Austria. By which I mean she found Austria almost too pristine, too beautiful, too clean, too perfect. Too ... *Sound of Music*-ish. Lucy liked the odd wart.

'It's almost forced, the beauty of those villages. They look as if they've been spring-cleaned for tourists,' she said more than once, as we drove Wolfgang past picture-book chalets, picture-book fields — and even picture-book cattle.

'Look at those cows, Lucy! Aren't they wonderful? They're so brown and creamy. And those eyelashes — I think that one's fluttering them at me!'

'Yeah, she's in love with you, Arnie.' But she had to admit that the cows were very appealing.

Austria always looks the way it does, and probably has done since the sound of the first yodel echoed through the mountains. A sound, I should add, that Lucy found irritating.

Which, of course, caused me to yodel whenever I wanted to liven up the journey.

'*Yodel-aieyee-dee!*'

'Stop it, Arnie. I hate it! Get away — ' And she would cuff me lustily across the head until I stopped.

* * *

On the slopes, Lucy had a graceful gazelle-like quality. To ski behind her was a constant joy, watching the growing confidence in her poise, the swishing turns as the flying figure in pink and pastel blue and green hurtled ahead of me.

Over the weeks she had gone from strength to strength, and by now she was taking the black runs like an expert.

Lucy had grown to adore the mountains and all they symbolised, endowing them with the same passion she gave to everything in life once she was committed in her mind to doing so.

Which, I'm glad to say, included me.

The healthy climate, fresh clean air, the exhilaration of taking your first breath on the slopes — when suddenly it really is a joy to be alive. Lucy took them all exuberantly to herself.

She usually wore a headband, which really suited her, allowing her long auburn hair to flow out behind her as the wind took it. My own pulse would pound with a heart-catching mix of pride and adoration as I followed in her tracks, often alongside her, keeping pace like a circus duo working out a new act.

'That girl's like a thoroughbred racehorse,' a close friend once confided. Watching her long mane in the wind, I couldn't have put it better.

Lucy disagreed.

'Arnie, I look terrible!'

It was my fault that I showed her the video in the first place. Some 5,000 feet up on the slopes of Lech, the up-market Austrian resort, we had skied the Arlberg Valley on a glorious Tuesday morning, accomplishing 18.78 miles and 21,600 vertical feet. We decided to relax and have an afternoon off from dedicated piste-bashing.

Lunch up the mountain (hot Goulash soup, large sausage in a roll, strong local red wine) at the popular Palmenalpe Restaurant on the Kriegerhorn, its terrace crowded with spring skiers sunbathing in T-shirts.

To make our afternoon descent into Lech more diverting, I said: 'Right, Lucy. Time for your latest personal appearance!'

I produced the video camera, complete with fresh tape.

'Oh, Arnie. We've done all this before. What now?'

Lucy was a 'natural' in front of the camera, and was able to reel off a very professional 'piece to camera' as soon as I pointed the lens at her. In fact, we had already videoed several hours of our odyssey, sending the tapes back to London when they were full rather than cart them around as superfluous luggage. Mostly they recorded resorts and events, some of them indoors — a dinner here, a speech there.

I had already videoed Lucy on skis, but nothing out of the ordinary. But now ...

'Let's celebrate our first million vertical feet,' I said.

It was true. The previous night Lucy had triumphantly written into the Black Diary the magic words: ONE MILLION VERTICAL FEET! In capital letters, complete with exclamation mark.

Now Lucy put down her glass, and frowned across the terrace at me.

'What sort of personal appearance?'

'To record your progress. You've come on such a lot that you're almost unrecognisable from the person you were four months ago.'

Her face lit up. 'Do you really think so — ?'

'I know so. Now — enough of the flattery. I want you to ski as you've never skied before.'

Well, she did.

I went ahead, taking up position at the foot of various suitable slopes, bellowing: 'Okay. Come on!' And following her through the lens, watching her as she swooped and dipped, her lithe, strong body somehow managing to look both elegant and effective.

'Very professional,' I said approvingly at the bottom station. 'We must have a look at that one.'

That same evening we found an obliging bar with a video system attached to the TV. At the cost of a beer for the barman, who hailed from New Zealand, the video was set up.

'Okay,' Arnie B de Mille sat back in the comfort of the Stube with his latest star find, and raised his glass. 'Roll it!'

Two minutes later, all hell broke loose.

Alright, I exaggerate. But a shriek rent the air, and Lucy was squealing: 'Oh, Arnie, it's dreadful. I look like a *sauterelle* — grasshopper.'

Perhaps she had tended to exaggerate the technique she had been taught where you shift your weight radically from one leg to the other to get through fresh powder and over the dreaded bumps.

'Does she look like a grasshopper?' I asked the Kiwi at the bar, who was looking appreciatively at the display.

'Well ... ' he said, unhelpfully. And he was drinking my beer, too.

'There, I told you.' Lucy tossed her head.

'Thanks a lot, friend,' I said feelingly, on the way out.

To me, Lucy would always be more gazelle than grasshopper.

*   *   *

The next day, we found ourselves in royal company.

A coffee at the bustling Rufikopf restaurant to warm up after the chair lift that had taken us up to 7,637 feet, and we were off on a red run on the winding five-kilometre piste down to Zurs. This is pleasant, relatively undemanding skiing, and would serve to put another few miles under our belts.

As we paused to take in the view, a tall, attractive woman in a powder-blue one-piece outfit came over the brow of the hill behind us, skiing with an instructor. We followed casually for a full half-minute before I recognised her.

Princess Diana skied well, and stylishly. She was loving every minute of it, possibly because there were no *paparazzi* in sight. Presumably they had called a truce for the day — or maybe none of them were good enough to keep up. William looked confident, too.

When they stopped to regroup, Lucy and I skied on past with a swift salute.

It isn't every day you get to ski with the future King of England.

*   *   *

We played another game on the chairlift. A word game called 'Ghosts'. It goes like this.

One player starts with a letter, and the second player follows with another — but you must never finish a word. Sample: I start with 'S'. Lucy follows with 'O'. I would probably go for 'C', knowing I'd trapped her. She would have a problem getting out of it without saying 'K'. S-O-C-K-E-T wouldn't count, because you'd already said SOCK. And if you lose three times, you've lost three lives. You're a ghost. And you're out!

I have to say that for all her basic honesty, Lucy could be very crafty. Worse, she would actually accuse me of cheating — while inventing a non-existent word herself, and swearing it was true.

'It *is* a word, Arnie!'

'No it's not. It's a French word, and French words are not allowed. You know that — '

'I'm sure it's a word.'

'Bullshit!' I'd say in the heat of the moment, quite often as we were coming to the end of the lift and getting our skis hurriedly together to heave ourselves out of the chair. The attendant would look inquiringly at us, hearing my bad language and Lucy's explosive laughter as she skied off. 'Bullshit to *you*,' she'd say. 'It *is* a word, Arnie. I win!'

*　　　　*　　　　*

'The rocks, Lucy. You're going to hit the rocks. Watch out! WATCH OUT!'

*　　　　*　　　　*

I was always aware that we had to keep our ski 'Mileage Account' in credit, using the good days to offset the bad.

It was in the Alps that we ran into serious trouble with our ski-dometers. Mike Browne, whose injuries had not prevented his triumphant return to the mountains to ski with us in a ski-bob, saw the problem at first hand. The metal spurs he had provided us with to attach to the back of our skis had worked well in America, where virtually all the lifts are chairs. In other words, you're in the air, not in contact with the snow.

But in the Alps, T-Bars or 'Button' drag lifts are often the order of the day. And, of course, those spurs would faithfully record every foot of the way — including the uphill haul.

To work out the calculations would be well-nigh impossible, and beyond even Lucy's masterly mathematics.

'We're supposed to be Downhill Racers, not Uphill Racers,' I said, when the truth hit me.

Instead we used my Avocet watch. By calculating approximately 1,150 vertical feet per ski mile — which we found to be the average during our trip so far — we discovered this did the job just as effectively.

An altimeter watch, for the uninitiated, is similar in principle to the dials you find in the flight deck on aircraft. All you have to do is to press the Start Button at the beginning of the day, and leave it to the wonders of modern technology to do the rest. The watch works on barometric pressure, records every inch you ski, and runs out every 299,000 vertical feet, when it automatically starts again at zero.

*   *   *

There can be few more exciting runs than the one we are going to do today. The Val di Mesdi, the Valley of Midday, is one of the classic off-piste runs in the whole of the Italian Dolomites, and there is one quick way to reach it.

By helicopter.

'I've never skied it myself, Lucy, so maybe you should just come and look over the edge. You can always turn back.' I was busy gathering my gear.

'Arnie, I'm not sure — '

I would never, ever, knowingly put Lucy in danger, and I could have left her on the easier slopes at any time. But neither of us wanted it that way.

So she came with me. And, when the gleaming silver dragon-fly whirred away into the sun and left us standing there in total isolation, we stood in awed silence for a full minute gathering our breath and our nerve.

We had Amin Momen with us, a friend from Bladon Lines who knew the Dolomites well. If anyone could get us down, Amin would.

Danilo, our pilot, hadn't helped our central nervous system by giving us the scenic ride — a mesmerising eagle's eye view of huge craggy pinnacles that tower above the Val Gardena like hostile sentinels, daring anyone to invade their awesome fortress.

Below us now I could see a wild and beautiful gulley plunging down between sheer rock faces into an abyss where there was nothing but space. Small stones rattled off the rocks, heading nowhere.

I wasn't sure Lucy was up to this.

'Are you sure we can both do this?' I muttered to Amin, out of Lucy's hearing. This, I realised, was going to be the sternest test of her skiing so far, if not her life.

'It's not as bad as it looks,' Amin assured us cheerfully. 'Just keep in my tracks.'

Lucy's jaw tightened in determination. Now I'm here, the message read, for better or worse let's get on with it!

As with all good guides, Amin's words proved right. The slope turned out to be steep, but not lethal. Just as long as you were a strong skier.

Just how advanced Lucy had become, I was about to find out. But I was still very anxious.

Lucy, edging her way across and down. Traversing where possible, performing tight turns to get back into the fall line with a dexterity that showed just how much her skiing had improved since New Year's Day a thousand years ago in Jackson Hole.

Amin visibly relaxed. So much so that he called a halt. And lay on his back in the snow to gaze up as if in a trance at the vast battlements soaring into the brilliant cobalt blue sky overhead.

Sometimes it gets to you that way.

I turned in mid-descent to see Lucy skiing fast. Too fast. For the first time in the trip I am frightened for her. I shouldn't have brought her to this place. Please God, don't fall! Somehow, she gets down safely.

I pull her close. Under her pink anorak, she is trembling.

'Darling, I'm so proud of you!'

She smiles.

'I still ski like a grasshopper!'

*   *   *

Over fresh crisp rolls, honey and hot chocolate, we discuss the coming weeks.

'Just think where we're heading, Lucy.' With only a week to go, our thoughts were full of our visit to India and Japan.

India was rushing up on us, fast. Soon the gravy days in exquisite Alpine resorts would be over, at least for a time, and we would be heading into uncharted waters. I felt the familiar frisson of excitement between my shoulder blades.

'I hope our hotel room in India will be clean!' said Lucy.

Mind you, it wasn't always clean enough for her even in her native France. In La Plagne, for example, Lucy was so upset with the lack of cleanliness in our apartment that she refused to go skiing until she'd cleaned it up.

'God, Arnie, it's tatty,' she said. 'Look how dusty and dirty it is.'

Occasionally we had rooms like that. At least there was a washing machine, which cheered her up slightly. I told Lucy it was unavoidable that in 365 days we would find ourselves in a tip every now and then.

'But I don't like it, Arnie. I must do something about it!'

And, already wearing her ski-suit, she got busy with the Hoover.

'This is crazy, Lucy. We must go skiing.'

I was beginning to sound like *her*.

'And just look at the bed!' It was misshapen, by which I mean that it was not quite rectangular, more wobbly oblong. The sheets didn't fit. The duvet hung down to the floor at one corner.

Lucy, hoovering away. Making beds. Not skiing for once.

To my delight, in Courchevel, where we were hosted by an old friend, Andrew Dunn, the boss of Ski Scott Dunn, my daughter Samantha, a TV producer, came to ski with us. I hadn't seen her for four months.

I'd sent her a silly fax: 'Dearest darling daughter, do decide dates damnquick. Daddy desires desperately 'dorable daughter's decision. Do dash Daddywards! Drop dead donkey!

Dankeshone! Don't delay! Daddy.'

How could she resist such an invitation?

One afternoon, after a picnic on the slopes, Mark Rowe, the Ski Scott Dunn rep suggested a plan that arguably had a profound effect on Lucy's skiing psyche.

Finishing off his last few drops of hot mulled wine and lodging the empty glass in the snow, Mark turned to us and asked: 'Who's for the *couloirs*?'

Couloirs — off-piste gulleys which trap wind-blown snow — are often quite extreme and not normally shown on official trail maps; resorts prefer not to lure recreational skiers into them. But Courchevel has three that are official. What Mark had in mind was to ski all three in a single afternoon. Two of them — Grand and Sous Téléphérique — I had skied before. But I had never got round to skiing the third, Emile Allais, named after a famous French ski racer.

Samantha had never skied a *couloir* in her life, and here we were, thinking about skiing three one after the other. With two precious and hugely loved women in my charge — both obstinately brave skiers — I felt a great burden of responsibility.

'What sort of condition will they be in?' I asked Mark.

'They should be quite soft,' he said.

In a *couloir*, soft is good. Icy is dangerous.

The problem was that to reach the top of these *couloirs* — even to find out whether the snow conditions were safe or not — involved skiing down a narrow, difficult path from the top of the huge Saulire cable-car. It would be difficult to get back again. So in a sense, once you reached the top of these descents, you were committed.

Mark went into the Grand first, and I followed. My skis made a horrible rasping sound on the snow. It wasn't soft enough. Suddenly, I was very anxious. Sam and Lucy stood at the top, waiting to see what I thought.

'*Don't come in,*' I shouted back at them. '*It's too icy.*'

Sam considered my advice for a moment, and then

slithered over the edge. Now she *was* committed! More guts than sense, I thought. Well of course, once Sam was in, there was no stopping Lucy. She wasn't going to be shown up by my daughter. It was a tense, tentative descent. But at the bottom, Sam and Lucy were ready for the next one.

'If you're sure,' I said.

They were sure.

Even I had never skied three *couloirs* in an afternoon, and when we turned to study Emile Allais from a distance, I didn't like the look of it.

'There's a nasty dogleg in it,' I said. 'Quite honestly, as I've never skied it, I think we should give it a miss. We've done two, after all, and got away with it.'

But Mark was keen to ski it and I must admit I was keen to add the scalp of Emile Allais to my list.

'Look, Dad, I'm going home in a day or two,' said Sam. 'You and Lucy have got another eight months of solid skiing. I'd like to do it, but there's no need for you to.'

That did it. I wasn't going to let Sam ski it without me. But I said to Lucy, 'Darling, be happy with the two you've skied. Don't do this one, please.'

Lucy thought about it, and — very reluctantly — agreed to rest on her laurels. As it turned out, it wasn't any worse than the other two. The dogleg's appearance was worse than its bite. And of course, when Lucy heard this, she was angry with herself.

'God, Arnie, I really wimped out there. I feel really cross that I didn't ski it with you.'

The thought haunted her for days. Even months later she would refer to it. Now, I sometimes wonder whether that memory of 'wimping out' on that spring day in the French Alps nudged her into plucking up the courage to ski that other fateful *couloir* in La Grave, a year later.

La Grave. A chill chisels its way down my backbone every time I say or write those two words. It was in La Grave that I was about to endure the most frightening descent of my life.

In the very ski area where Lucy herself would have her catastrophic accident.

It wasn't the first time I had met Olivier Laborie. I had enjoyed his company and some adventurous skiing with him in the past. Today, less than a third of the way into our mission, he wanted to give me the ultimate treat: skiing a run that was on the very edge of my capabilities.

All day long, as Lucy and I enjoyed our day in one of the world's most exciting ski areas, there'd been a gleam in his eye.

He knew I liked being pushed to my limits. And I knew he knew.

He'd selected a 'special run' that in his mind at least, would give me the ultimate buzz. In fact, it scared me to death. With Lucy waiting anxiously way below us, unable to see the drama taking place high above her, I had mentally frozen on a terribly steep traverse on the way to the run Olivier wanted me to ski : the Pan de Rideau — Edge of the Curtain. I was desperately afraid. And I didn't mind telling the *FT* readers that.

When Lucy died in La Grave a year later, the *Daily Express*, seeing the irony of the situation, was quick to quote what I had written before.

> *'I was stranded like a disorientated mountain goat on the edge of a snowy chasm. Opposite, spring avalanches thundered off the sun-baked shoulders and flanks of the mighty Meije.*
>
> *The terrifying traverse on which I now stood was above two or three precipitous couloirs which merged into a sheer gully hundreds of feet below. I knew that one slip would result in certain death. Below me was an impossibly steep gully which fell away almost vertically. I pictured myself tumbling hopelessly down and down, bouncing off one cliff after another, until I reached a frozen grave*

thousands of feet below.

A guide at La Grave is highly desirable. But perhaps not a guide who seduces you into exploring your own threshold of fear. It would be a quick death. A scream would be undignified. Silence would be better.

Sometimes a short, risky and heart-stopping section like this is the 'entrance fee' you must pay for the most sublime and exciting skiing. But this was more than a challenge. This was coming face to face with the inner demons which haunt all skiers who mix skiing with mountaineering.

The two of us were now teetering on the brink while he struggled to get a rope round my girth without either of us falling. Then he began driving in a piton in the rock above me. As he hammered, the sound was so clear that I thought it must carry all the way to Lucy, who was awaiting our descent on the glacier floor more than 1,000 feet below.

Having secured the rope through a karabiner, Olivier asked me to push the rope through the piton, retrieve the karabiner and lower myself back on to the traverse. This was madness.

What did I know of karabiners? These were the tools of climbers, not skiers. They were completely alien and frightening to me, and spoke of people who actually enjoy being suspended over vertiginous drops.

But I did it, and inched — no, centimetred — my way back. At last we were out of danger. I was going to live.

In front of us were thousands of feet of supreme powder. The skiing was ecstatic. We

*both shouted in the direction of the rock where
we had arranged to meet Lucy. Our voices
echoed emptily among the moraines and seracs.*

*Fearing the worst as the sun began to set,
Lucy had found her way down, without a guide,
to raise the alarm. The manager of the
téléphérique, armed with strong binoculars had
spotted us making our way back through green
fields carpeted with crocuses. From half a mile
away I waved at Lucy and she waved back. We
were overjoyed to see each other.*

*Over a beer in the Castillan Hotel bar, I
asked Olivier how often he took clients down the
Pan de Rideau. 'You were the first,' he said. 'I
like to push clients beyond their normal limits.'*

*When he said that, Lucy and I looked at
each other. Little did we realise that I was going
to have a second day of terror in La Grave. Far
worse than the first.*

*   *   *

We lay in bed together, Lucy's head cradled in my arms. She
stared past me with heavy-lidded eyes, out at the great bulk of
Mont Blanc hunched like a sleeping giant against the star
spangled night sky.

We were staying with our friends Colleen Olianti, the boss of
one of my favourite family tour operators, Collineige, and her
gravelly-voiced husband, Jean-Marie, a high-mountain guide.

Mont Blanc is to the Alps what that other Great White is
to sharks: the most formidable, most respected and to us
mere mortals surely the most revered peak for its sheer
awesome presence.

Skiing Chamonix means skiing the Vallée Blanche. Which
in turn means scaling the Aigulle du Midi — the legendary
'Needle' pointing its snow-capped finger to the sky 9,000

dizzying feet above the town. Once the cable car deposits you on a wind-blown platform, you tramp off through a series of rock tunnels and over a bridge suspended between two icy peaks — to the incredible glacier of the Vallée Blanche itself.

Lucy knew France's celebrated resort as well as I did, if not better. I didn't have to tell her that we needed a guide for the hazardous descent through scenery that almost defeats the imagination, with its staggering views of Mont Blanc and its spectacular ice columns carved out by nature in a moment of sublime inspiration.

Apart from the safety factor, and not wishing to vanish down a crevasse on the unpredictable, constantly moving glacier, if you have an accident without a guide the rescue costs are horrendous.

We took a guide.

Now, safely back with another unforgettable memory and another 6,500 vertical feet to add to our days together, we were exhausted, but drowsily euphoric.

'Lucy — '

'Umm — ?' Her eyes were closing.

'If you could travel in time, would you go forward or back?'

A pause. Then her sleepy voice: 'What would *you* do, Arnie?'

'I'd go back. I'd like to be there at all the momentous historical occasions. I'd like to see what really happened to Jesus on the Cross. And you — ?'

'I'd want to go into the future.' She was tailing off into a whisper. 'I'd like to see what's going to happen to me ... '

And Lucy slept.

Chapter 9

May

*Will we be able to drink the water on the Air India jet?
And will there be any jumping snakes in the Himalayas?*

Lucy Dicker, Geneva Airport, 5 May 1994

India was always the wild card in the pack.

We stared gloomily out of the car window at the raging cacophony of dust, hooting car horns, shouts from vendors peddling their wares, barefoot children scampering through muddy puddles, the odd long-horned bullock dragging a cart, and a general atmosphere of overall squalor.

'Arnie, is this what they call culture shock?'

In the rear seat beside me, Lucy shuddered.

'Do you know what this makes me want to do? To grab a big broom and duster and sweep the whole of India clean single-handed!'

I believe she meant it.

Our arrival in New Delhi had not been exactly auspicious, either, though we couldn't fault the Air India flight from Geneva, via Rome, that had landed us on Asian soil shortly after dawn.

In Europe, we had given ourselves as much ski time as was

humanly possible. But we had known all along it was going to be close. We'd had a frantic rush up to the departure lounge to catch Air India Flight 174, leaving at 15.15hrs.

The flight would take ten-and-a-half hours, including a 75-minute stopover in Rome, before touch down at Indira Gandhi Airport at 06.15hrs.

Flying into the sun meant a short day and a short night.

With snow to find at the end of it.

At least we had the privilege of flying Executive Class, seats 1a and 1b in the front row immediately behind the curtained-off flight deck of the giant Airbus. There was no First Class on that run, but from the treatment we received you'd never know it.

'Are you sure it's OK to drink the water, darling?' asked Lucy.

She had no such qualms, however, about accepting a glass of Bollinger champagne from a sari-clad stewardess with the graciousness expected of those able to afford £1,559 for the one-way ticket.

Lucy worked out our vital statistics.

'In all, we have skied 1,664,253 vertical feet, and 1,460 miles.'

That called for more champagne.

We had also managed to dispose of a goodly quantity of luggage. Hauling fourteen bags and four sets of skis around India was not our idea of fun.

'Okay in the days of the Raj,' I said. 'Servants, elephants, and all that. But I believe those days have gone.'

We drank to the Raj, to elephants, to plenteous snow in India, to the vertical feet we had descended — 'And may there be many more to come' — and to the willing hands who had helped us lighten our load for this leg.

Thanks to our friends, we had in fact been able to drop bags off in several places where we planned to return. Mostly full of papers and resort information, and we had bought empty holdalls to replace them. Thus, one case had stayed behind in Jackson Hole. A second was pushed under a bed in Dillon, Colorado. A third had gone into a locker in Kolsass

Weer, Austria, while four weighty holdalls were stored in a cupboard in the Oliantis' chalet in Chamonix.

Now, with only seven bags between us (plus skis), you could say we were travelling light. The wheels of Flight 174 screeched on to the tarmac at Indira Gandhi Airport shortly after dawn on the morning of Thursday 5 May. I arrived with jet lag and a hangover, in a temperature of 23 degrees Centigrade, or 75 degrees Fahrenheit. On either reckoning, it was warm.

'Just be grateful we're not wearing our ski outfits, Lucy. Then they really would know we're crazy!'

She burst into giggles.

*   *   *

Destination: Manali, situated in the foothills of the Himalayas in an area encouragingly known as the Valley of the Gods. I had never heard of it, and I would presume the same applied to the citizens of Manali about Arnie Wilson and Lucy Dicker, Skiing the World.

'I just hope they smile down on us,' I muttered. 'Actually, we could be in for something interesting. The Solang Nala ski basin is the primary area for winter sports in India.'

There was yet one more flight.

Jagson Airways produced a plane whose fuselage, in cigar terms, was a Wills Whiff compared to a Churchill. The flight to Bhuntar ('As in Billy, Lucy?') took two hours, after a ninety-minute delay before take-off from Delhi.

The plane finally staggered in four hours late. By which time my shins had been kicked mercilessly by a small Indian boy sitting opposite me swinging his legs, without taking his eyes off me for the whole flight.

'We'll never make it to the snow.'

Squashed in the back of the plane in seats made for the vertically challenged, my knees ached, my head ached, and the jet lag was producing a growing torpor, broken only by a kick from Mowgli across from me.

Arrival in Bhuntar. Time to wake and stay awake. Somewhere, we had to find snow.

It was 2pm.

I would have liked to have whacked him with my ski bag as we embarked, but instead I settled for a dark look at his grinning face as he scampered off into what passed for the Arrivals Hall.

Now, in the centre of Bhuntar, we sat in the mother of all traffic jams, listening to the hooting and hollering that seemed to symbolise a sub-continent in turmoil.

I felt turmoil of a different kind. We had three hours to get to any trace of snow in daylight. Or else ski the Himalayas in pitch darkness.

A cheerful brown face in the front passenger seat on the driver's left turned and beamed at us.

'May I at last introduce myself fully.' He was gaunt and lean, with an enviable thatch of jet black hair for someone who must be approaching his fifties. 'My name is Bushan Lal Bhat, I am your guide, and it is my wish to make you happy.'

Delighted, I'm sure. I smiled back at him through my jet lag, and was rewarded by one of those nods which means neither yes or no and is as indigenous to the sub-continent as curried rice.

'I have had strict orders from my boss to make certain your wishes come true, and I am determined, now that he has instructed me in this, to make sure that you have everything you need.'

His head moved on his shoulders from side to side like a metronome. Tick-tock!

'How about snow?' I said. 'We could do with snow —'

'Indeed, sir. We will find you snow.'

Mr Bhat had met us in the Arrivals Hall at Bhuntar Airport, holding up the familiar piece of cardboard with our surnames scrawled in thick black ink.

After much shouting and hand waving, together with

quantities of rupee notes pressed into outstretched palms, our luggage was safely packed aboard a large limousine that looked as if it had been freshly polished, just for us. Which undoubtedly, it had. There was even a VIP flag fluttering from the offside wing in a bright shade of green and white.

I was impressed. Just one thing, though. 'Look at the tyres,' I muttered out of the corner of my mouth. I didn't want to upset our guide and mentor who was scurrying around, supervising the loading of seven bags in the boot and four sets of skis (which went on the roof).

'What — ?'

'The tyres!' I hissed.

They were as bald as Kojak. Great for hairpin bends, I thought.

But somehow we were out of the streets at last, and on to the main highway heading for the foothills of the Himalayas, some hundred kilometres away. Correction. For highway, read country lane.

Our driver had resorted to the tried and tested remedy of hitting the horn and the accelerator simultaneously. It worked, as it seems to all over India.

We were on our way. But not for long. Thud-thud-thud!

'What's that, Mr Bhat?' But I knew, and so did he. One of our almost bald tyres had sprung a puncture, off-side rear.

The driver pulled into the side with noticeable reluctance. I had the feeling he would rather have gone bumping happily along on a rim and a prayer. But he unloaded our luggage from the boot, without apparent effort or hurry, wheeled a fresh tyre out, and hammered it in place.

I looked at the spare as he slammed home the hub cap, and winced. Kojak, Mark II, bald as a coot.

Another half hour lost. And when we finally drove off, I couldn't help noticing how our taciturn driver kept glancing out through the window, making sure the 'new' wheel was still with us.

Even more frustratingly, we kept stopping at various wooden huts which housed uniformed figures. Each time Mr

Bhat leapt out, waving papers in one hand, vanished into the interior, and emerged again several minutes later brandishing the sheets in triumph.

'What is it, Mr Bhat?'

'Permission, sir. Our vehicle is from the Bhunthar district.'

'So — ?'

'They think we are depriving local taxi drivers of custom, sir. Every region, we have to get permission. But I tell them who you are. And that I want you to ski, ski, ski.'

'Thank you, Mr Bhat. That's what we want, too.'

'I know it, sir.'

It was proving a long haul to the snow. By now Lucy and I were getting really anxious.

The road wound through bare hillsides of mud, rocks and shale, climbing with every bend. The air grew noticeably colder. Outside, a wind had sprung up, whistling eerily. Our driver drove steadily but unhurriedly along the narrow highway, right up to the hill station of Manali — a famous back-packers' centre where we would be staying.

And then, eventually, joy! Relief! The first hint of white glimmered through the rock-strewn slopes, lying in dirty white patches like soiled sheets.

'Do we really have to ski on that, Arnie?'

'Well, it's snow!'

'Let's stop the car. Please!'

Mr Bhat translated. The driver sought the brake, and our four bald tyres slewed to a halt.

'This will have to do.'

I looked out at terrain strewn with large boulders and small stones, as if the Great Gambler in the Sky had tossed them in the air and let them fall haphazardly like dice on an uneven green baize cloth.

But at least the patches of snow were interlinked enough to ski that slope. We would have our work cut out to get more than a hundred yards at a time, but skiing beggars can't be choosers.

'I have to tell you, Lucy, that this is not exactly the way I had envisaged telling people back home how we had skied the Himalayas.'

'Be grateful for small mercies, Arnie. A little snow goes a long way.'

The sun was dipping behind the foothills, turning the sky into a crimson furnace. If we didn't want to be skiing in darkness we had to take what was on offer which wasn't exactly Himalayan in proportions.

A hut advertised: BOOT, OVERCOAT AND GLUB ON HIRE. For the princely sum of 120 rupees, which is around five pounds Sterling to the likes of you and me, tourists from India's deep south, many of whom had never seen snow before, could hire red wellington boots, artificial fur coats and gloves to scramble up and slither down the foothills. We had some slithering to do, too.

'Come on, Lucy!'

We scrambled out of the car, and the driver and Mr Bhat helped drag our skis off the roof. A man in a fur jacket was sitting on a rock by the roadside, strumming a sitar. Small children with chocolate-drop eyes stared at the strangers in their midst, unblinking.

Down the length of the street, the red coals of burning braziers had sprung up like fireflies. An aroma of roasting meat filled the air, alerting our taste buds.

In that world of rags and no riches, Lucy looked like a creature from another planet in her purple anorak, colourful sweater and blue jeans.

'You couldn't be causing a greater stir if you were Madonna — '

'Don't you wish I were!'

We snapped on our skis.

'Race you to the bottom!'

The bottom was all of three hundred yards away, or one hundred and eighty vertical feet by our altimeter watches.

Also, as I pointed out, the slope was festooned with

slippery rocks and small stones that had rolled down from on high to entrap the unwary, poking unsportingly through the thin layer of snow like a minefield of trip-wires.

'On second thoughts, I can't say I like the look of this, Lucy. Take it carefully.'

She watched as I skied off gingerly, with caution in every limb. And at the bottom: a stream I didn't see until too late, hidden behind a snow bank. I was in it, freezing up to my ankles, before I could stop.

'What was that you were saying, Arnie?'

I looked up at her, hastily changing my glower into a vapid grin.

'Wasn't that fun?' I said.

But now, since there seemed to be no such thing as a drag lift in this corner of India, we still had to get back. On foot.

'Lucy,' I said. 'There's only one thing for it.' I drew a deep breath.

'*Yodel-aiyee-dee!*' The echoes spun down the valley.

'Stop it, Arnie! Stupid monkey!'

But I caught her smiling. Most important of all, we still hadn't missed a day.

*　　　　*　　　　*

In their wisdom the Indian Tourist Office in London, who had organised this phase of our trip, had booked us into the Evergreen Hotel.

'Look, Lucy. Something's missing — '

It was the roof, actually. Despite its exotic name, the Evergreen Hotel still had its top floor unfinished, and from all appearances would seem to have precious little chance of ever completing the task.

In India, staff quarters are often located on the top storey of provincial hotels, lending an uncomfortably impoverished look to what would otherwise be a two- or three-star establishment.

'It's a bit like finding a shanty town on top of the Hilton,' I said, rather unfairly in the circumstances as our driver unloaded our luggage on to the pavement while the indefatigable Mr Bhat whistled up a phalanx of porters.

Among those sleeping on the roof was a young waiter with staring eyes who had, poor chap, been delegated to look after us. He took his mission rather seriously, knocking on our door every morning at 5.30am, saying with his Peter Sellers accent: 'Good morning, *madam*. Good morning, *sir*. Coffee is served.' Then, just as we were dozing off again, he'd be back to pick up the empty cups and saucers.

What seemed like immediately afterwards, there'd be another knock on the door. 'Your breakfast is ready, *sir, madam*!'

After a while this got a little tedious.

'God, Arnie, I can't cope with this!'

We'd only asked for an early morning call for one particular morning when we'd planned to check out another area. But it was raining so hard that we went back to bed. Ever since then, he'd woken us up at dawn every single morning.

'You don't need to,' we told him.

'It is my duty to serve you,' he said.

We discovered later that he rarely got to bed — if indeed he had a bed up there on the roof — until about 2am anyway. And *then* he couldn't get to sleep worrying about whether he would wake up to give us the early morning call we didn't want anyway! Poor chap. Lucy and I felt sorry for him, even though he was wrecking our sleep.

*   *   *

Every day we saw shanty towns.

Bundles of depressing shacks lined the road, hovels inhabited by Tibetan refugees who had arrived on the outskirts of Manali after the Chinese invaded their homeland in 1959. By 1962, they had been given official refugee status which included state handouts, thus making them potentially better off than India's indigenous poor.

'God, Arnie, how do they remain so cheerful?' Lucy had noticed it too.

Like Sheru, our Tibetan driver, they seemed full of smiles and bonhomie. They greeted us from the doorways of their shacks with broad grins spread across their seamed faces. They appeared to have no animosity about their plight, and behind the thin plywood walls I could detect no signs of a pending revolution or plans for a forced march back to claim their homeland.

As in so much of life, it's what you settle for.

Moreover, and this was important, not once did we feel threatened — even though we were the only white faces, and with our colourful ski outfits and trendy tinted glasses I felt that we stood out like aliens who had stepped off another planet.

'They're a proud people,' Lucy said, impressed by their dignity.

*   *   *

We christened our four regular runs Waterfall, Hairpin, Roll-on (as in roll on Japan!) and Eagle (this last after a glorious bird of prey we spied performing stately circles above us).

'Just as long as it's not a vulture,' I commented, after a tumble when I looked up to find it circling high in the sky above me. I could sense its beady gaze sizing me up.

To pass the time on the long journey to the snow (at least an hour a day), we invented a new game. Some people play Scrabble, others, Trivial Pursuit. Or if you're in a car, I-Spy keeps the children amused.

We played the Ski Resort Game.

It's very simple, really. On a given signal, you both shout out the name of a ski resort beginning with the letter 'A'. Then move on to 'B'. And so on, all the way to 'Z'. The one with the most names wins that round. Play five rounds, say, and the winner is the one with the grand total at the end. I have to admit to a certain advantage — namely, that I had skied 440 resorts, while Lucy was only on about 100.

'It's not fair,' she pouted after the first time, as a passing yak peered in through the driver's window before ambling on with its cart-load of hay. 'I should have a handicap.'

'You have,' I said wittily. 'Me!'

'Very funny. Anyway,' she said, 'whoever heard of Zug?'

That little village in the Arlberg was my trump card. That is, after Zermatt, Zurs and Zell-am-See went to the wire.

*   *   *

'Guess what, Arnie? Last night I dreamed about General de Gaulle.'

From the bathroom, I called back: 'You what?'

'Yes. I was with him on the Champs Elysées. In a parade of some sort, standing next to him. Taking a salute. There were thousands of people all round us, cheering us. My parents will be so proud!'

'And I thought I was supposed to be weird!' I said.

I dream, too. One recurring dream throughout our globe-trotting year was a little strange, I have to admit, but probably a gift for those dream analysts to mull over.

I'm in this single chair swinging from the cable, in full ski gear, riding to the top of a high mountain with skis dangling from my boots as usual.

There's only one problem. There is no snow, not a sign of it anywhere. And, at the grassy top, no link either with any other chair lift. And nobody else around. I am left standing there, quite alone.

Lucy had this other dream: she was taking part in a bizarre competition in which she had to make a chocolate mousse while skiing.

'What does it mean, Arnie?'

'I daren't guess.'

I stroke her cheek, then kiss it goodnight.

'Sweet dreams, Lucy.'

'And you, baby.'

Other dreams are not so sweet.

This one recurs too often, spiralling out of my subconscious. Visiting me again and again after the accident, like an uninvited spectre. And it will not go away.

I am standing in my blue ski outfit on a bare stone platform in the open air. A chill wind is whipping around me, sending spirals of snow dust swirling at my feet. I know it must be cold, but I feel nothing.

A steel hawser hangs above me, its thick grey rope snaking away up the mountain into a pale mist. I am alone in a silent vortex of nothingness, waiting.

It dawns on me that I must be standing at a cable car station. Sure enough, out of the mist, a large gondola materialises, its squat steel outline taking solid shape as it draws nearer, the windows clouded.

I stand patiently with my skis, waiting. The gondola stops. The doors slide open. Inside, Lucy lies crumpled on the floor. Her face and her body are covered in blood, her ski suit soaked a dreadful crimson. The blood is everywhere. Spattering the windows, the floor, even the ceiling.

I stare down at her beautiful, fragile, lifeless body. And I start to scream, my mouth agape in horror ... But no sound emerges.

That's when I wake up, sweating.

*   *   *

There's a mynah bird outside our window. We call him Dickie, which I have to acknowledge is short on originality. Dickie mimics blackbirds, as any starling back in the UK worth his salt can do.

Much to Lucy's amusement I wave the Bear at him through our first-floor window overlooking the lush tropical garden. Dickie hops across the balcony towards us for a closer look, curious and unafraid. He tucks his head on to one midnight wing, giving the Bear an unblinking stare as I wave a small brown paw at him through the glass.

'I don't trust that bird. He'll have the Bear for breakfast, and still be hungry!'

So I put our small companion away in a drawer for his own safety, give him a friendly pat on his backside, and returned to our breakfast of lychee juice and cornflakes by the window. Delicious. As long as you like lychees.

From the Evergreen Hotel, the slopes are at least 20 miles away, a daily slog through snarled-up traffic, then mud, then grey slush. At this time of year, the snow in this part of India has a curious film of mossy slime on the surface, which does nothing for our skiing and not a lot for our skis, either.

'We'll have to get them thoroughly overhauled once we reach Japan.'

'You mean once we get back to civilisation,' Lucy wrinkled her nose. She wasn't altogether enjoying the Indian Experience. 'I can't wait.'

In all, we would spend only six days in the sub-Continent, though it felt more like six weeks.

*   *   *

From our improvised ski slopes we can see the towering Himalayas in the far distance, gigantic snow-covered triangles gleaming like white-spangled wedding-dresses in the morning sunshine and soaring more than 20,000 feet into the heavens as if they owned the whole world.

We ourselves have been skiing at a modest 7,000 feet, strictly no contest. There are no lifts working anywhere that we can find, so we ski downhill, and plod back up again.

A curious oddity: the closer we are into the foothills, the harder it becomes to glimpse those enormous peaks from the road. But sometimes a break in the clouds occurs. It has to be at the right moment, when there is a similar gap in the high green rock-strewn banks around us on the winding road. Then it hits us, almost physically, like a blow to the body — the timeless mystique of the Himalayas, as the bulk of an enormous unknown peak looms above us from nowhere, filling the sky like a giant white Buddha, watching and waiting, benign in repose, lethal when scorned.

Everest we couldn't see, because the Solang Nala Valley is several hundred miles to the west of Katmandu. But its omnipresence permeates throughout the gigantic range.

'Can't you feel it, Lucy?'

Only imagination, of course.

But somehow we both felt that mountain's power.

*   *   *

Like our friend Dickie, I became quite good at doing impressions. Only mine were of our unfortunate waiter, not the local bird-life.

'Good morning *madam*,' I'd say, eyes staring, to Lucy. 'Your breakfast is *ready*.'

'*Don't*, Arnie!' she'd say, stifling a laugh. 'The poor man!'

Mr Bhat didn't help. Although extremely considerate to us, he gave our waiter a really hard time.

Every morning at breakfast he would lecture the poor chap on our requirements for the rest of the day. 'For packed lunch — you must get *bread ... butter ... omelette*.'

And when Lucy asked if she could have less butter on her daily bread, Mr Bhat would yell: 'Bread ... Omelette ... but *very* less butter!'

Then he'd issue the instructions for our evening meal. 'Dinner!' he'd cry. It was usually the same. 'Soup ... beef curry ... lychees.' Once we asked for fish.

'Rather difficult,' said Mr Bhat. 'But I'll try.'

We were duly served something vaguely fishy. Lucy was convinced it was snake. We washed it down with something called an 'English Wine' which turned out to be neither.

*   *   *

A knock at the door. Mr Bhat had come to take us for our final day's skiing. Outside, in the teeming streets, I could sense that Lucy shared my relief that it would be the last time we battled through this hooting, honking, shouting mêlée.

A battered old bus lurched by, packed to the rafters with passengers. They were even crammed together on the roof, hanging on for dear life.

A Vespa with three youths clinging to the driver buzzed past, swerving like a suicide squad in front of our silent driver, who didn't even flinch at the wheel. The smell of burning rubber, spices and sweat filled the dusty air.

'Last time I saw anything like that, it was in a circus,' I said.

'There are no traffic rules in India,' said Mr Bhat, from the front. 'If a driver can pack more people on his vehicle, he'll do it. That's why you see so many on the roof of the buses. Soon they'll be putting two people in a coffin!'

Indian humour.

*   *   *

Before we leave for the airport, Lucy dashes off half a dozen post cards. 'Is the postage for other countries the same?'

'The same for all,' Mr Bhat informs her. 'Except for Pakistan. That is much cheaper.'

'Oh? Why's that?'

'Nobody wants to send letters to Pakistan, so there is no point in charging full price for stamps!'

More Indian humour.

'Well, goodbye, Mr Bhat. Goodbye, Sheru.'

Our Tibetan driver takes my hand in a strong, silent grip without removing his glove. His face breaks out into a big grin. As he wheels our piled-high trolley into the departure hall, shouldering the remaining bags on his broad back, I prepare to proffer rupees in gratitude.

Mr Bhat shakes his head. 'No need, sir. He is only too pleased for your happiness.'

'Thank him for us, will you, please?'

'Of course, sir. It has been our pleasure.'

Our doe-eyed waiter is waiting to see us off. We are not sure if he will be better or worse off with our departure, so we give him something to cheer him up. He'd told us he only received the equivalent of $10 a month. We leave him three months' wages. Lucy very much approves.

'I know you're not supposed to leave big tips in India, but the poor chap ... '

We head through the gates. Mr Bhat steeples both hands together in a final salute, a silent prayer to see us on our way.

'Don't forget to send me faxes. And photos. And video,' he implores.

Faxes? You'll be lucky, I think. Not with the power cuts you have here!

'So, Lucy, last thoughts on India?' I ask as we board the Airbus, bound for Tokyo.

'I never want to go back,' she said. 'I felt very over-privileged, so I didn't feel comfortable. And I hated those poor people treating me like royalty, as if we were from another planet. These two people, skiing with their nice new ski equipment and going up the mountain in their private jeep. It just didn't feel right.'

*   *   *

Air India Airbus AI 302 soared into the evening sky from Indira Ghandi airport at 6.30pm, heading east. The flight arrived in Japan at 8.00am. By the time we touched down at the gleaming steel and glass palace that is modern Narita Airport, Lucy had finished her sums, and brought the Black Diary up to date.

India's tally amounted to a modest 8,665 vertical feet, and an even more modest 8.45 miles. In a week!

'Pathetic,' I said from the depths of my Executive Class seat. 'Just as well we've got a healthy few miles in the kitty. But we'll still have some catching up to do when we get to the States.'

I lifted a glass to one culture shock behind us, and another to come.

*   *   *

Having left the poverty of India behind us, we were now impoverished ourselves. For some reason — not lack of funds — none of the cash dispensers Lucy tried at Narita Airport would recognise any of our assorted cash cards.

Lucy would stand first by this machine, then that, racking her brains for the various PIN numbers she carried around in her head, getting nowhere and nothing.

'I don't believe this,' came the familiar Lucy cry. And of course, the more she failed, the more frustrated she got, wondering eventually whether she had forgotten every single PIN number or was going mad.

'Maybe your brain was wiped clean by an Alien during the flight!' I suggested.

'Very funny.'

'Or maybe you had too much English wine in Manali.'

'Arnie, this is *serious*.'

She was right, of course. Being without money in Japan, of all places, is a nightmare.

Fortunately, we had clung on to a $20 note from our American travels, which at least enabled us to afford our train tickets to Lalaport, where our hotel was. Although we were five bags lighter now, it was still an exhausting journey.

'I'll guard the bags while you go for the trolleys,' said Lucy.

'Sorry, Lucy. There are no trolleys.'

'A porter, then?'

'No porters. We have to carry our own.'

Our total baggage had somehow crept back to eight, plus four sets of skis.

'*Arnie*!!' A mixture of disbelief and fatigue. 'How are we going to manage all this?'

'We'll have to leave two bags and one set of skis here, take the rest a couple of hundred yards or so, dump that, come back here, and so on.'

'That's crazy, Arnie! Our bags won't be here when we get back!'

'Oh yes they will,' I promised. 'We're not in Europe now.'

It was a tried and tested luggage technique: this was my third visit to Japan, and I was an old hand at hauling myself around Tokyo with a surfeit of luggage and no trolleys.

The concourse was a teeming human anthill.

'God, Arnie, look at them!' Lucy had never seen so many people rushing around under one roof.

As Lucy and I staggered clutching the first consignment along a corridor even more endless than the kind we habitually traipsed along to get to our average hotel room, we found ourselves struggling against the flow of a constant stream of commuters.

'God!' said Lucy. 'They don't exactly make it easy, do they? We might as well not exist!'

'Ah, but they have one saving grace,' I puffed. 'They may be inscrutable and indeflectable, but they seem to be scrupulously honest. I've never known anyone trying to steal your bags while you're retracing your steps to collect the rest of them.'

As for actually skiing today ... we decided to take the easy way out.

The real snow was five hours away on the Bullet Train, and we would still have to get through the rush hour traffic into the heart of Tokyo to catch it. And if you have never seen this city in the rush hour, you have never seen a traffic jam! We would never have made it. So we settled for the Ski Dome on the outskirts of town near the Minami Funabashi station.

The Ski Dome is a massive indoor stadium with a great curved roof like a railway station, and six parallel lines of downhill skiing, reached by high-speed quad chairs — a huge investment for what could hardly have been much more than a 200-yard ride.

Our ski will be 'legal' because we'll be on artificial snow — not plastic, which would have created a moral dilemma as we were trying to ski the world fair and square. But in my book this was no different from other ski resorts in the world that survive on artificial snow, like all America's Banana Belt resorts, for instance.

The Ski Dome was fair game.

The building is enormous, overpoweringly so. From the outside the Ski Dome resembles the launch-pad of an Apollo space craft, with the rocket and the tower on its side, and the rest of the building stretching away into a maze of concrete.

The inside is like a giant echo chamber rather less than half the size of Wembley Stadium or the Hollywood Bowl. Loud Oriental music blares from the tannoy, interrupted by frequent announcements in a high-pitched metallic voice that are incomprehensible if you don't speak Japanese, and probably equally so if you do.

The Ski Dome is the biggest indoor skiing area in the world.

As we got on the lift there was a great deal of jabbering about fastening this and clipping on that, emanating from small figures in yellow oilskins and white helmets, busying themselves around us like bees at a hive.

'It's called safety awareness, Lucy,' I said wearily, before the quad took off for the rarefied air beneath the domed glass roof.

'Arnie, it's ridiculous! It's hardly as if we're going to fall very far even if we did slide off,' Lucy said.

'Just be patient. Remember we're in toytown, but as far as they're concerned it's a major mountain.'

It was certainly a major dent in our budget. They charged us about £30 each for two hours.

The next day the cab we took into the city cost us one

hundred pounds. Sitting in mute frustration in one of those almighty traffic jams, watching the meter beside the driver whirling like a one-arm bandit — which, in effect, it was — is enough to give anyone a coronary.

Has anyone ever talked about taxi rage?

The plan was to breeze into the capital, a mere 13 miles away with all our luggage, check in at our next hotel, wander across to the *FT*'s Tokyo Office to say hello, and then go to the Tourist Office to chat about our Japanese schedule.

We hadn't bargained for the mother of all traffic jams. Not only were we now running disastrously late, the meter was eating up our cash at such an alarming rate that we realised our last 8,000 yen was not going to get us even into the city centre.

Short of climbing out of the cab in some obscure Tokyo suburb, our only option was to change course and head for the *FT* in the hope that they'd be able to cash an English cheque!

The problem was that our driver had been carefully briefed by our friendly ski instructor, Shike Kitahari, to take us to our hotel and the *FT*'s address was in my jacket pocket. And my jacket was in the boot with the rest of our luggage.

'We've got a problem, here Lucy,' I said, as the traffic built up. 'How do we explain to him that we need to stop, open the boot and change our destination?'

'We're virtually at a standstill anyway,' said Lucy. 'Just do it with hand signals.' The driver guessed that something was afoot. During a serious snarl-up, I gestured to him to let me get out and retrieve my coat.

And then: 'Not going to hotel: *Financial Times*. You know *Financial Times*?'

I think he got some of the message. At least he knew there was a change of plan. All I knew about the *FT*'s location was that it was opposite Otemachi Station. But which exit? When we finally found the station, the meter had gone into hyper-warp drive.

'My God, Lucy. It's like some financial doomsday machine. You'd better stay here in the cab to keep the driver happy, and I'll try to find the *FT*.'

'Yeh, but — come back quickly and let me know what's happening. Otherwise we're going to blow the entire budget on one cab fare!'

I decided the only way to find the right exit was to walk down to the vast complex which honeycombed the subterranean station. As I raced down, I realised we were in bigger trouble than I thought. It was like a city down there. Like a rat searching for a way into a maize rather than out, I darted this way and that. My task seemed hopeless until in a panic I asked a homeward-bound businessman for directions. To my astonishment, he did an instant U-turn and rushed to a map of the labyrinthine complex. When I explained that, above ground, Lucy was waiting in a cab whose meter was about to go into orbit, he broke into a trot.

'Maybe you could tell the driver how to find the *FT*?' I suggested. He was happy do so, and after that I assumed he would be on his way. Not a bit of it. Our saviour, refusing the comfort of riding with us in the taxi, spent the next twenty minutes jogging in his pin-stripe suit up and down various streets, returning to our cab to to give us breathless updates until finally we had located the *FT*'s offices. Can you imagine an Englishman doing the same on the London underground?

'I have never known such extraordinary kindness from a complete stranger in any other city,' I said. 'Perhaps you would join us for dinner this evening?'

Politely, he declined. 'I too have been helped in a similar way during my travels,' he said. 'It was nothing.' And he disappeared like the Lone Ranger into the streets of Tokyo.

Finally, we went in search of the real mountains.

The sleek silver pencil of the Bullet Train slid into Platform 1 of Ueno Station. We were bound for the snows of Hakuba Valley, venue for the men's Olympic downhill at Happo One (pronounced Hap-Pony) in 1998.

The *Shinkansen* (Bullet Train), pride of the Nippon railway system, stops with its sliding doors positioned precisely opposite a red line painted on the platform. All you do is stand on that red strip, and shuffle forward in an orderly line.

A voice from the loud-speaker above our heads brings an unforeseen hiccup. The Bullet Train will remain in the station for one minute, it announces.

Ever tried getting on a train with eight bags, four sets of skis — and ski boots — in sixty seconds? Not even allowing for the passengers who wanted to get out before we could get in. Unseemly scenes took place as desperately I jammed a ski across the doors to prevent them closing.

'Come on, Arnie!' Lucy, inside, was grabbing the bags as they rained in.

That day the *Shinkansen* was a full minute behind time leaving the main station. The Station Master watched us from the platform as his great train snaked out like a silent wraith, before picking up a speed that would eventually touch 160 mph and more.

'Oh, Arnie, did you see his expression?'

'I'm afraid so. The Bullet Train is never late. Much loss of face.'

I handed her the three-day tickets I had purchased in the bustling basement concourse. Her eyes widened.

'Eighty thousand yen! How much is that?'

'Close to £450, ' I told her. 'This is not a cheap country.'

The Japanese ski the way they do everything: to order, in regimented ranks. They dislike and discourage skiing off-piste, which means they jam the slopes in their thousands. Which in turn means that when they collide, which they do frequently, the results are spectacular.

'Look, Lucy. Over there.' Bodies were littering the slope, the sounds of collision punctuated with shouts and laughter. 'I can count ... three ... eight ... fourteen! Today's record!' Now we had a game on our hands!

'Arnie, stop it! You can be very unkind — '

'I'm hereby christen this slope Kamikaze!'

Lucy let out her thunderclap laugh.

'Dawn to dusk, Lucy. Just watch them. They join the queue at the bottom, shuffle to the head of it, up the mountain, straight down — and back into the queue.'

She sighed. 'Don't they ever relax?'

'They *are* relaxing!'

*   *   *

Lucy loved the cleanliness and order she found in Japan. It was a tremendous relief after India. The people are delightfully hospitable, certainly in the mountains, where Lucy's smile radiated a warmth that was returned on all sides.

Lucy loved to investigate the legends which abound in Japanese mythology and folklore. One in particular, I remember. She came across it in a book in a small street market in Nagano, the 1998 Winter Olympics HQ.

'Look at this, Arnie.' She stood by the stall, reading aloud:

> *When a Samurai warrior left his home to follow his lord and master to the wars, it was the custom for his household to serve him a special farewell dish — baked tai or perch, which had to be served up on a big leaf of the tegashiwa shrub. The leaf was then hung over the door, as a spell, to ensure the Samurai's safe return.*

'Isn't that lovely? I'll hang a big leaf out for you, Arnie, when you go away to the wars.'

'You're sure you don't mean fig leaf?'

I ducked away, grinning, as she swung her bag at me.

Lucy also found their hi-tech mania had its absurd moments, while developing a taste for sushi, vegetables in their own juice, rice wrapped in leaves, and cold fish.

The two came together in the YuyuSha snack-bar at the base of the Goryu Toomi resort. Outside, an icy wind carrying snow across the Sea of Japan all the way from Manchuria splattered white bullet holes on the windows. It was cold out there, but oven-hot inside as we settled down to a light lunch.

'Why, Lucy? What are you laughing at?'

She had her hand to her mouth, trying to suppress pending hysterics. 'Over there — '

I followed a gesturing chopstick, and finally caught on. A rotund Japanese skier had arrived, shaken the snow off his anorak and was babbling into his mobile phone, clutching the lunch menu in his free hand. It transpired that he had dialled his wife, who was still struggling through the blizzard out there like Nanook of the North, clutching her own mobile phone. And now her thoughtful husband was chattering away to her, going over the dish of the day before she arrived.

'Now that's what you call inverted take-away,' I said. 'Now I've seen everything,' Lucy's voice was choked. She wiped her eyes with a tissue.

Lucy always could see the silly side of life.

*   *   *

Next day, with 40,565 vertical feet and 35.51 Japanese ski miles behind us, we were on our way south-east to America.

One quick run in the Ski Dome, and we bade *sayonara* to the snows of Japan, both real and unreal. An hour later we were checking through the American Airlines desk at Narita to catch the 5.40pm flight to Los Angeles, in time to reach Mammoth Mountain the next afternoon.

To achieve our ten days in Asia we had travelled 6,600 miles by air, road and Bullet Train. We had skied barely 44 miles. This meant that we had travelled almost 150 miles for each mile skied! We were going to have to do better than this. A lot better!

Chapter 10

June

There's a tendency for you to be critical at the wrong time, with the wrong person, in the wrong place. All this is an innocent expression of the really deep motivation in your psyche to be a perfectionist.

Personal horoscope for Lucy Dicker

*B*uenos Dias, amigos!
That's how Lucy started her letters, post cards and faxes home to celebrate the fact that we had finally set foot on South American soil.

'And also to show off a little, Arnie. I mean, just look where we are!'

We are in Chile! More precisely, we are in the spacious forties-style bar of the Portillo Hotel. We are sipping Pisco Sours with the owners, Henry Purcell and his younger brother David, along with their black labrador Sally, who is on milk.

We have reached this point in our travels after zig-zagging across the Western Hemisphere — and now, down to the Southern — in the past two weeks, clocking up 27,354 miles by air, 3,115 miles by car, and 279 miles by train. Oh, and a paltry 244 miles on skis!

Lucy logged the statistics meticulously.

From Tokyo, good old American Airlines had taken us to

Los Angeles — via Seattle, and an enormous 4,000-mile dogleg to Chicago and zig-zagging back to San Jose on the Pacific coast.

'It's the scenic route, Lucy.'

'I know, Arnie. It can't be helped.'

'You realise that theoretically we'll be younger when we arrive than when we left Japan?'

This was all thanks to the International Date Line, which allowed us to arrive in San Jose, California, at 10.55am on the morning of the same day we had left Narita at 5.40pm.

'Even if we don't feel it,' said Lucy, closing those green eyes of hers to the world and settling down for the long journey.

More travel details. At San Jose we connected with American Airlines at 12.45pm to fly on to Orange County, arriving at 2.04pm. Then at 4.25pm, the short hop to Los Angeles, arriving at 4.49pm to connect with the final flight up to Mammoth that left at 6.45pm.

And all in one day, give or take the Date Line!

We skied Mammoth that evening to keep our record intact, enjoyed a few easy skiing days to recover, then headed for Austria. Summer skiing in the Swiss Alps: Saas-Fee, Diablerets, Verbier, and then golf with Lucy's parents, who had driven all the way to visit us. A joyful, carefree reunion! Then a race to Frankfurt (departure time: 5.30pm) to catch an Air New Zealand flight back to Los Angeles, arriving at 8.30pm the same day.

Can you wonder we are somewhat out of breath?

Flying down to Chile? Easy. We ski Mammoth (yet again) at dawn, then jet down to Santiago (via Miami), arriving at 11.40am. We have twelve hours to find snow. Portillo, near the top of the spectacular Uspallata Pass, is about one hundred and ten miles away, and our rental estate does it without a hitch.

In the bar of the Portill. I asked Henry Purcell, a quietly spoken, bespectacled New Englander in his sixties, 'Any relation of the composer? They're about to celebrate the 300th anniversary of his death.'

'Not a close one,' replied latter-day Henry mildly.

All the same, it seemed only right to toast the great man's memory. Solemnly, we raised our glasses of Pisco Sour. 'To Purcell!'

For the uninitiated, a Pisco Sour is a lurid yellow concoction hailed as Chile's equivalent to Mexico's salt-rimmed Margarita, 'But four times stronger, and an absolute killer,' Henry informed us amiably, on the second round.

His hotel, built in 1949, stands close to the old Caracoles Station, where keen skiers used to alight from the Trans-Andean train to head for the hills. The railroad was completed in 1910 by a small army of labourers led by English and Scandinavian engineers. Sadly the rails no longer ring to the thunder of the great locomotives. It became part of history when the mountain road leading up to the heights of Portillo was transformed into a highway linking Santiago with Mendoza, across the border in Argentina.

In its day the Portillo attracted the rich and the famous from both continents, and became Chile's answer to the Kulm at St Moritz, the Palace at Gstaad or the Sun Valley Lodge. With its walls tinted bright yellow and blue, the ornate building stands out like a child's painting against the mountains and the glistening frozen mirror of the Laguna del Inca close by.

Myth has it that the Inca Illi Yunqui buried his princess there after she was tragically killed on a hunting trip. According to the legend, at that moment the lake water 'turned emerald, dyed by the colour of the eyes that the son of the Sun could no longer awaken.'

And did it turn emerald again the day you died, Lucy?

*   *   *

Ever since my schooldays, I had always regarded Chile as a thin, brown bootlace running down the left-hand side of South America. More poetically, it is also known as 'The Tear From Peru'.

Only on closer inspection does one realise just how enormous the distances are. The 'bootlace', running from Tarapaca in the north, down to Tierra del Fuego in the south — the other end of the world — is around 2,500 miles long. We could never make the world's most southerly ski area of Punta Arenas, tempting as it would be to say we had been there, done that, in a place where the next sight of solid land beyond Cape Horn is the Antarctic ice cap.

As we travelled along the main Pan American Highway due south, the Cordillera, pinkening in the evening sun, kept us company for mile after mile. The journey was a mesmerising mixture of fantasy and nightmare. Heart-stopping scenery by day. Heart-stopping traffic at night.

As dusk fell, it was like driving along a completely unlit motorway with pedestrians, dogs and cyclists (who for some reason ride towards you on the hard shoulder on *your* side of the motorway) — mere shadows in the night — trying to cross your path at every opportunity. At the same time, huge trucks and assorted coaches — Chile Bus, Pullman Norte, Fenix — bear down on you at 80mph.

'My God, Arnie! These cyclists are a menace. He came out of nowhere! Thank God he swerved at the last minute! Why are they on the wrong side of the road?'

'I don't know. It's insane. And they haven't even got lights!'

More road. More mad cyclists. More wandering pedestrians. And dogs — we'd seen at least four dead dogs lying in the road before we'd even left the outskirts of Santiago. And more mountains.

Many of the mountains we'll be skiing from now on are volcanoes, some of them still alive and dangerously well. Llaima, for example, our mainstay as we criss-crossed the Andes between Chile and Argentina, has erupted ten times this century, most recently just a few weeks earlier. Chile has 55 active volcanoes, some of them ski areas. Our resources are limited, yet we plan to take in sixteen resorts here and across the border in Argentina.

And who knows what we'll find there?

*   *   *

Like rats on a treadmill, we're always on the run. Running for planes, running for cars, running for slopes, running for ski lifts. We lit a fuse under ourselves, and now it's burning so fast we can't stop.

But tonight, we do stop, the wheels of our first Chilean car, Andy (named after the Andes), flailing hopelessly on the frozen, pot-holed track only ten short miles from Thermas de Chillan. We *had* chains, but the thought of trying to put them on in the middle of nowhere on a cold Andes night was too daunting. Let's face it, I had failed to fit them in the middle of a French town six months earlier!

There was nothing for it but to retrace our steps — or at least the last 70 kilometres — back to the town of Chillan, birthplace of Chile's first president. A man — thanks to his Irish diplomat father — with the unlikely name of Bernardo O'Higgins.

Every town has street named after him. There's even a Chilean football team called O'Higgins. They weren't doing too well during our visit. But we noticed that two teams that reminded us of home — Everton and Rangers — were doing rather better.

The lights of the Gran Hotel were still blazing when we finally arrived at 2.30am.

*   *   *

I couldn't sleep. So I started thinking. It's very easy with hindsight to say it was destiny. I had this great scheme to ski the world. Lucy turned up at the right moment, we did it together and she was my inspiration.

But now ... I would like to think that Lucy and I were destined to meet, but that may be wishful thinking. I mean, how does one know? I'd just love to think it, that's all.

*   *   *

As our travels continued I would find myself behind the wheel ever more frequently. In the end, I took over almost entirely, unless I was dropping with fatigue.

My choice. I'm not a model passenger. All right, I'll be honest. I'm a very bad passenger. I had begun to find Lucy's aggressive driving harder and harder to deal with, and when we took turns on the long drives so that I could snatch some sleep, I would frequently jolt awake in mild terror, in certain knowledge that we were about to hurtle off the road.

Silly, really. In some strange way it was a reversal of our skiing roles, where as the better skier I usually took the lead. I was a little reckless on skis, but almost a wimp behind the wheel. Whereas Lucy was a combative, stylish driver, but more cautious on the slopes.

Sitting restlessly in the passenger seat of the four-wheel truck which we had borrowed for the high mountain driving, she chewed away at her fingers.

'Lucy, will you stop that!'

I slapped at her hand, half playfully.

Whereupon she hit me back. 'Give me a break, Arnie! Just let me be!'

Basically I was worried about the suffering she was causing herself, but it was also beginning to get on my nerves. 'Look, you stupid woman. You've drawn blood.'

Her fingers were bleeding as she tapped away on the Palmtop while we drove.

She chewed some more, just to make me mad.

'I've got a good bit here. Lemme do it, lemme do it! Just let me get this good bit — '

'Lucy, don't!'

In the end, reluctantly, she fished in her purse and brought out one of the small Mickey Mouse plasters she had packed back home in London. 'All right, Arnie. You win.'

But I knew I hadn't. Because even when she drove I noticed that sometimes she'd have one hand on the wheel, the other in her mouth, gnawing away at those fingers again.

*   *   *

'God, I'm cold!' Lucy lay in bed, fully dressed in her ski outfit, shivering.

'Me, too. It's perishing.'

Our tiny room in the refugio was freezing. Bare wooden floor, no carpet, just a small coal-burning stove for warmth. Both taps in the single wash basin produced a trickle of ice-cold water.

Arnie and Lucy, braving spartan conditions. And none too happy about it, either.

'Did you know,' I said, 'that Scott of the Antarctic insulated his hut with seaweed and sackcloth?'

From the depths of the blanket, Lucy bestowed a withering glance across at me. 'Didn't he freeze to death there?'

End of that conversation.

Lonquimay, the third largest of the country's skiable volcanoes, is located somewhere up in the north of Chile's mountainous spinal cord. Or, put another way, in the middle of nowhere. The windswept summit stands at 9, 482 feet, and has been described as 'the most inviting of all Chile's volcanoes'. From where I lay beside Lucy, it occurred to me that only those hardy souls who like nature in the raw should accept the invitation.

But on a sunny day there are magnificent views of three other volcanoes — Llanin, Villarrica and Llaima — and the headwaters of Chile's longest river, the Biobio, rising nearby.

The lifts only cost eight US dollars for a full day pass, which is a bargain in any language, and I felt we'd earned any reward just by getting there.

Today, unhappily, had not been a sunny day. The volcano itself was shrouded in white mist, the slopes were bleak and deserted, and the snow had turned to rain on the lower slopes, sending us scuttling back to our refuge hut. But not before we had skied until the lifts shut.

At least I had put our video camera to good use before the heavens opened, photographing Lucy skiing against the incredible araucaria groves, more familiarly known as monkey puzzle trees, whose long spindly arms and sharp needles are another of nature's spectacular surprises in these parts.

Now, after arriving back wet and cold for a tepid shower in the refugio, we huddled together under a sheet and two blankets in fresh dry clothes, searching for warmth.

Often I would warm Lucy's hands and feet in bed with a long, languorous massage, which she relished like a cat being stroked. But this time she insisted on keeping her socks on. It was that cold.

'There's only one thing I can suggest to warm us up!'

'Oh yes, Arnie — and what could that be?'

'A large whisky each!'

There was a communal dining-room for the few guests who had braved the elements.

I clambered out of bed in full ski regalia, and found my warm fur-lined Sorel boots. At the door, I turned.

'Lucy?'

'Yes, darling.'

'I may be gone for some time.'

Lucy put her head under the blanket and snorted.

*　　　　　*　　　　　*

'Where are we?'

In the course of the year, we must have said this a score of times, probably more, and not just when we had taken a wrong turning and were roaring off down some highway in the wrong direction. But now, on a dark mountain-side in the depths of Argentina, we really didn't know.

We had left San Carlos de Bariloche an hour before in our Russian four-wheel Lada, which we had nicknamed the General, after its origins in the Chilean village of General Lopez. The locals could not have been more friendly, and our initial misgivings had evaporated at the first border check on the Uspallata Pass from Portillo. And we needed a friendly face — because the General finally pulled rank on us, and called it a day.

San Carlos de Bariloche, on the fringe of Patagonia, is South America's most popular winter holiday spot, a Mecca for skiers from Buenos Aires boasting its own Club Argentino de Ski. It is described as the only resort in the entire continent with a 'ski culture'. Which means they are geared for snow, with Swiss-style architecture, clusters of chalets, and ski promotions visible on hoardings and in tourist agency windows all over town.

The place itself dates back to 1902, when two German brothers named Wiederhold started trading with their fellow countrymen on the Chilean side of the border, and the local populace became known as 'the people from behind the mountains'.

Right now, in the middle of the moonless Argentinian night, we had joined their ranks. Unwitting and unwilling. The General seemed to be a stretcher case.

'Arnie, what's happened to it? Can you get it started?'

'I don't know.'

'Where are we?'

'Somewhere on Planet Earth. Beam me up, Scottie!'

'Arnie, it's not a joke.'

Snow had turned to driving rain. It had been raining, or snowing at the higher altitudes, for twelve miserable consecutive days, and both of us were feeling edgy, soggy and scratchy.

But at least, on 22 June, we had reached two million vertical feet on skis — or almost sixty-nine times a descent of Everest. Mr Bianco — that's me — celebrated with white wine. Madame Tinto with a full-bodied Chilean red.

I had been steering the Lada at a careful pace back towards Temuco and big city sanity, squinting through the running rivulets on the windscreen at a lonely road with only ourselves and Vivaldi from the tape deck for company.

That's when the General surrendered.

We sat in the dark, alone and miserable.

'Arnie, look — ?'

Away to our right, through the stair rods of rain, a glimmer of light.

'You stay here, Lucy. I'll go and get help.'

It was a small garage, with a single two-star pump, and a family gathered round the TV set, watching football.

A leathery little man with lined features, together with two women in black, and six children whose ages ranged from around fifteen to almost nought, sat crammed into a tiny front parlour. They eyed me curiously as I went through the gestures of a breakdown — the General's, that is, not the driver's although it wouldn't have taken much.

Thanks to Lucy's improving Spanish, we explained the problem. The owner donned an oilskin, trotted out into the rain and trotted back five minutes later. $2,300 was his estimate for repairs.

Lucy joined us, hopping through the puddles like a rabbit, and drying herself off with a shake of her hair that sent droplets splashing all round the small living-room.

It was Lucy who had the brainwave. 'It would be far cheaper to get the General repaired back in his home town than pay $2,300 to get him fixed here,' she said.

Crazy, but true.

Because we were dealing with not only two countries but four different regions, it was going to take no fewer than four different breakdown trucks to get us back to Temuco.

Thirty minutes later the sounds of rattling chains and clattering implements filtering back through the downpour, indicated that the General was being winched up on the back of the *grua*. The driver reappeared, his face running with rivulets.

The world's longest tow was about to commence. Would we qualify for the *Guinness Book of Records* in a way we hadn't planned?

Out of San Carlos de Bariloche. Past the long expanse of Lake Nahuel Huapi. Into the mountains. The vertical exhaust of the second *grua* belching black fumes as we re-crossed the Puyehue Pass.

Because the driver had a friend in the cab with him for this section, Lucy and I had to travel in the General, which squatted at about 45 degrees, its nose pointing high in the air, with its rear wheels resting on the road.

Like two astronauts preparing for blast-off, we sat for the next three hours with our faces pointing skywards, the scenic view interrupted only by the rear of the tow-truck taking us out of Argentina and back to Chile.

Briefly, the rain had stopped. The stars came out. Somewhere up there, the Southern Cross was wheeling overhead.

'Hey, Lucy. Do you remember that line from *Sweet Charity*? "If friends could see me now."'

'They'd never believe it,' she said softly, echoing the line. 'Oh, if only they could see us now, Arnie.'

At the border, a long pause. Then the first Chilean *grua*, driven by a delightful man called Cesar — by far the sweetest of the four — arrives.

Lucy and I are in good spirits. Lucy is on record as saying: 'Arnie is a very easy going, cheerful person. He's always singing on the lifts, and telling jokes. *I think he is the best travelling companion any woman could have.*' And yet — she didn't always think like that!

It was while we were waiting for their fourth and final breakdown truck to arrive that the day began to turn really nasty. Believe it or not, when Lucy was asked later by our friend Nigel Lloyd — the man who had inadvertently brought us together three years ago — to describe the 'lowest point of the trip' for an article in *You* magazine, she chose not the poverty of India, the hardships of skiing at night, or nodding off over her Palmtop, or even my catheter. She chose the row about the fried egg sandwich!

It happened near a place called San Jose de la Mariquina. This is how she herself described it. I think it revealed a great deal about Lucy and her conflicting passions. When I read it, I loved her all the more.

> *It was lunch time, and some comfort food was needed. There was no sign of the fourth grua. The only thing to do was to investigate the small hosteria, a rather shabby-looking building. It was raining and the restaurant was very grim — dark, dank and very basically furnished. We were the only clients apart from a group of men in overalls standing by the stove. The waitress seemed puzzled by my request for a cheese sandwich and came back to announce that there wasn't any cheese. We ordered a steak sandwich which Arnie found delicious, but I couldn't share his enthusiasm. It was disgusting. What I wanted more than anything was a cheese sandwich. I then had a bright idea. What about a fried-egg sandwich? We were in luck. But as soon as we had ordered, we saw that the Temuco grua had arrived. We paid in a hurry, then dashed into the pouring rain.*
>
> *In my haste, and to my deep regret, I didn't tip Cesar, the last driver, who had been so kind. I was punished with my first bite of the sandwich when runny egg yoke spurted all over my hands, trousers, and the Lap Top computer on my knees. Yuck! it was horrible.*
>
> *I was so stressed by then — all the pent-up*

frustrations of the last few days came to the fore and while I ranted and raged, Arnie had an amused grin on his face which infuriated me even more. In disgust I put the egg sandwich in a plastic bag and threw it on the floor. To top it all, Arnie fished it back out of the bag and ate it. I was so furious and angry that he would do this!

And the poor driver, stuck in his own cab with two passengers arguing vehemently in a foreign language, pretended not to notice, and put some Chilean Folk Songs in the cassette player. I felt like crying.

We finally arrived in Temuco after dark in the pouring rain, panicking about how we were going to ski without any transport. Our only option was Llaima volcano, 50 miles of bad road away — the last 25 mostly unpaved and badly potholed. Feverishly we rang every taxi company in town. All refused to take us. Then, just as we were beginning to think the unthinkable — that the trip was all over — we managed to rent a truck. A desperate drive through flood waters, weaving through abandoned cars, brought us to the snow-covered flanks of the volcano where we skied a few hundred yards in torrential rain — and survived to ski another day. It was the closest call of the entire trip.

It had been a very tense time, with so much to lose. Later, I said to Lucy "God, that was a close one. Imagine failing six months into the trip — after all we've been through to get this far. It doesn't bear thinking about. Supposing we'd had to swim for it, with our skis on our backs?"

'Don't be ridiculous, Arnie' she'd said, slightly mockingly. 'You sound like Tintin!' Tintin, now, was it? First Dan Dare to her Digby. Then Neil Armstrong to her Buzz Aldrin. Now I was reduced to Tintin!Tintin or not, I like to think that if there'd been no alternative, I, at least, would have swum to the slopes. If it had come to the crunch, Lucy would probably have swum for it too. Fortunately, we were never put to the test.

That night, when we finally reached our hotel, Lucy wrote in her diary, 'We argued even more violently than we had done during the day. Arnie threatened to sleep outside in the truck, then told me to go home as he didn't want me on the expedition any more. I cried myself into an exhausted and troubled sleep.'

Needless to say, when I read her words later, it broke my heart.

Chapter 11

July

We are often asked if we thought it was sheer madness,
what we were doing. And we used to answer:
yes, we're probably mad. Because it was fun to say it,
and that was what they wanted to hear.
But maybe it was true. In a way, we were mad.

Arnie Wilson, July 1994

One of Lucy's great joys was to tuck me up in bed. 'Time to undress you, beauty!'

After a long day on the slopes or behind the wheel, I would always be the perfect gentleman, allowing her to use the bathroom first. Meantime, the Sultan of the Slopes would lie back on the bed, and glance through the schedule for the next day or catch up with an old newspaper.

Often by the time she emerged I was dozing off. Still fully clothed.

But Lucy actually relished the prospect of undressing me. 'Why not, Arnie? It's your little treat. And mine, too!' It was almost her version of my reading *Alice* to her. And just as innocent. Coming from a household of women — one wife, four daughters — I was fairly well used to being mothered, and acquiesced to these attentions quite happily.

Oddly, there was no sexual connotation, no particular

undercurrent of sensuality about it. It became a personal challenge for Lucy to undress me seamlessly and get me into bed without my actually getting out of bed. It was like a little girl undressing a doll.

A foot on the floor would be deemed as failure. So first she removed my shoes. Then she lifted my legs in the air so that she could slip off my trousers and underpants, rolling me sideways and back again so that she could pull back the sheets. I just lay there half-dozing and chuckling like a baby, loving every minute of it.

Finally she would put a strong hand behind my back and heave me up so that my shirt came off. Then, on with my night shirt (though most nights we both slept naked) and one sleepy boy was tucked up without actually having left the bed.

I would watch her through heavy lids as she carefully put my shoes away side by side in the wardrobe, then folded my clothes neatly over a chair.

'That's what I call a labour of love, darling.' I mumbled from my pillow.

'Everything in its right place, beauty.' Lucy was a stickler for tidiness.

'You're spoiling me.'

'I know. And don't you love it?' A knowing Provençal laugh. Well of course I did.

Those were the nights when we didn't make love immediately. Instead we would sleep with our arms flung across one another, or simply with our fingers entwined under the cool sheet — somehow it always seemed terribly important that we were in physical contact.

But we would make love at any time during the night. Depending on who made the first move — and the reaction to it. And if we'd missed out, there was always the morning.

'Do you know, Lucy, I read a survey before we left England. Eighty per cent of couples make love first thing in the morning rather than last thing at night.'

'Are we on it?' she said, raising an eyebrow above the pillow.

'In about twelve seconds,' I said. 'We're going to be.'

As a lover, Lucy was everything a man could ever dream about — and for me, so much more. From profound tenderness to clawing wildcat, loving or lustful, she explored the whole spectrum of sensuality with me so that at the end of it I was left with that curious, wondrous paradox of being physically spent and emotionally recharged.

Sometimes, when we had locked horns in some argument — whether Grand Guignol Rows or just nasty little spats — and lay silent with a gulf like the Grand Canyon separating us, I knew I would never get to sleep.

'Lucy, are you awake?'

'Yes, Arnie.'

'I'm sorry — '

'That's okay, baby.' Followed by two kisses blown from pillow to pillow. There were always two, like quotation marks.

*   *   *

In that year when we spent every single day of every single week of every single month together, saw each other's faces last thing at night and first thing in the morning, and were scarcely out of one another's sight for more than a few minutes, something had to change. In each of us.

Me, I became a much neater person. Lucy? She simply became obsessed with skiing.

I had always been relaxed about tidiness, never really feeling comfortable if things were too squeaky clean, but certainly never letting my flat degenerate into a tip. Okay, I lied about that.

Lucy, while never being heavy-handed about it, exerted a subtle influence on me, if only by example. And on this kind of expedition on which we were embarked, it was essential that everything was in its right place. Including me!

So I became most definitely neater.

When we came down from the slopes after a day's skiing, I

had hardly wrenched one ski boot off when — before even unbuckling her own — she started doing up the clips on mine. Then she would tuck both of my boots away in their usual place at the back of the vehicle, saying: 'Your hat, darling. Your gloves? And your neck,' (as she called my neck-gator), 'where is your neck?'

'No, don't put it there. Here, give it to me. Let me do it. No, they don't go *there*, Arnie. *Really!*' And so forth.

Yes, Lucy really liked to 'know where things are'.

> *I wake up with a start, fully dressed, lying on a strange bed in the darkness. A sliver of light shines through the gap where the curtains meet, faintly illuminating the room. My shoes are lying on the carpet in the middle of the floor, carelessly flung there. Funny. Lucy usually puts them away? And why hasn't she undressed me?*
>
> *I feel a cold draught brushing at me through my clothes, a creeping chill of foreboding that is not purely due to the time of night. A small travel clock with a luminous dial stands on a table beside the bed. Two o'clock.*
>
> *Then I remember. The pub last night. Much forced jollity and too much beer at a friend's 40th birthday. I came home alone to a room kindly loaned by a friend, and lay down on the bed for a few minutes. I must have dozed off. Because, of course, Lucy isn't here any more. In the darkness, I feel terribly alone. And there is no one to call out to.*

*   *   *

We were on our way to another volcano — Villarrica. I looked it up in our guide book:

> *'The first ski area was located on the north face*
> *due to the ease of access, and a refugio was*
> *built there. But on October 18 1948 Villarica*
> *erupted, and the lodge desparecio totalmente.*

'In other words, Lucy, it disappeared completely!'

'That's nice, Arnie. I'm really looking forward to seeing the hole in the ground — '

I continued:

> *'The new ski resort was built by Carlos Urzua,*
> *grandson of one of the pioneers, where the*
> *volcano is less likely to cause problems. Now the*
> *challenge is to find skiers to fill the lonely*
> *slopes.*

'Oh, now, isn't that sweet? And rather sad.'

'Very.' Lucy concentrated on the road, brow furrowed, following a sign off the main highway.

The road became a track. The track became a dead end, half a mile from where a curious orange glow hung in a thunderous sky. It looked like stage lighting in an open-air theatre.

We were on the edge of the notorious Volcan, and its bubbling centre was just over the rim. But at least there was snow.

Outside, the wind the locals called El Puelche was making an eerie wailing sound like a pack of hyenas in pain. Snow was whipping off the desolate landscape, exposing icy patches and lumps of lava.

This godforsaken place gave me the shivers.

'Look!' I pointed at a hut that was visible on the next bend. A windsock was flapping from a pole by the fence. 'Civilisation.'

I squinted more closely as the truck crawled nearer. 'That's not a sock. It's a bra!'

It was, too.

'Ho! A windbra!'

'We'll ski here.' It would be a short run, and as the guide book had warned, a lonely one, in gale-force conditions.

'We'll name it Spock — after the Volcan!'

But as I helped Lucy down with her skis from the roof rack — crack! The rear door flew open, jolting me first on the elbow, then slamming on to the middle finger of my right hand, up near the fingertip.

'Arnie!' Lucy's voice came above the wind, high-pitched and anxious. 'Are you all right?'

All right? It hurt like hell. 'Let's get this run out of the way!' I knew the finger was broken. The slope had been gauged out by an ancient lava flow. It felt primaeval.

It didn't take long, and we were happy to leave the inhospitable mountain.

'I'll get you to a chemist, Arnie. If that finger really is broken and sets crooked, you'd have to have it broken again.'

The pain was sending waves of nausea through me. But within ten minutes, we had found a cluster of shops, along with the familiar red cross on the awning outside.

The chemist confirmed the finger was indeed fractured, and advised me to report to the local Pucon Hospital for proper dressing.

'We haven't got time,' I said. I thought for a moment. Then, 'All I need is a splint to immobilise it in a straight position.'

The chemist obliged. He fished around in a drawer, and finally produced a wooden lolly-pop stick.

'*Tenga*!' he exclaimed in triumph.

Three minutes' swift work with the stick and a roll of pharmaceutical tape, and I had my splint.

'*Gracias, amigo*!' And we were on our way.

Well, it was preferable to a catheter.

*   *   *

Although the General had finally been given the once-over in Temuco, and pronounced fit for active duty, Lucy and I had to travel on without him. That meant heading 500 miles north up the spine of Chile to Santiago by train.

In all probability, you've never seen a train quite like the one that clatters its way north from Temuco to Santiago.

Actually, at first it doesn't clatter — it trundles, like a combine harvester, gradually speeding up as it gets closer to the capital.

There's rather a good reason for this, as I discovered later.

The condition of the track further south along the 'Tear of Peru' is, apparently, rather dodgy, to use a second-hand railway carriage dealer's vernacular. In other words, they only let the train speed up to something like its normal potential as it gets closer to civilisation and better maintained track.

It wouldn't do at all on the Eurostar route!

The train itself was an extraordinary amalgam of a sort of decaying Orient Express and an old British Rail diesel.

The pre-war rolling stock, heavily clad in mahogany, was shabby and antiquated. But there was still a fading hint of elegance, which spoke of a sedate if not glorious age of steam.

Lucy and I booked a private *dormitorio* (two-berth sleeper) instead of one of the corridor beds, which, as Lucy pointed out, with their heavy brown velvet curtains, were very similar to the beds in the movie *Some Like It Hot*.

We wanted a little more privacy. This was our first night on a train together since we had travelled back from Les Arcs at the beginning of our romance more than two years ago. After the recent crises, and some of our more wretched rows, we badly wanted to kiss, cuddle and make up. And we were certainly hoping for better things on the menu in the wonderful old dining car than fried egg sandwiches.

But before dinner, Lucy was determined to do her stint of 'reporting' on her Palmtop:

> *Phew! What a relief when the train pulled out of Temuco with our belongings safely on board.*

The night porter has locked our most bulky
possessions, including our skis, in a cupboard.
The train has seen better, more glorious days. Its
mahogany panels no longer shine, and there are
letters missing on the doors of the dormitorios.
Our loo smells nausiatingly of chemicals, and
our antiquated shower looks as if it has never
been used. At the end of the corridor is a cubby-
hole housing the heating system for our
carriage: a rickety gas boiler dating back to the
Ark, with a heavy coating of dust, and full of
spiders' webs.

Reaching the dining car involved braving the cold night air as
we leapt across the sometimes yawning gulf which separated
the carriages as they clattered northwards beneath a full
Chilean moon.

Hercule Poirot would not have felt out of place in the
quaint old dining car, where white-jacketed waiters from
another age fussed over the immaculate arrangement of anti-
drip napkin collars on bottles of Chilean Chardonnay.

Later, we slumbered fitfully as the ancient train built up
speed on its way towards the Chilean capital, and dreamt of
volcanoes and condors.

*　　　　*　　　　*

'Arnie, do you think we'll ever get tired of travelling?' Lucy
murmured. She was psyching herself up for the longest leg of
our odyssey — to New Zealand. Via Tahiti.

'You know, Lucy, I don't seem to have stopped since I
was four.'

I told her about my father.

How, as a young composer of Lithuanian extraction, Bernard
Wilson Koschecowitch had become aware of the chaos in the
music business immediately following World War II, with old

orchestras losing their members and never recovering, and new ones being formed everywhere to fill the gap.

My father, who had run his own orchestra in Hampstead, when the celebrated French horn virtuoso Dennis Brain had been a member, realised that there must be masses of forgotten orchestral parts lying around in dusty attics, many out of print, and that if he could lay his hands on them there would be a big market for them, not just for orchestras, but universities all over the world and, not least, the BBC. He took to the road with my mother (herself an accomplished pianist) and me, aged four and with no great musical talent — well, they do say it can skip a generation — and toured the European capitals and cultural centres, where my father would buy up old music and manuscripts, and send an annual catalogue to universities around the world.

From 1948 onwards, at least once or twice a year, I'd find myself exploring the ravaged cities of post-war Europe, even going behind the Iron Curtain to the Leipzig Trade Fair in what was then East Germany in 1952. At one stage we even moved the family business to Glion, a pretty mountain village above the shores of Lac Leman in Switzerland.

Being bitten by the travel bug that young, when you have no choice anyway, must surely turn anyone into something of a nomad at heart. Despite having created a happy and secure home life for my own daughters, Samantha, Lara, Amber and Melissa (my 'grand SLAM' as I used to call them), I never lost the thrill of packing my bag, shutting the front door behind me and heading for the airport.

But never in my whole life had there been a trip like this one, or an undertaking with such commitment and so much at stake ...

'No, Lucy. I don't think I'll ever get tired of it. And you?'

She stared through the windscreen as the high rise granite blocks of Santiago loomed up, her eyes far away on other horizons.

'No, Arnie, I don't think so either.'

*   *   *

Somehow we had to get from South America to New Zealand on successive days and ski on both those days. I was aware that international airports are not normally close to mountains.

So this is how we did it. In Santiago's noisy, bustling air terminal, we checked our luggage through at the LanChile counter (LanChile is one of the country's two national airlines), keeping our skis, poles and boots with us. Then we rushed off to pick up another vehicle.

I spotted a white Chevvy. 'That one?' I immediately thought, with a pang, of Spud.

'No, señor,' said the booking agent, laboriously copying out my driving licence. I had told him where we were headed. 'Not white. Very dangerous. You would be invisible in a white-out.'

White-out? It hadn't worried the Avis people when we rented Spud..

We settled for a highly visible blue Subaru Impresa. Lucy nudged me in the ribs. 'Look at the number plate. LD.'

'We'll baptise her Lucy. What else?'

Twice, huge trucks on the wrong side of the road came close to forcing us off the highway as we made for Chapa Verde, a ski area built dramatically above one of the world's largest copper mines.

'Look out, Arnie! Look out! God, that was a close one!'

Then, as usual, we got lost.

We could have followed the smoke signals.

'My God, look at all those factory chimneys belching out those murky grey clouds,' said Lucy. It wasn't what you'd expect at a ski resort.

'It doesn't do much for the scenery,' said Lucy.

The chimneys formed a huge bank of smog which almost obliterated what would have been an outstanding view of the Andes.

'They'd never allow this in the Alps, would they, Lucy?' I said.

Later, mission accomplished, in the VIP lounge at LanChile, Lucy was busy with the Black Diary again.

'Arnie, get ready for this!'

'What's that?' I was nursing a gin and tonic after the long drive.

'We have skied 2,531,085 vertical feet. That's eighty-seven Everests.' For some reason, Everest had remained our psychological yardstick.

'It's wonderful, Arnie. We've done 2,230 miles over 2,553 different runs. Driven 22,248 miles, and flown 76,355 miles. And — '

'And how many times have you fallen?'

She grimaced, then grinned. 'All right. You have fallen one hundred and fourteen times.'

'And you?'

'Well ... one hundred and thirty-one, if you must know.'

'I'm catching up on you, baby!' She was, too. And she wouldn't fall again for the next twenty-three days. Which would work out at three hundred miles of solid skiing, without a tumble.

I was proud of her.

*   *   *

We took off from Santiago at 6.00pm, heading into the sunset with the blue Pacific turning dark beneath us.

For the second time, the International Date Line loomed on the horizon. It also loomed large in our plans, because it affected our time-scale crucially.

When trying to avoid the tripwires of chance and natural disasters to ski every day — every Calendar day, that is — we realised immediately where the biggest headaches lay: in the enormous distances we would have to travel south of the Equator.

The itinerary that we had worked out involved LanChile and Air New Zealand, the two national airlines of their respective countries. From Santiago on Sunday, battling the head winds to pass close to Pitcairn, we would land on Easter Island and then fly on to Tahiti, arriving at 0.35am in the early hours of Tuesday.

So we'd miss Monday completely. And we knew, rather like a leap year, that we'd have to ski on 1 January to fulfil our mission. Oddly enough, it was a full moon that very night. Now why did that seem significant?

'Rather like Ray Milland in *Lost Weekend*,' I suggested, after we touched down 4,995 miles later at Papeete. 'Except that we've only lost a day.'

'Does that make us younger or older?'

'Do I look like Einstein? I'm still trying to figure it out.'

The Date Line can drive you mad! Quite often all I got was a headache wrestling with it, and gave up.

The world map will show you how the IDL bisects the Pacific on the 180-degree longitude from the South Pole, running north through Scott Island in the Antarctic, zigzagging to avoid New Zealand, up through Tonga and Samoa and on again through the Bering Sea on its way to the North Pole.

After that, it slinks over the top of the world and back again, transforming into zero degrees through Grimsby, Greenwich and East Grinstead to leave the white cliffs of Sussex behind at Peacehaven, with no further change in the date for us mere mortals to worry about.

Somewhere above the inky Pacific, supported by another glass of full-bodied Chilean red wine, I got down to basics with an airline map spread out on the plastic tray.

To the east of the Line, the calendar date is one day earlier than the west. So far, so good. In even more basic terms, after ten hours in the air we arrived on the IDL at midnight on Monday — to encounter Tuesday rushing at us from the west, and engulfing us the moment we crossed that invisible barrier

... to find ourselves twenty-four hours older!

By the time the tyres of the giant jet were sending dust spurting from the tarmac at Papeete Airport, I was feeling my age anyway. The flight had been an endurance test, even for us.

Following that lingering sunset which set the whole Pacific aglow, we had flown in darkness the whole way, cramped into economy seats at the rear of the huge, whispering jet. We were paying for this flight. In spite of our planning, we had to occasionally!

Now we faced a further five-hour flight to get us down to New Zealand at 7.00am, to be followed by a drive to the nearest ski slope — a dot on the map called Whakapapa that I had never seen, and wasn't sure even how to spell, least of all pronounce.

The full moon that had danced attendance on us for most of the flight had vanished over a far horizon. I watched the lights of Tahiti swim out of the blackness as we circled our approach, and chuckled involuntarily.

'What, Arnie?'

'I was just thinking. I remember a friend of mine getting married on 21 June. I sent them a telegram: 'THE LONGEST DAY. THE SHORTEST NIGHT. DIDN'T ANYONE TELL YOU?' When they read it out at the reception, he laughed his head off. She didn't.'

'What happened?' Lucy was almost too tired to ask.

'They're divorced.'

'Oh.' She didn't sound surprised.

'Well, this is our longest night — '

'That's for sure.'

Through the window of the bungalow-style airport, I watched our skis being trundled on a luggage trolley from the hold of the LanChile airliner into the cargo bay, and thence to the equally massive bulk of the Air New Zealand flight that was waiting on the tarmac.

With three long hours to wait, we took a stroll around the

quiet airport concourse to clear our heads and stretch stiffened limbs. Outside in the warm night, there was no-one around, not even a taxi. Hand in hand we walked along the approach road, drinking in the honeyed scents of tropical flowers under the palm fronds flapping lazily overhead.

'I think we've stepped into a time warp,' I said. 'What are we doing in Tahiti?'

'Listen!' said Lucy. 'I haven't heard that sound in years — '

It's odd how you don't notice it at first — the unceasing background chatter of crickets in their hiding places somewhere in the lush foliage.

'All that noise just from rubbing their legs together.'

'Just like *La Cigale et la Fourmi*, Arnie.'

Reciting *The Grasshopper and the Ant*, the classic de la Fontaine fable about the ant which refuses to give food to the grasshopper during the winter after it had chirruped all summer, was Lucy's party piece.

I inhaled a heady fragrance redolent of white sand beaches and blue lagoons, not forgetting the occasional hula maiden.

'You can see why Captain Cook was seduced by this place. And the crew of *The Bounty*. And Gauguin. I wish we could stay here a month! Or maybe forever.'

'There's only one thing, Arnie.'

'What's that — ?'

'They weren't going skiing!'

And one of her thunderous *éclats* echoed around the palms, and temporarily silenced the crickets.

But *we* were.

Chapter 12

August

Let's face it, out there on the surface of this globe,
right now there are millions of women.
And one turned out to be the perfect partner for me.
But it often crosses my mind how arbitrary it all is.

Arnie Wilson, April 1995

Whakapapa. 'Sounds like paternal abuse,' I said, just
for laughs. Silence. So I had to explain it. 'Whack-
a-papa?'

'Very funny,' Lucy was lost in the map spread out on
her knees.

Sometimes, as every aspiring comic knows, the audience
can be heavy going.

Whakapapa, a wonderful Maori name, is the biggest ski
resort in the whole of Australasia. To find it after our
mammoth flight, I was back behind the wheel, my broken and
temporarily splinted finger aching but bearable, as we
ploughed along through freezing New Zealand rain.

At least it had washed the Chilean mud from our suits.

We were back in Spock country. By which I mean
volcanoes. The twin triangles of Tongariro and Ngauruhoe
loomed out of the mist on either side of the road to glower

189

fitfully at us before receding into their grey shrouds. And there, alongside them, was the one with all the skiing — Ruapehu.

They call Whakapapa the Magic Mountain — nothing to do with mushrooms, despite scenery that is so spectacular we felt we could easily have been hallucinating.

'Arnie, look at this notice.' In the Grand Château Hotel, I was more interested in bed than reading the sign on the back of the door. And by bed, I mean sleep.

We had checked in, dragged our bags along another interminable corridor and ourselves after them to locate our room and headed back to the first slope we could find, moving like automatons. Twenty-eight hours door-to-door across the Pacific is a long hop, but still we had to get our skiing in, however short. And the lifts were about to close down for the night.

We made it in a white-out, snow that turned to driving rain, and like drowned rats crept back to warmth and sanity.

'What about the notice?'

Lucy read from it. 'In the event of a *lahar*, guests should proceed calmly to assembly areas.'

A *lahar* is a local word for mud-slide. It is an Indonesian expression describing a torrential flow of water-saturated debris that is channelled into the valleys during an eruption, pouring its deadly cataract down the mountainside at speeds of thirty miles an hour, and more. In other words, something best to avoid.

Until the spectacular eruptions of 1995 and 1996, by which time I was back in England, the last big mud-slide here happened in June 1969. In the event of another one, guests are urged: do not attempt to leave the village. Remain calm and wait for the all clear. Lucy read, and looked pensive.

Remain calm? There was enough rain performing a drum-roll on the windows to send a warning flicker of unease up our spines. We both knew that the twin volcanoes — plus the Godfather of them all, Mount Ruapehu (9,175 feet) — were high on the active list. Changing the subject, I took off my sodden socks and waved them gleefully in the air.

Being a clean-living girl, everywhere we went Lucy's number one priority was a washing machine. Her first question to a hotel at the reception desk never changed. Is there a washing machine anywhere in this hotel? And if not, anywhere in this town? Otherwise, is there a launderette?

It was all part of her obsession with cleanliness. Lucy hated to have dirty clothes hanging around, and insisted on getting everything washed every night if it was humanly possible. I would actually see her eyes light up when she spotted a launderette. Or, better still, a washing machine in our room on the occasions when we were given the five-star treatment with our own kitchen complete with all mod cons.

'Why not use the bath, Lucy?' I would ask wearily, as she left the room bound for the hotel laundry annexe with a bag of dirty washing slung over her shoulder. 'Most people do.'

'I am not most people,' she would retort. 'It has to be done properly.' And the door would shut smartly behind her.

She could be quite stern about it, as if dealing with a child with a nappy problem. And, almost always, it was done properly.

Hygiene, of course, was always going to be a potential worry. When you're traversing the globe the way we were it was bound to come into the equation. More days than not we travelled in our ski clothes — and that meant a spot of nose-wrinkling when we took them off. Especially my socks. But Lucy, being Lucy, always found a way to keep the party clean.

Well, almost always.

'Remember that day — ?' I waved the stained socks some more, like a cheer-leader.

'Remember Mammoth?'

'Arnie, don't! Give them to me — '

She hated to be reminded of it, because it was the one lapse in an otherwise blameless career of Keeping Arnie and Lucy Clean.

Back in June we had hitched a lift on a private jet to whisk us the three hundred miles from Mammoth to Los Angeles Airport to catch a vital connection to the Alps. We had left the Mountain Lodge in a hurry, rush-rush-rush, with no time to wash yesterday's clothing. I had bundled it all into a 'used' duffel bag.

At Mammoth's small but perfectly formed (and very busy) airport, what did I find but our friendly host Randy McCoy helpfully stowing the bag away in the nose cone of the resort's jet, close to the front passenger seats.

Fortunately, the whiff of the Wilson socks did not permeate the plane during the spectacular 40-minute flight. The tyres soon screeched on to the tarmac at LA Domestic.

Back in London I had in fact packed forty pairs of socks, all purchased from Marks and Spencer in Marble Arch on one mammoth shopping spree, along with ten pairs of bottle green boxer shorts. I also had two pairs of long johns for the really cold climates.

Battling with the ever more insoluble problems of travelling light for a whole year, Lucy was suddenly struck with what she thought was a brainwave.

'Arnie, I've got it! Disposable underwear!'

'What?'

'Throw it away as we go.'

I wasn't about to indulge in papier maché underpants, and told her so. She giggled.

As it was, by the time we flew into New Zealand, half my sock supply had disappeared into the limbo of forgotten hotel drawers, washing machines, under beds, or simply thin air.

'Odd, Lucy.'

'What's that?'

In our hotel room in Whakapapa, I held up a handful of socks. 'Do you notice something?'

'They're clean.'

'That, too. They're also all different colours. Blue, green, red, but only one of each. The only socks that are still pairs are brown.'

Brown is my least favourite colour, and I had hardly worn them. Which no doubt explained why we had a full house in brown and a very oddball collection in other colours.

'As long as they fit, Arnie.'

It still felt odd.

*   *   *

Meantime, we had a volcano or two to conquer.

The Magic Mountain of Whakapapa has everything on offer. Happy Valley is a separate area for beginners. For extreme skiing, you make for the *couloirs* and chutes of Front Stage, visible to everyone relaxing on the sun terraces far below watching safely through binoculars as you do the dicing-with-danger routine.

The alternative is going Back Stage, where no audience is present to laugh at you digging yourself out of a deep powder burial chamber after a wipe-out.

North Island is often dismissed by skiers as the poor relation to South Island. This is a myth. True, South Island has more ski areas and more mountains than the North. But the resorts of Whakapapa and Turoa on either side of majestic Mt Ruapehu are each bigger than anything their Southern sisters can provide. And when they get good snow it really is magic!

One thing the North Island doesn't have is the kea. A brownish-green Alpine parrot (*nestor notabilis*, if you're in the ornithology business), it waddles and hops its way around every ski area like an arthritic clown. Its lack of fear is matched only by its curiosity and greed. It simply cannot resist sinking its huge beak into anything malleable.

There is no escape from this extraordinary bird, known to every South Island Kiwi by the nickname 'Charlie'.

Picture the following scene, for example, outside the ski lodge at Mount Robert.

'Get away!'

I was in a primitive loo, a wooden hut with a gap above the

door, which was where the draught was coming from.

Have you ever had the feeling that someone — or some*thing* — is watching you?

From my squatting position on the low wooden seat I became aware of a presence in the confined space. I looked around.

Then I looked up.

Hey! There, hanging from a wooden slat, upside down, was Charlie, giving me the beady eye.

'Out! Out!' From my irrefutably vulnerable position, I picked up the first thing I could lay my hands on, and flung it at him.

The toilet roll. Only — God, he moved fast — to see him snatch at it, and flap off through the gap, trailing a stream of loo paper from his beak. Which left me with nothing but yesterday's newspaper.

Later we heard frightful tales of the dreaded kea from a new-found friend, one Arthur Tschepp, a sprightly 67-year-old from Croatia who was now patron of a primitive ski club field called Awakino.

'One of those darned birds hopped inside a lift operator's rucksack, and ate all his sandwiches while the guy was standing there, utterly oblivious, just a few feet away.' Arthur rocked back in his chair on the sun terrace, chuckling like a pixie.

'They'll go for anything, those birds. Ski gloves, cardboard cups, picnic leftovers, you name it.'

In our case, loo paper apart, stop-at-nothing Charlie had gone for the rubber clips on our ski rack, and left them hanging in tatters. These Alpine parrots frequently gnaw their way through the rubber seals of car windscreens, and for an encore rip off the rubber insulations around ski-lift electric circuits. They have even been known to demolish car seats!

'Charlie's beak knows no bounds,' I intoned with solemn respect. 'You mess about with him at your peril.'

'I have to tell you something,' Arthur leaned forward

confidentially, his accent thick from another country and another hemisphere. 'A lot of people round here would gladly shoot 'em. But it would cost them.'

'How much?'

'Around $30,000 NZ dollars.'

That's £12,000 to us. 'A lot of protection money,' I said.

'More than that,' said Arthur. 'A European tourist was caught trying to smuggle a couple of keas in aluminium tubes stuffed down his trousers! He got a huge fine, and he was lucky he didn't go to jail. They're worth £50,000 apiece to a collector.'

'With those beaks?' I said incredulously. 'That takes a brave man.'

'Maybe the customs heard it squawking,' Lucy joined the debate.

Well, those keas do have a loud voice.

Arthur learned to ski on barrel staves in the hills above his home town of Zagreb. He also knows a thing or two about cannibals, having worked with them in Papua New Guinea in 1954 to clear up the havoc after the eruption of Mount Leamington, when three thousand people were killed.

'They had an old piano in their village, this tribe,' he shouted above the roar of his ancient Land Rover.

He was giving us a ride along a rocky, unstable track which crossed a tumbling waterfall to the top of his mountain in the oldest, noisiest Land Rover in the country. It clattered like an old tug-boat as it neared the Awakino Ski Lodge. 'They let me play it. Whenever I sat down, they all shouted the same thing: "Hit him strong, make him cry!" So I did. I could work with those people — they're less difficult than some of today's teenagers.'

Suddenly we are back to basics.

Awakino Ski Lodge. A large wooden hut, primitive rooms, no central heating, and back-packer atmosphere.

Also very cold indeed.

The notice on the walls said it all.

> *GUIDE LINES: Ensure showers are kept to three minutes each. No candles and no cigarettes in the bunk rooms — there is no fire brigade. Generator off by 10pm. Use Gaz lamps after that.*

And, allotting duties:

> *Cooks rise at 6.30am, make sure lunches are taken up the hill. Slushies*[Kiwi for washers-up, or washer-uppers] *empty ashes, light oven fires, get in fuel, get stove roaring for a good hot breakfast, clean bunkrooms, loos, sweep floors, hose out, scrub and disinfect loo seats. And then at last, if any energy left: Ski Yer Heart Out!*

'Who'd be a slushie?' Pinned to the wall of our small room was a sheet of paper with a childish scrawl on it.

'Otematata School outing. The ski instructors kissed us all goodnight (yuk!) We all liked the times Mr Gulliver and Mr Gray fell over.'

'Poor old Mr Gulliver, no more travels for him. And no elegy for Mr Gray,' I mused.

'Lucy — ?'

She was asleep, in a bulging sleeping bag under a blanket on the lower bunk. Inside, fully clothed in her cold-weather Degré 7 ski suit against the biting chill, breathing gently.

Arthur, the sweet man, had lent us his double bunk. I pulled back the blanket, kissed the tangled blonde hair that was all I could find of her. 'Ummm ... ' from inside.

*　　　　*　　　　*

I became a member of the 'One-Ski-in-the-Grave-Club'. This is a jokey outfit started up by some elderly skiers based in Christchurch, open only to those hardy souls who reach the age of fifty-five and still get a kick out of falling down mountains for fun.

Actually, I didn't join so much as 'I was admitted'. Because I still had five years to go.

'Do I look fifty-five?' I wasn't sure whether to be flattered or furious.

'We're making an exception. Be grateful.' Arthur grinned. 'With all this travel, you are regarded as a veteran. Welcome aboard.'

Rather than an accolade to one's prowess on the planks, this was much like getting a bus pass, or becoming a Senior Citizen of the Slopes. Though in reality no one pays you any attention if you look pathetic and try to move up a pace too many in the queue for the lifts, whatever age you happen to be. Have you noticed?

'Yes, Arnie. Be grateful,' Lucy chided me with a smile that said: Hey, Arnie, I've got ten years on you!

'I am,' I said. 'And I can read your thoughts, Lucy. So just watch it.'

The three of us raised a glass to my new status, and we stared out through the window at a view that can bring a dizzying rush to the head for the unwary.

*   *   *

During our stay with John and Jennie Fairbrass, our hugely hospitable hosts at the Porter Heights Ski Lodge, we visited their home a few miles away and helped them carry a bag of coal up to the lodge in the back of our vehicle. I thought no more about this until I found that day after day the big toe on my right foot emerged looking black after skiing. At first I said to Lucy: 'My God, I've got frost-bite! I didn't realise it was that cold.'

'Silly Monkey!' she said with one of her big grins.

True, my toe didn't seem to be any the worse for wear. When it kept happening, it suddenly dawned on me — some coal-dust from the Fairbrass's sack had got into my ski boot. So for weeks every time I went skiing my right sock — and my foot — kept turning black!

The Nugget Point Hotel in Queenstown perches on the lip of a dramatic vertical cliff dropping four hundred feet down into a gorge carved out by the broad, serpentine sweep of the Shotover River. Legend has it that two farm hands started a gold rush here after collecting a solid nine ounce pebble of gold with a tin dish and a knife in one single afternoon back in 1862.

The man in charge of the Nugget Point Hotel was Philip Jenkins and his own place in the great canvas of history is, sadly, not legend but hard fact. Philip is a former British Army officer whose father Trevor, the Commissioner of Police in Kenya at the time, had to break the news to the Duke of Edinburgh in 1952 that his young wife's father, King George VI, had died.

'When the news came though to Treetops where the royal couple were honeymooning, the rest of their tour scheduled for Australia and New Zealand was cancelled on the spot,' Philip recalled. 'My father told me how the royal party had to drive to an air strip to get to Nairobi for the flight home, and how men from the East African Rifles lined the route, their heads bowed and rifles reversed. In the rush, my father carried the new young Queen's jewellery in his lap.'

Philip himself was not born until two weeks later. When, years afterwards, he was finally introduced to the Queen, she said to him, wittily, 'I believe we nearly met on an earlier occasion.'

At Nugget Point we find a glossy book in a small bedside cupboard. I opened it at random:

> *It was rock 'n' roll, the emblem of an uninhibited society, that threatened the safe world which post-war New Zealand parents had erected for their families. Stodginess permeated*

> *national life. There was little tolerance of*
> *diversity, clothes were drab, short back and*
> *sides haircuts were part of the national male*
> *uniform, and rugby, racing and beer represented*
> *for most men the extent of recreational options.*

Or, as the writer Colin James once put it: 'Men drank beer and whisky. New Zealand was a place of no choice, and none needed. Small, rich and bland beyond boredom.'

That's until snow-boarding came along.

This is a recent phenomenon, and they have the Japanese to thank for escalating it. This, it seemed, was the first year in which large groups of Japanese youngsters had spent the entire winter in New Zealand as ski bums, kids in their late teens or early twenties, living for the snow.

I have mixed feelings about snowboarders. They can be extremely hazardous in the wrong hands — or feet — and while the expert can do anything from somersaults to cartwheels and still come up smiling, the same doesn't apply to a terrified beginner skier who simply wants to get down the hill without being flattened.

'Look at this, Lucy!'

I spread out that week's copy of the local paper, the Mountain Scene. On its front page, a big story.

' "JAPANESE SNOW BOARDERS AT CENTRE OF GLUE SNIFFING SCANDAL." How about that? We have blundered into Sodom and Gommorah.'

And another one. 'A mugging. The suspect was dressed like a Japanese snow boarder!'

'What does that mean? A mask and goggles?'

'I'll bet he threatened his victims with a snow board,' I said.

But these are worrying times for snowboarders in NZ. Complaints are rife. The local *Mirror* reported that fifty 'Long time skiers' at Treble Cone, one of the South Island's top resorts, were lobbying the management to make the slopes for skiers only.

Times are changing in New Zealand — on the slopes and off.

'You know that joke, Lucy?'

'Which one, Arnie?'

'The plane from London, packed with passengers, is on its descent into Auckland. And the captain is saying over the loudspeaker: "Ladies and gentlemen, we are about to land at Auckland. Welcome to New Zealand. Would you please put your clocks and watches back fifteen years?" '

'Arnie, that's not nice.'

But slightly true, perhaps.

*   *   *

The dream again. Recurring. But this time it's different. Terrifyingly, heart-stoppingly different. There's been a collision, and I start to move, as the slippery sides of the couloir slide past and I pick up speed. I try to gain leverage, to brake — but it's not working. My skis scrape and scrabble on ice. It's so steep!

Now there's the desperate sound of the ski edges biting into ice, but not deep enough to make any impact. And I'm sliding, sliding, sliding ...

And suddenly I know where I am, and I want to cry out. I'm inside Lucy's head! I am her! Watching it happen through her eyes, helpless as the vicious rock walls stream past, and the blue-grey ice abyss yawns ahead of me.

The rocks roar up. The dogleg. Turn to the right. Got to get round it. Got to get round —

But I've fallen. I'm on my face, my back, my face again, tumbling like a circus clown ... ... and into the rocks.

They say you never reach the moment of your death in a dream. We fall, and we fall —

but never the dull thud, or the explosive impact
at the end to betoken the end.

    Somehow we always wake up, or change the
dream. But what if you're inside someone else?
    What then?

*   *   *

We were not great night-clubbers. *Après-ski* in our language usually meant getting back to our hotel for a shower, finding a decent restaurant for an intimate supper, then back to the room to write up the day's events, and make love.

'You know what you are, Lucy? You're gorgeous. Something else I always remember — '

'What's that, Arnie?'

We're in bed, and my fingers are reaching for the light switch.

'The way you dance. It's sublime.'

*   *   *

I remembered a disco. Somewhere in France, I think it was Val d'Isère. And something like two o'clock in the morning, one of those nights when we hadn't wanted to go to bed early but just sat together in a candle-lit basement club talking the night away over black coffee and cognac.

Suddenly Lucy was getting up and walking — no, stalking — on to the empty postage stamp dance floor and starting to move. Like a cat. By herself.

I just sat back (since I'm no great shakes as a dancer) and watched the performance.

She was wearing a little black number with thin shoulder straps, the kind of figure-hugging dress in which she always looked terrific, and to me, mind-numbingly sexy.

Lucy had a great figure — and as they say, if you've got it, flaunt it! She'd got it, and she flaunted it, but in a subtle way that was never cheap.

And I basked in her own powerful sex-appeal, a proud man showing off his woman to the world.

And never more so than now. She stayed on the floor through five numbers, and no one dared disturb her. The dozen other couples seated at small tables around the dance area watched in silence, riveted as I was.

I've seen moments like that before, coming out of nowhere, when the spotlight is on one single person, an entity commanding a space that simply cannot be violated.

This space, and these minutes, belonged to Lucy. She danced for herself. Drifting in her own world, unhurried, sexy as hell, a small smile on her lips and a look in her eyes that was focused faraway on something that I might never know.

*   *   *

Jennifer Rush was pouring out *The Power of Love*; Chris de Burgh with his heart-aching *Lady in Red*; Whitney Houston and *I Will Always Love You*; Sade singing *Your Love is King*.

And still she danced, but not for me.

Finally, her eyes came back into focus, and she danced to seduce me, sitting there transfixed with love.

To the words of *Butterfly*, and Lenny Kravitz:

> *You are the most beautiful thing I've ever seen,*
> *You shine just like sunlight rays on a winter snow,*
> *I just had to tell you so ...*

She smiled, and from my seat in a dark corner my heart turned over.

Lucy had enormous style. She poured her money into clothes that were very expensive, very chic. She could have been a model, and more than once men asked her if she was. To which she would reply with a toss of those auburn locks: 'No! But thank you for asking.'

She knew how to flirt, too, as we have already mentioned. As someone once said: You can take a girl from France, but you cannot take France from a girl.

Lucy was one of those women who could never look rumpled, even if she tried. Her favourite outfits were jeans, small velvet waistcoats, and denim shirts. And black leather trousers, for show.

But in ski attire, now, that was something else. She had the curious ability to be beautiful — and look a bit dotty at the same time. Especially in the hats she chose.

'Do you know, Lucy, you remind me of those ladies who pioneered flying the Atlantic.'

'What do you mean, Arnie?' A fleeting danger signal.

'No, no. It's just — ' I searched for the word.

'Yes — ?'

'You look like ... an adventuress!' Saved by the bell.

She smiled. 'Why, thank you, Arnie.'

*   *   *

I chucked the lollipop splint away. After ten days, my finger was as healed as it would ever be, and if it was sticking out at a slightly strange angle, too bad.

We were often asked during TV and radio interviews if we had had any injuries. To which Lucy would reply: 'No, we've been very fortunate.'

And if I would add: 'Yes, we've got away with it,' she would shush me with a warning look, and afterwards turn on me.

'Arnie, don't say that. You're pushing your luck.'

She was genuinely superstitious. 'Please, Arnie. Don't tempt fate. Not until our last day. Then it will be all right.'

Why did she have to say that?

Chapter 13

September

We ski any time, any place, if necessary.
At midnight, at dawn, in a field, off a cliff.
If there's snow, we ski it.
If there's not, we find it.
If we can't find it, we ask someone to make us some.
Our daily priorities are simple:
ski, breathe, eat — and then ski some more.

Arnie Wilson, every day

By now I was calling her the Red Baron. In her bright red ski suit, which she wore more than the purple or yellow and grey outfit, Lucy hung on my tail down the slopes with ever-increasing confidence and skill.

In the early days, she had stayed a cautious fifty yards behind me, and I would find myself waiting around for her to catch up. As the weeks passed, the distance narrowed.

Often there are just the two of us on the mountain. This is our world, the world we have made our own.

'Come on, Arnie! Move it!' Her joyous shriek from a few feet behind spurs me on. I accelerate away through the powder.

We have reached Australia, a comparatively short visit of

less than three weeks, to find the resorts and runs have typically colourful names like Perisher Valley, Mount Baw Baw, Blue Cow and Thredbo.

For Thredbo, read threadbare. Us, that is. After two hundred and fifty days (and five hundred vertical miles) of skiing, the toll is beginning to tell. If not on us, then on our equipment.

'Your skis are just about blown out, mate,' Alex Herbert at Fleet's ski repair shop in Thredbo ran an experienced and somewhat jaundiced eye over our battered Salomons, and reported back with the traditional Aussie aptitude for the *mot juste*. 'They're screwed.'

Well, he used another word, but it meant the same.

It also meant a three day stopover in Thredbo while said skis were unscrewed, but that was okay. No hardship. Thredbo is a busy resort in southern New South Wales, in the Snowy Mountains, a prime target for Aussie enthusiasts who flock in their scores to enjoy the slopes. When nineteen people died in a mudslide there in 1997, it knocked the heart out of the New South Wales ski industry.

*   *   *

Our spirits soared as we came upon vistas of white with the dots of skiers moving down them like ants. While Alex got busy on our skis with file and screwdriver, giving them a full MOT (bindings included) we took to the slopes on our spare Salomons, and hit the Crackenback Supertrail.

First day: 19,600 vertical feet, and seventeen miles. Second day: 16,640 vertical feet, and fourteen miles. Third day: 14,460 vertical feet, and twelve miles.

Fair dinkum!

Our days skiing Thredbo's extensive terrain gave us some of the best skiing of the month, as well as finding ourselves on the highest vertical drop in the whole of Australia.

We took the Tube, more mountain railway than London

Underground, to Perisher.

Perisher achieved its name when two cattlemen, trying to round up their herd before winter set in, found themselves on horseback battling through a blizzard. One of them noted later:

> *We rode out to the west face of the mountain to look down along the Snowy River to see if the cattle were there. The frozen snow was beating into our faces. Jim Spencer's beard was white with snow. Turning to me, he said: 'This is a perisher'.*

On such small acorns of inspiration, oak trees of nomenclature grow and thrive.

*   *   *

We were arguing again.

This one began in Perisher, lasted all night and the best part of next day, and finally fizzled out in Charlotte Pass, a small resort reached by bus and snowcat from Perisher and having the distinction of being the first ski area with modern lifts in Australia.

What lit the fuse this time?

I blame our room in the Barrakee Lodge. Not for any lack of atmosphere — it was a small, cosy chalet where all the guests shared tables at communal meals (which encouraged a buzz of conversation, even if you were feeling un-neighbourly, and didn't want to talk).

Besides, we were guests yet again of the resort, and you don't look a gift kangaroo in the mouth. Our finances were in their usual parlous state, despite money from the *Financial Times* for my regular reports about our progress.

No, it was lack of space. For a start, there was no telephone in the rooms.

'That's all right,' I said. 'I can get some work done with no interruption.' We weren't expecting calls, anyway.

Then I switched on the lights.

'God, Arnie, it's tiny!' Our room was indeed little more than a box-car. And the bulb in the ceiling was so faint it was impossible to read by it. Small bed, one wooden chair, no table. Which meant nowhere to rest my word processor.

Except one place. Where the light was good enough, just. I sat on the loo hunched over my laptop, typing by the single-bar strip light over the wash basin. Lucy stayed in the bedroom, propped up on two pillows, doing her best to fill in her daily diary with her Palmtop processor and succeeding more by guesswork than judgement.

I suppose the row was my fault, because this time I was the one who lashed out.

Lucy muttered something from the bed.

'What was that?'

'I said, *merde*! I keep making mistakes. Stupid room — '

'Don't be so ungrateful. It's not costing us anything.'

'What do you mean, ungrateful? What's there to be grateful about?'

The temperature was rising.

'You've got the bed, for a start. I've just got the loo!'

'Well, I can't see properly. How can I keep up the diary?'

'You're just being a prima donna! If you don't like it, you know what you can do —'

'What can I do?'

'You can always go home.'

I didn't like the silence that fell after that. Or the fact that neither of us broke it for the rest of the night. It was the first time we had gone to sleep without making up.

But at least by the time we headed for Sydney and the airport, we had skied our ill-temper out of our systems and left it on the slopes.

*　　　　*　　　　*

In all, we spent just seventeen days in Australia, skiing the Great Divide and the Alps and the Snowy Mountains. We had found hospitable resorts on Mount Buller, Mount Buffalo, Mount Hotham and even Mount Baw Baw where the only ticket you needed for a friendly handshake was a capacity to enjoy a good joke and drink copious quantities of beer.

But we had a schedule to meet. And that meant the 11.30am Air New Zealand flight out of Sydney and across to the South Island back in New Zealand. Arrival time at Christchurch: 4.20pm.

No big rush. It would be after dark before we could make it to our target: the slopes of the legendary Mount Hutt. But we had skied at night before, and it held no terrors. Just one field by a car's headlights would be enough to keep our record intact. Or even a long strip of snow by the roadside, as we had once done in Argentina.

We stayed overnight in Sydney at the home of Lucy's best friend, Sandra Dunne and her boyfriend Mark. Lucy and Sandra, former colleagues in the travel business, had exchanged gold chains at Heathrow some years earlier when Sandra had left for a new life. Lucy wore that chain every day as we skied around the world. For a while, after the accident, I wore it myself.

Next morning, a hearty breakfast with our hosts at a hotel overlooking Sydney Harbour: scrambled eggs and smoked salmon, preceded by muesli the way Australians do it. Unlike Britain, where my favourite cereal is dry and served with milk, the Aussies have copied the Swiss way, soaking their muesli all night in cream so that it is marvellously gooey by the time you sit down to it.

We hugged all round, and set off for the airport, ready for anything the day would serve up.

Well, almost anything.

'Sorry, sir. The flight has already gone.'

'What?' It was only ten o'clock. I waved our Air New

Zealand ticket, issued in London and reconfirmed in Los
Angeles back in June. It was so long since our flights had
been booked, the timetable had changed!

His voice was implacable. 'It was rescheduled for 8.00am.'

'When the hell is the next one?'

'To Christchurch? Not until tonight.'

Which meant we wouldn't have a cat's chance in hell of
making any snow whatsoever today.

We raced over to the Air New Zealand desk, and in a few
crisp sentences told the startled Customer Services assistant of
our plight. 'We're skiing the world ... you're sponsoring us ...
we're stuck ... not our fault ... whole expedition hangs by a
thread ... help!'

And so on.

She got the gist of it immediately, that lovely lady whose
name I never did know, reached for a phone, and did some
fast talking. Then she looked up, and smiled.

'We can get you on a flight for Wellington, and make a
connecting flight to Christchurch. You'll have to hurry. It
leaves in half an hour!'

Not for the first time — nor would it be the last — Lucy
and I found ourselves running along endless corridors towards
a departure lounge that, like our hotel rooms, seemed by sod's
law to be furthest away.

Heart pounding. Mind full of doubts. Was all the baggage
on board? Had they remembered the skis? It was too late to
worry now. Just catch that plane!

We did just catch it. Skin of the teeth, but we made it.

As we watched Sydney Harbour Bridge and the giant shell
of the Opera House pass beneath us into history, I felt a flood
of relief wash over me.

'That was close, Lucy.'

'Too close.'

'I need a drink!'

*   *   *

The day wasn't over yet. I had that nasty feeling that fate was wiggling its fickle finger, but hadn't quite yet decided to point it at us. We were ahead of the game, but only just.

We had to get to snow.

The bright September spring sunshine burned down on us at Wellington, on the southern tip of North Island, and an hour later at Christchurch, mid-way down on the east coast of South Island.

We rented a luxurious Toyota van, and headed for the hills.

This time it was the pressure that sparked off another row. We were starting to argue too much. Over little things that became big things.

'Are you sure you know the way?'

'Will you leave it to me, Lucy. I've been here before, so just keep quiet and let me do the driving.'

She didn't like that, and I can't blame her.

Inevitably, I got lost.

Everything was fine until we got to Methven, a neat little suburban town, buried in the foothills. But then it all started to fall apart in one of the worst nights of our entire year.

First off, the drive should have taken ninety minutes, but somehow went on for close to three hours. During this time Lucy sat in sullen silence, nibbling at her fingertips.

I saw blood welling up in the wounds as the main street of Methven loomed out of the gathering dusk.

'Let's get a quick snack.' I parked outside a café. While Lucy ordered coffee and sandwiches, I hurried across the road to catch a pharmacy before it closed, to buy some fresh plasters.

Inside, I spotted something on one of the shelves. A small bottle of liquid, no less, that parents put on the fingers of their children to stop the kids biting the tips.

Wonders never cease. 'I'll have that!'

I crossed the road back to the café, and proudly showed my purchase to Lucy sipping coffee inside. 'Look, Lucy! For your fingers — '

She turned on me like a jungle cat, green eyes glowing with fury.

'Arnie, will you stop trying to run my life! You do not control me. You do not tell me what to do. Just leave me alone. If I want to bite my fingers to the bone, that's my affair!'

There were times when it was wise to say nothing. I walked out into the street, crossed the road, and asked for my money back.

It got worse.

The café proprietor gave us directions for Mount Hutt.

Thirty minutes later I was peering blindly through the windscreen into darkness that reached out like an all-enveloping black glove.

'Arnie?'

In adversity, we were talking again.

'Are you sure we're right?'

How could I be sure of anything? There was no moon, no stars. Not even the tiniest glimmer in the sky. Usually in the mountains you can expect some kind of glow, whether it's moonlight reflecting off the snow or perhaps the crystals in the snow itself.

But never this impenetrable, inky blackness that had closed in on us like a dark suffocating shroud.

'Arnie, I'm worried — '

So was I, but I wasn't going to let it show.

'We'll be fine. Can you see snow?' It would be enough to stop the car, put on our skis, and slip and slide a few hundred yards down the road. The headlights showed only grass and rocks.

Lucy wound down her window, then wound it up again. 'No.'

That was when the first hail stones hit us in a cacophony of sound like a thunderous drum roll.

'God!' I slewed the car instinctively to a halt, then proceeded ahead more cautiously.

The heavens opened. Small round ice cubes bounced off

Clint Eastwood, who surprised Lucy by chatting to us (in French) about our dream when we met on the mountain at Sun Valley, Idaho only a few days into our mission.

Top: A spectacular and unexpected mountain-top welcome for us at Heavenly Ski resort in Lake Tahoe, California.

Bottom left: Ski the Summit, Colorado – our main sponsors – devised this logo for the celebratory T-shirts handed out when we returned to Breckenridge in triumph.

Bottom right: Lucy and I in Tignes, in the French Alps, a few days before our departure for Jackson Hole in December, 1993.

Princess Diana – or is it Lucy? At least one American tourist confused them!

Top: A cartoon prepared by the *Financial Times* to illustrate my final despatch after completing the challenge. In the end the newspaper used photographs of us instead. Thank goodness, although it flatters Lucy.

Bottom: Embarrassing but fun – crowned 'King and Queen of Skiing' on the final day in Breckenridge.

Top: Lucy meets a skier in wolf's clothing in Portillo, Chile.

Middle left: On the 'General's' lap – the Russian truck which made our lives a misery, but was also our salvation.

Middle right: All smiles at Ski Butler, Kentucky.

Bottom: Me on the slopes at Jackson Hole.

Top left: After stopping by a Chilean lake to pick a sprig of mimosa, Lucy didn't get the chance to pose. I caught her natural smile to produce my favourite picture of the trip – this photo is on her grave.

Top right: The final day – it's all over!

Middle right: Come rain or shine. Lucy gets soaked in Goryu-Toomi, Japan.

Bottom: We skied on several active volcanos, and in the Southern hemisphere.

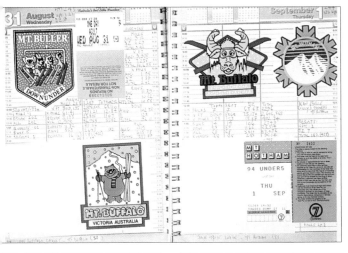

Top: A life in the day of ... Lucy and I. Just one section of our diary for 1994, with skiing statistics and lift ticket.

Bottom left: Sunshine at last: An appetising scene at Valle Nevado, Chile in August – mid winter!

Bottom right: Olivier Laborie, the high mountain guide on the expedition to the Couloir des Triffides where Lucy lost her life.

Top left: Peter Hardy, still recovering from the severe injuries he received from Lucy's fatal accident.

Top right: A celebratory kiss on New Year's Eve.

Middle right: Carol Thatcher's ski instructor boyfriend, Marco Grass, does his party trick on skis for Lucy.

Bottom left: The Bear – and proud owner.

Bottom right: Lucy poised to ski the Val di Mezdi in the Italian Dolomites. I was frightened for her safety, but it was too late to turn back.

the bonnet like lead shot, threatening to dent the metal. Worse, they were cracking against the windscreen with a ferocity that had us cowering back in our seats.

I remembered something. From three years ago, the last time I had been to Mount Hutt. Roads to most ski fields in New Zealand are unpaved, with hairpin bends, sheer drops and no barriers.

I was aware that people — and I mean people in cars — had been blown off that road by fearsome gusts of wind that came from nowhere. I had even witnessed the skeletal rusting wrecks down the mountainside that bore testimony to nature's power when roused.

At least Lucy wouldn't be aware of the metallic carnage below the road as we crawled round those hairpin bends in the driving hail, ever higher into the hostile night.

And then, as suddenly as it had started, it stopped. The drum roll finished. The wind eased off into eerie silence, and only the sound of our engine and the wheels scrunching over hard mud and stones filled the night air.

'Look!' Lucy flung out an arm, but I had seen it too. There was light ahead, a brilliant whiteness. I couldn't help but remember that scene in the film *Close Encounters of the Third Kind* where Richard Dreyfuss had his first experience of a UFO in dead of night while waiting at a rail crossing. These lights were like that, dazzling in the firmament, maybe half a mile ahead and above us.

'What is it, Arnie?'

'It means we're in luck, darling!' Relief filled me like the kiss of life itself. 'They're snowcats, grooming the slope.'

Now we could see the snow, and the huge lumbering insects crawling like giant slugs across the face of the mountain. Two of them, moving in unison, grooming the piste for tomorrow's skiers.

And their sound came to us too, a constant grinding sound like a mincer, churning and flattening, churning and flattening ...

We came round the last bend, with our tyres now

scrunching over snow and came upon a scene that could have come from a science fiction movie. A huge hangar big enough to house an airliner stood open, with bright light spilling out on to the snow. Rock music blared off the mountain from a radio in the cab of another huge snowcat parked nearby, its door open, and no sign of the driver. No sign of anybody, in fact.

'Welcome to Mount Hutt,' I said. 'Let's go skiing!'

'Yes,' said Lucy. 'Let's. But how?'

I clambered out of the car. It was late, and we had only an hour or so to go before the whole mission would have been rendered worthless.

At last we found someone — John Millington, the maintenance director in charge of operations, working throughout the night and every night during the season.

'The lifts are closed, of course. But I can get a couple of Cats to take you up the mountain.'

Now that was an offer we couldn't refuse.

'John, thank you.' Two drivers, Carl McHugh and 'Chance' Sullivan were assigned to the task of making sure that Arnie and Lucy survived the dark slopes of Mt Hutt to ski another day.

I climbed into one cab, Lucy into the other. With searchlights blazing ahead of them, the twin monsters, breathing menace and power, crawled slowly to the top of the main piste.

We snapped on our skis.

'Arnie, I don't like this!' Lucy's voice was low and uncertain. Of course. I remembered, but it was too late now. On the very day we first made love in Les Arcs a million years ago, an Olympic speed-skier had hurtled into a moving snowcat and had been killed.

Lucy was scared of snowcats. Especially at night.

'Stay between them! They can escort us down in their headlights.' I shouted and gesticulated to the drivers, who nodded in what I hoped was understanding. 'Okay?'

More nods.

But Lucy hated the idea. One snowcat on her tail was bad enough. Being sandwiched between the two was a nightmare. We decided to ski ahead of them. Of course, we went too fast. Much too fast. And once we had skied out of the pool of light, there was nothing but the blackness of the mountain — and then we were skiing by pure instinct.

'Stop!' My shout carried across to her. 'Wait for them to come over the brow of the hill!' That would illuminate another section and give us some light, at least.

The rumble of the caterpillar tracks followed us down that mountain like a storm brewing. We stayed ahead.

More importantly, we stayed out of their way.

And on that crazy and frightening descent, I think Lucy grew a little — in confidence, in courage, in the ability to conquer her fear and face her demons.

It took us ten wary, uncertain, minutes. But we made it to base camp, where John was waiting to offer us a handshake and strong black coffee with a slug of brandy in it for warmth and comfort.

'Are you sure,' he said. 'That you two are doing this for fun?'

'What time is it?'

He looked at his watch. 'Almost midnight.'

'Will you do us one more favour? Can we go up again!'

That put a second run under our belt.

*   *   *

That night, at the luxurious Powderhouse Hotel in Methven, we received a message from Fran. My mother, Joan, who had died the previous May, had donated her body to Science. Science, it seemed, had now benefited all it could and Joan was about to be cremated. Unfortunately, the date they chose was 15 September.

15 September. Lucy's birthday. Virgo.

Virgos are unquestionably dependable and

sincere. They are fastidious and exacting in grooming, eating, working and romance. They also have very precise ideas about health, little patience with laziness, and very few illusions about life and people, even when they're in love. Virgo is the sign of the Virgin, but you can't take that symbolism too literally.

Thank you, Linda Goodman, for your unnervingly accurate star signs.

Lucy was forty-one. And beautiful.

I bought her a dreamcoat of a jumper in her favourite colours, blue, purple and mauve, all in beautiful pastel shades. A bottle of champagne was waiting on the breakfast table at the Edgewater Resort Hotel on the romantic shores of Lake Wanaka, nestling in its ice bucket. Our friends Minty Clinch and Neil English had brought it with them. They had interrupted a tour of New Zealand to ski with us.

So where did the day go wrong?

'Arnie, let's go skiing!' Lucy was like an impatient colt, itching to be out of the paddock and into the fields. Little patience with laziness.

'No hurry, darling. It's your birthday. Let's just relax for once — '

'No, I want to ski. Hurry up!'

The third time she said 'Hurry up', I blew my top.

'For Christ's sake, Lucy, just take it easy. We've got all day — '

'I want to ski!'

Sulkily, I downed the remnants of my glass, too fast to enjoy the bubbles, and followed her retreating back to the door and out to the car.

On the way to Treble Cone, my irritation got the better of me. God knows why, because after all it was her birthday. But on a mountain bend, I stopped the car, and pulled out the key.

'What are you doing, Arnie? Where are you going?'

Wordlessly I got out of the car, found the nearest rock, and plumped myself down. I sat there for five whole minutes, staring out across the mountains. I must have looked like a spoiled child deprived of his last sweet.

Finally we went skiing, but it was a tense day.

Much later, with great sadness, I read what Lucy had written in her diary for that day:

> *My birthday was a mixed affair combining a bitter-sweet mixture of pleasure and pain. The pleasure at discovering a bottle of champagne at our breakfast table was followed by anger and sadness when Arnie objected at being asked to hurry up and go skiing. I still fail to see how my eagerness could have created such a crisis ...*

We made it up, as we always did. This time with the sheer exertion of skiing through heavy mist that made visibility practically nil down steep, treacherous paths to the cafeteria at the base. To raise another glass, this time of warming brandy with our coffee, and a toast.

'To you, Lucy. Happy birthday. I'm sorry, darling.'

'Thank you, Arnie.'

'Forgive me?'

'Yes. I forgive you, Bull-ron!'

We were friends again. But the entry remains in her diary, and the diary is with me for ever. Her last birthday had burned into my conscience like a branding iron of remorse.

Chapter 14

October

Every day I talk to her. Lucy, I don't know if you can
hear me or not. I know you're out there,
buzzing around and being brilliant.
You know I adore you. And one other thing:
Life without you is unutterably sad.
Please wait for me, even if it takes twenty years.

Arnie Wilson, July 1995.

We hit three million vertical on Friday 7 October, at
Broken River. Three million vertical feet, that is.
And 2,674 miles of actual skiing.

I needed the boost, a shot in the arm of fresh adrenalin. We
both did. Because some days, especially when the rain was
performing its dull incessant tap dance on the windows, I felt
like an old campaign veteran who has forgotten why he is
fighting any more.

'If we finish this mission, we'll keep moving endlessly on
to other resorts across the globe, committed to everlasting seas
of snow like the Ancient Mariner.' I grumble into the pillow.

'Poor baby! Just relax.'

I felt Lucy's fingers expertly digging into my shoulder
blades. She was massaging Tiger Balm into my bruised and

battered muscles, and I have to admit that after several minutes of this treatment my grumbling had turned into muffled moans of pleasure filling the room.

'Shush, Arnie. They'll hear you.'

'I don't care — '

'Arnie! The walls are so thin. What are they going to think?' A light Provençal giggle. 'We'll be thrown out.'

'Don't care — '

Lucy always cared for me, though, and more than I ever took care of myself. By now, my body was showing the strains of the expedition, an inevitable legacy of our huge endeavour but painful all the same.

Start at the top of corpus Wilson. Not a pretty sight!

I had injured my left shoulder a few times. It's strange how one injury compounds another, and I always seemed to be falling on it. My left hand had sustained a nasty ropeburn on a contraption known as the 'nutcracker' lift at Awakino. Just imagine a large steel nutcracker that you snap on to a moving rope to drag you up a slope, and you've got the picture. It can play havoc if you miss clipping it on at the correct moment. Timing, as a wise man once said, is everything. Get the nutcracker wrong, and you either plummet face first into the snow, to ribald laughter from the onlookers, or, like me, unthinkingly grasp at the rope, with dire consequences.

Other ski-mata: my thumb was bandaged after I cut it on the rusty lock of a mountain hut. My big toe nail had finally come off after constant rubbing against the inside of my ski boot. And my finger was still deformed after that nasty argument with a car door in Chile.

Apart from that, everything was just fine.

As for Lucy, what was the medical report? She had a toe nail hanging by a thread, too. Bruised ribs. And a nasty welt on her shin caused by a fall on a rock protruding from a treacherous ice slope the previous day.

All in all, we are the walking wounded.

'Tell me, Arnie,' asked another curious local radio

interviewer, 'what's your motivation for this trip?'

'Motivation?'

'I mean, how have you approached it?'

Motivation, inspiration. 'We ski any time, any place. At midnight, at dawn. In a field, off a cliff. If there is snow, we ski it. If there is not, we find it. If we cannot find it, we ask someone to make us some!'

Now that, I thought, sums it up admirably.

'Has anyone tried to tell you folks that you're a little crazy?' Many times, I tell him feelingly. Many times.

*   *   *

Our most hilarious moments in New Zealand were probably waking up in Peter and Shirley Foote's bungalow at Fairlie, which is where they ran their ski area (Mount Dobson) from. They had generously allowed us to spend a couple of nights at their home, but even so we were not prepared for the cacophony of activity which broke out long before dawn — Peter and Shirley prefer to start their hectic day from base camp rather than at 5,000 feet!

At 5.30am, No 30, Alloway Street struck me as being a little like the opening sequence of the movie *Amityville Horror*, in which various domestic gadgets suddenly swing into action of their own accord. Fax machines whirred automatically, sending messages to all corner of South Island. Telephones rang. Answer-phones were triggered, seemingly all over the house. At 6am a cuckoo clock cuckooed manically. The answer-phone message echoed down the corridors with Shirley Foot's slightly shrill Kiwi message: 'Conditions above the valley cloud are clear and calm!' (unlike the conditions at No 30!)

'There's two centimetres of new snow' she continued. 'The main runs are groomed and there's excellent skiing on packed powder. Chains are required today!'

Shirley records two new messages every morning, while

still in her nightie, and triggers the fax machine in its helter-skelter hook-up with various radio stations, sports shops, hotels and lodges, while Peter organises his staff on the mountains via short-wave radio. Our short visit gave us a wonderful if slightly comical insight into one of the best-run private ski fields in New Zealand. And at the end of the day, Lucy and I skied fresh powder for a magnificent 3,000 foot descent of the face of Mount Dobson — one of the most exhilarating runs of the whole year. Our tongue-in-cheek Amitieville Horror had become a Mount Dobson Dream!

*   *   *

The dream again.

Rocks rushing up, poking through the ice like sharp beckoning blades. I am consumed with the helpless knowledge that nothing is going to stop me, and I hit them head on. But there is no pain. Just a dull, spreading thud.

And there is Arnie, his face contorted with shock, launching himself from the spot where he had been waiting for me fifty yards below the dogleg. The dogleg where you mustn't fall.

Arnie has caught me, his strong arms clutching me in a flying rugby tackle, holding on in a desperate grip as if he will never let me go.

But it's too late.

Too late.

We tumble like pierrots in a circus, bouncing in a last macabre dance of death.

Arnie, please hold me close!

And he does, as best he can, as we cartwheel together, bouncing four, five, six feet into the air with every dreadful impact like two rag dolls clutched together.

But at last we're wrenched away, and our

helter-skelter ride slithers to a halt as we lie in
the snow at the foot of the couloir, *the final*
corridor.

And I look into Arnie's horrified, staring
eyes, see his outflung arms stretched towards
me. Curiously, I know that I am dead, and that
the sorrow I feel is for him.

'Lucy!'

I wake up in my borrowed London bed. The pillow is wet.
But it is sweat, thank God, not blood.

*   *   *

We went bird-watching. Of the feathered kind.

Now I happen to fancy myself as a bit of an ornithologist,
which started as a hobby when I was about twelve years old.
First, I went bird-watching with a school friend. Then I started
taking books out of the library. Then I started buying them.
(Books, that is.)

I became so fascinated with African birds that once when I
found myself on a trip to Botswana led by my old friend
Colonel John Blashford-Snell, I somehow became official
'Bird-spotter' for the group, listing sightings on a special
form which was dispatched to the Government.

So now, everywhere I went skiing I had a bird book with me.

'How come you're allowed all those bird books, Arnie,
when you wouldn't even let me take *Alice*?'

'It gives me something extra to write about, Lucy,' I said,
rather lamely. But it did.

Besides, I wanted to educate her in the joys of identifying
Icarus in all his myriad forms.

The only bird that Lucy could identify in the field was
the robin.

I thought, misguidedly as it turned out, that if I taught
her the plumage and song of one new bird at a time, she

might come to enjoy a little bird-watching. We never got past the chaffinch.

In Chile, we had spotted our first condor. At least Lucy could tell that wasn't a chaffinch!

'My favourite is still the *robin*,' she announced one day as I was thumbing though a book on bird life, looking for whatever we might find next on our grand adventure. 'I love his sweet little red chest.'

She peered over my shoulder, down at the pictures of a large cockatoo. 'Hey, Arnie — he looks just like you!' And she gave one of those huge *éclats* of laughter. Or was it a cockatoo-like screech? After a moment I joined in. I couldn't help it.

Then there was the Pied Currawong, which woke us in Australia with his extraordinary song. *Quardle, Oodle, Ardle, Wardle, Doodle*! Or something like that. Skiing in the Australian eucalyptus trees was full of ornithological surprises. When did you last see a flock of crimson, blue and green rosellas fluttering in snow-gums weighed down with fresh snow in Les Arcs?

*   *   *

Wednesday 26 October, noon. It was time to bid our farewells to New Zealand, and indeed to the Southern Hemisphere, and head north. Which, of course, meant encountering our old friend the International Date Line for the third and last time.

'Do you realise that we're leaving spring and heading into autumn all in one day?' I snapped the Air New Zealand route map shut, and settled down into the roomy upholstery of armchair comfort. The only trouble about travelling First Class is that it spoils you for anything else.

'When we get to the Date Line,' I said, 'Get ready to say Hello and Goodbye in one breath. That's all it takes — and we're both a day younger.'

'I'll never get it,' Lucy sighed.

'Don't worry,' I told her. 'When I say when, we'll both say it together.'

I contemplated my first glass of champagne as the 747 Jumbo lumbered into the pale blue sky above Auckland, both its engines on maximum thrust. Down below, the spring flowers were poking their heads above the earth for the first time, sniffing the breeze. The sun had shone on us from a great height, with the promise of a warm day.

With summer beckoning, it was hard to leave. As for us, we were heading back to the snows. Having skied on so many volcanoes in the southern hemisphere these past few months, we almost felt we owed it to our delightful host country on that last day to climb Ruapehu in a ritual farewell. One for the road, so to speak.

We wished we hadn't.

Ruapehu has a lake in the crater. Sometimes it is like a beautiful shimmering coin dropped from the sky to lie in a rocky cradle with its silver surface calm and unruffled, reflecting the white peaks in the still waters like shark's teeth biting into gunmetal. Other times, the lake bubbles ominously.

'Is this a good idea, Arnie?' We were tramping up the steep incline from the Far West T-Bar above Whakapapa, boots scrunching on hard snow that was freezing into solid concrete. The weather was becoming progressively worse — mist, rain, finally hail.

Eventually, a complete white-out made us, and the mountain, invisible.

If you have never been in a white-out, my advice is: don't bother. Unless you are the kind of person who likes to drive down dark country roads with the lights turned off.

The world disappears. You can become totally disoriented, lose all sense of direction. Sometimes, when the mist lifts for a split second or the clouds roll back, I have found myself looking at a different mountain altogether from the one I was expecting. Or maybe at a fresh grove of pines that shouldn't be there because they weren't in evidence ten seconds ago

when I skied into that wall of clinging wet gossamer mist.
That's a white-out.

'Arnie, where are you?'

Her plaintive cry from just ten feet away.

'Here, darling. I'm trying to keep up.' The Sultan of the
Slopes, lagging behind his Sultana. We had to ski this
'Volcan', then get to the airport for our major flight across
another ocean to America.

Just as long as we didn't get lost. Or fall in the lake.

'Try to follow the footsteps, Lucy!' Others had been here
before us, the imprint of their boots etched deep into the
shifting snow. We had trudged up to the rim of the volcano,
and the smell of sulphur hung in the air like bad eggs,
growing stronger by the minute.

The only way I knew we were on any sort of track was by
following the outlines in the snow like some kind of
bloodhound.

'Okay, this is it!' The slim silhouette of a signpost loomed
out of greyness. One arm pointed downwards to 'The Lake'.
Another to 'Far West', which meant the T-Bar. A third to
Whakapapa, where our car was.

Since we couldn't see the lake and could hear only the
menacing hiss of the volcano emitting its steam, we decided
to quit while we were ahead. We took a slow, cautious descent
back to base camp.

At least we had skied that day. Adding a few more precious
feet to our New Zealand figure of 695,960 vertical feet skied
in the North and South Islands (or 24 Everests) and, now, a
grand total of 3,209,965 vertical feet under our skis since
leaving Jackson Hole.

'Er, falls, Arnie?' As if I'd tried to cheat. But I could have
fallen a dozen times in the mist yesterday and Lucy would
never have known.

Ah yes, falls.

'What about them?' The red wine from the McWilliams'
vineyard close to Auckland in North Island was pleasantly

smooth. I relaxed back in my armchair in First Class, allowing mock leather and euphoria to steal over me. It had been a long day.

'Do you want to know how many?'

'Go on. Surprise me — '

'You've fallen 152 times. I've fallen 158. Only six more than you! I'm catching up.'

She was, too.

Fact: at noon on 26 October we were flying over a volcano in New Zealand. At precisely the same time and date our 747 was starting its descent into Los Angeles International Airport. Amazing!

Travel, I have to say, was definitely agreeing with Lucy. Her cheeks were glowing with health, her tan was enviable, and her body was just marvellous, muscle-tone perfect, moving with ever more feline grace whether she was encased in her various ski outfits or relaxing *après-ski* in a trouser suit or dress.

In the plane, up front, I said cheerfully.

'Do you realise, darling, that people were writing us off almost before we began? They said we wouldn't be talking to each other after six weeks.'

'Silly monkey. Of course we are.'

And that was the great thing about our relationship. We talked. And we talked. All the time. On chair lifts, in cars, trudging through snow fields, sitting close in cosy bars over candelight dinners, splashing through strange slushy streets in strange slushy towns. Somehow, there was always something to say. How many marriages can boast that? They said when Lucy died that we'd crammed more time together into a year than some married couples do in ten years.

Marriage. I had made a note before we left England, all those months ago. Our friend the Chinese horoscope had something to say on this score. Now seemed as good a time as any, cocooned above the dark Pacific Ocean, to locate it. I fished around in my case until I found the slip of paper, unfolded it, and read it to her:

> *If the Monkey married the Snake, they may have a tendency to bring out each other's mutual weaknesses. He will be extrovert and imaginative; she will be hard-working and stylish. Both have imposing personalities, and so they may find themselves in frequent disagreement because they are naturally cautious.*

Uncanny!

'Yes,' Lucy said seriously. 'It is rather.' And she fell silent for a while, staring into her glass.

'Did I tell you that I love your scents?'

Lucy had so many. And like most women, she went through phases. Subtle light hues, heavy perfumes that left you swooning. She chose them with extreme care. I chose them too, occasionally, when I found myself at a counter and on impulse bought something that looked right, mainly I confess because of the shape of the bottle. The assistant would dab a spot on her wrist and I would bend and sniff and say, 'Yes, I'll take that one.'

There was a big triangular bottle which I still have, its remnants swimming in the base. Liz Claiborne, Eau de Parfum spray. After the accident, I went through her belongings and found literally dozens of small, intimate bottles of scent, many unopened. To this day I still don't know her favourite.

'More wine, sir?' The stewardess poured more McWilliams into my half-empty glass. Her gentle Kiwi twang, an accent I had come to enjoy, was friendly and uncomplicated. Like her.

'Why not!'

Trains and boats and planes. You confide in strangers, in human ships that pass in the night, never to be seen again despite the swapping of business cards or addresses and the best intentions of keeping in touch. Of course, you never do.

But Lucy and I were two vessels interlinked, travelling together through an ocean of time and space, never to be separated.

Please God, never to be separated.

*   *   *

Time for drowsy assessment, as the Pacific night passes us by and we head back into another hemisphere. Another world.

We have slept in king-size beds in luxurious hotel suites, in single bunks in freezing mountain huts, aboard rickety old trains and even in a Russian truck. We have fled from hotels and refuges where Lucy found the accommodation unsuitable through cleanliness, or lack of it.

We have been transported to the highest slopes imaginable by helicopter, ski planes, high-speed quads and low speed single-grip rope tows, on an assortment of four-wheel drives, snowcats — and all too often, on foot.

We have skied in fresh, feather-light powder, clinging crud, breakable crust, over and round huge moguls, windpack, suncrust, man-made snow, frosted powder, hoarfrost, rime, and potentially lethal ice. But we still loved skiing, and each other.

Avis have loaned us fourteen vehicles (by coincidence the same number of TV stations to which we have given interviews). We have spoken on eleven radio programmes, and to fifty-six newspapers — including one in Japan that we never could read.

And the questions. Always the same.

How long will your skiing every day of the year last?

Well, er, every day of the year. That's right.

Or: But you don't ski the day that you fly?

Oh yes, we do.

Are you getting married?

Probably, but not yet.

*　　　　*　　　　*

'Do you realise, Lucy, that by the time this is all over we will have skied over one hundred Everests in more than two hundred resorts, travelling the equivalent of four times round the world — at an average speed of fourteen miles an hour?'

'Go to sleep, Arnie.'

But I saw her make a note on the Palmtop, as we came into America for the last great gasp.

Chapter 15

November

Roll on the cruisers, the bumps, the ice, the powder.
I'll take it all. It's my challenge and my relaxation,
taking my mind off the enormity of the task.

Lucy Dicker, November 1994

S ki resorts in America usually open on Thanksgiving
Day, traditionally the last Thursday in November. We
got there early. And we had to ski.

The actual arrival date had been 26 October. We headed
straight for Mammoth, taking the easy way out to keep our
record intact. And there would be snow, be sure of it!

But first, at Seattle airport, a major hiccup. We were
searched for drugs. And I mean, searched!

I saw this dog wearing a waistcoat, on which were printed
the words: AMERICAN AGRICULTURE. Actually, there
were two of them, a pair of benign-looking canines, Starsky
and Hutch on four legs. Brown, with deceptively sad eyes and
alert nostrils.

Okay, my fault. Stupid even to ask. But I did.

'Hey, that's a nice looking dog. Are they trained to sniff
out drugs?'

'Yes, sir.' The burly shaven-headed handler in his crisp

blue uniform had the initials LAPD on his rolled-up sleeves. 'Do you wish to declare any?'

The dog suddenly sprang into the alert position, paws splayed, sniffing round our bags the way most other dogs sniff around lamp-posts. The result was that we were body-searched!

'Marijuana, Mr Wilson. Grass. The dog found traces of it on your luggage.' In his small office behind the frosted-glass windows, the supervisor looked up at me with a bleak gaze. 'Are you sure you haven't been in contact with anyone who might be possessing this illegal substance?'

'No way. And neither of us touch the stuff.'

In fact the last time we had to our knowledge been anywhere near an illegal substance was back in Manali which we were later informed was the marijuana capital of India. The malady lingers on.

A personal search can be quite intimidating. A cramped, cell-like room. No windows, no signs of ventilation. A burly man in uniform runs practised hands over my body. A tape recorder on a small table is whirring softly, marking this dubious event for posterity.

'I am now searching your private parts, Mr Wilson.' As if I didn't know. I knew Lucy was in a neighbouring cell, going through the same ordeal, and the thought made me sweat with a mixture of impotence, frustration and fury. His fingers exploring my sensitive areas.

Finally: 'Thank you, sir. Sorry we had to put you through that. But you understand, we have to carry out our duty. Can you think how you could have picked up the traces?'

I was too tired even to have a theory. Besides, if I mentioned India we might both have been put through the ordeal again.

'No idea, officer. No idea at all.'

'Thank you, sir. Skiing the world, eh? Good luck.'

'Thank you,' I said.

Afterwards I thought: who is thanking who? And for what? God bless you, America. We're back! Have a nice day!

232

*   *   *

That day, or night, we skied Mammoth at four o'clock in the morning in order to get to our next resort: Keystone, which shared with Mammoth the distinction of being the only ski resort we could find in the whole of the USA with lifts operating this early in the season.

'Hey, don't you guys ever ski in the day time?' Out on the moonlit slopes teams of snow-makers, working all night, are monitoring the snow-guns blasting three trails with a fresh carpet of instant snow: they are called Fascination, Broadway and Far West.

I explain our own mission. He listens, fascinated. 'You've really skied every day?'

'And night, when we have to.'

'Jeez!' He is much impressed, and escorts us down to the hut that is open like an all-night Motorway café, except that we are the only things moving on the icy slopes outside. Plastic tables, a row of thin plastic seats. In the corner, a single bunk, presumably for casualties.

Hot, steaming coffee.

Three other men, big jovial figures in ski jackets, join the conversation. These are the people the world never sees. The dark side of California's moon. The men who are on call throughout the night, just in case. In case of what?

'Anything.' Tim Russell, our new-found friend, enlightens us. 'Could be someone lost out there. Or we get a few drunks decide to put on skis and maybe break their necks unless we stop them. Snowboarders, inner-tube toboggans, ski surfers, you name it. We get them all. Last week we had four guys turn up with a bench, which they upended and used as a toboggan. They walked near a quarter-mile up that slope, and almost killed themselves on the way down when the thing dug its nose in the snow, and sent them all somersaulting over a cliff. Luckily the drop was only twenty feet down, and they landed in soft snow.'

Tim Russell reflects the great bonhomie that exists among skiers the world over. We are experiencing it yet again, at first hand.

So if a couple of freaky people are trying to ski round the world — I was beginning to see it like the Resistance Movement in World War II — we will get help wherever we go.

*   *   *

Tim and a colleague, Eric Gehrung, complete with snowmobiles and helmets, equipped, miner's style with lamps, took us zooming up to the top of lift 1. Then, as we skied down, our two ski chauffeurs followed us, their headlights sending our shadows across Broadway as we made fresh tracks in tomorrow's new snow.

Dawn found us heading off by road for Los Angeles in a blizzard. In Colorado, too, autumn leaves had been sent swirling into creeks and ditches by the first real storms of November. Another winter had begun in the Rockies.

Mainly, people seem amused by our trip. Or envious. Impressed, too, when they finally grasp what we're doing. Sometimes there's a hint of disbelief at the corner of their eyes, and the hidden question: Why? What are you getting out of it?

Simple: the tremendous kick that we were doing something no one else had ever attempted in history.

Other interviewers ask the usual questions: 'Hey, are you two planning to get married at the end of all this?'

To which we keep a brave face and the stock answer.

'Maybe. We're thinking about it.'

Lucy put it more succinctly than anyone. In her diary, dated 10 November:

> *'We are getting on so well together. From my
> personal view, I've come to rely on Arnie as a
> friend as well as a lover. Getting so very close to
> him, and trusting him, the relationship has got*

> *deeper. I am not sure if marriage would make it*
> *better or not. After all, my experience of*
> *marriage hasn't been that great, has it?'*

*   *   *

Our route across the world, and across the United States in particular, was like joining up dots on one of those play-it-by-numbers games we all played as children. The dot on the map for Thanksgiving turned out to be Aspen, Colorado. The resort that five months later would plant a blue spruce in Lucy's memory at the top of the legendary Aspen Mountain.

Under cover of darkness, so that no one would see me cry, I went to see that spruce, and said a little prayer beside it, when I could finally bear to set foot in Aspen again.

Lucy and I celebrated Thanksgiving, America's answer to Christmas, with John Norton, Senior Vice-President of Aspen Ski Company, and his delightful wife Robin.

Aspen has achieved its name and its fame as the St Moritz of America, or maybe it should be Gstaad, when it comes to après-ski, with its surfeit of jet-setters, fur coats (real, not artificial, which does not exactly endear it to the environmental lobbyists) and high-decibel cocktail chatter in the night clubs and chalets of the rich and famous. But there's another side to Aspen when you get to know it. Friendly, ordinary, even unassuming. I've got to know the place so well, I often see more of that side than the glitz.

Earlier, we had helped the Nortons and their three daughters chose their Christmas tree from the backwoods beyond Woody Creek, a valley made famous by Hunter S. Thompson, of *Fear and Loathing* fame. Thompson, founder of the so-called Gonzo genre of journalism, lives in Woody Creek, and was once touted as an unlikely mayor of the ski town.

The valley is, in many ways, the antithesis of Aspen's Roaring Fork Valley: remote and unpretentious, with its celebrated Woody Creek Tavern, where the décor and food are funky and functional rather than the normal up-market Aspen ambience.

John Norton, a zany, larger-than-life character, whose arrival from neighbouring Crested Butte was like a breath of fresh air when he was hired by what had become a slightly stuffy Aspen Ski Co, had already lured Lucy into the whiskey bar at the Caribou Club, arguably Aspen's most exclusive watering hole.

I was there too, smiling in attendance, as Lucy let her hair down and supped vintage Scotch and sucked on a cheroot as if she was a saloon girl in a Western movie.

She would always pay her round, insisting on it, even when we were close to being dead broke.

'It doesn't matter, Arnie. We must pay our way — '

And the drink flowed that night.

At the Norton homestead, we were treated to a huge dinner. When it comes to food, America never does things by halves, and certainly not the Nortons.

'John!' I raised my umpteenth glass of wine. 'Robin! Lucy!'

Californian white Burgundy, made from original imported French grapes, from the Napa Valley. 'Here's to the light at the end of the tunnel!'

We drank to each other, to skiing the world.'Just as long as it's not a train coming at you, Arn!' Typical Norton humour.

We drank to roast turkey, Cranberry sauce, all the trimmings, and to an English Christmas we would never see.

We slept on Thanksgiving Night in the Jerome Hotel, the oldest hotel in Aspen, where the miners used to celebrate silver strikes in the bar and the atmosphere reeks of the Old West and the pioneers who made it all happen.

'Statistics, Lucy?'

She was bent over the Black Diary, face intent, immersed in higher mathematics.

'We have skied 3,671,560 vertical feet. That's 126 times down Everest.'

Our great yardstick.

The magic four million was in our sights. As long as we

didn't break a leg.

Although Lucy always wanted to pay tribute to me — 'Oh, it was Arnie's idea, this whole thing ... Arnie is a better skier than me ... But I'm getting better ... ' — she didn't like it one bit when someone ignored her role. Occasionally, someone would give me a gift and not her, which would leave her furious and insulted. It happened at the Jerome. They left a blue Jerome T-shirt on the bed for me. But not for Lucy. 'It's as if I don't exist!' she snapped.

*   *   *

We received a fax from Dave Watts, Editor of the *Daily Mail Ski Magazine*: CONGRATULATIONS, YOU'RE GETTING THROUGH IT. FAME FOREVER!

We wish, we wish.

We are, admittedly, getting a little light-headed about the prospect of finishing. We are also getting a lot of radio time, and TV too. Lucy provides the glamour, I'm the archetypal Englishman.

'Together,' I announce grandly, 'We are much greater than the sum of the individual parts.'

'The French have a word for that,' says Lucy. '*Synergie.*'

'We're a bit like Richard Burton and Elizabeth Taylor: we can't ski together and we can't ski apart. Burton and Taylor on ice, that's us!'

There is one nagging doubt, that we keep to ourselves. We are still behind our overall target.

'We're only on 9.9 miles per day, Arnie.' Lucy raises an anxious face from her paperwork. 'We've got some catching up to do.'

It might not sound much to be adrift by, but it's so late into the trip that it all adds up. Multiply 0.1 by 300 and it makes us about 30 miles short.

'We'll do it,' I say confidently. 'We're in the States, remember?'

But the doubt, albeit a small one, remains.

*   *   *

The 24 Hours of Aspen Ski Marathon is about to take place. This is one of the most dramatic events you can hope to witness in the United States ski calendar. Twenty-four hours of downhill racing. Day and night. The great sweeping escarpments above the town are floodlit, as twenty of the world's finest racers set out to ski Ajax Mountain from noon to dusk, and through the night till the sun comes up again. Round-the-clock, non-stop. Incredible, when you think about it.

'I mean, Lucy, how do they stay awake?'

Malcolm Erskine was one of two British entries, the other being Bill Gaylord, fresh from the British team. Lucy and I found ourselves in the company of these skiing stalwarts on a late run up in the Silver Queen Gondola. They would hit ninety miles an hour on their descent, again and again, even under arc-lights in the middle of the endless, freezing night.

Lucy and I stood at the base as they came hurtling in, checked out their time on the electronic scoreboard, and headed back for the Silver Queen. It was exhilarating for us, exhausting for them.

'Do you realise,' I said, as we headed for bed at midnight, 'That those two will ski in twenty-four hours the same distance it has taken us two weeks to cover?'

Sobering thought.

In the morning we were back at the finishing post. The crouched figures were still hurtling down the slope, skidding, like zombies now, into the roped area for another pit-stop. As they dive into the gondola yet again, a sea of willing hands — still on duty after the long, cold night — reach out to offer food, drink, heated polar-packs, blankets and even plastic bags and buckets for skiers who need to answer nature's call.

I shook my head in wonderment.

'And people think *we're* mad, Lucy!'

*   *   *

I got frostbite, for the first time in my life.

The odd — and dangerous — thing about frostbite is that you never know you've got it until it's too late. Jack Frost sank his freezing fangs into me on an unshielded peak 12,000 feet up in the great Ten Mile range above Breckenridge.

High up and alone, with a furious gale blowing and the wind-chill factor intense, Lucy and I traversed a wild and wintry slope with our skis scrabbling for purchase and the wind blasting frozen snow into our faces like ice bullets.

You have to walk for half an hour from the top T-bar to reach Peak 7, and this through deep, ungroomed, freezing snow. The moonscape terrain stretches away into huge snow-fields, looking golden and ghostly through my tinted goggles. Knowing what we might be in for, we had worn thermal underwear and a warm sweater under the distinctive all-weather purple Degré 7 suits. We wore our anorak hoods over our ski hats. It should have been enough.

The wind howled across that lonely plateau like a pack of ravaging wolves. There was no one else in sight. Half-way across that great pitiless slope, I felt a tiny shiver of unease.

Then my goggles started to ice up. Just at that moment, Lucy fell. Unable to see her properly, I started to panic a little, more for her than for me. Trying to help her up, I fell myself. Talk about the blind leading the blind! We were now both almost entombed in deep snow and the wind was howling louder than ever.

I had also forgotten something. When it came to protection, I omitted one part of my anatomy. My nose. First, it went numb.

Now this may sound funny, because I was totally unaware of anything unusual happening to me, until when I had finally managed to haul myself and Lucy out of the snow, she alerted me.

'Arnie, is your nose alright? It's gone white. Quickly, you must rub it, baby!'

Lucy, wet and cold, caught in a potentially dangerous

situation at high altitude on a treacherous mountain, worrying about me more than herself. Can you wonder that I loved her?

Between us, we put some colour back into the whitened flesh.

'Arnie, is it all right?'

'I don't know. We must get out of this wind, Lucy. Come on!'

The run wasn't easy. Lucy, in particular, found the deep, heavy snow difficult to manage. But at last, skiing defensively rather than gracefully, we were down.

As my nose began to thaw out in the warmth of the base lodge, it started to tingle, then burn, then hurt like hell.

An unsightly scab on the left side of my nose would stare back at me from the mirror for months. And even today, when the temperature dives, you can see where the flesh has never quite recovered. It's still the first part of my face to turn white in sub-zero temperatures.

So be warned, fellow traveller.

Frostbite hurts.

Stick to holidays in the sun.

Or ski in the summer!

Chapter 16

December

*When Stephen Cameron was stabbed to death by
a motorist on the M25 in May, 1996, his fiancée
Danielle Cable said, 'I wish I'd died as well.'
I felt the same.*

Arnie Wilson

Leave the best till last, I always say. We are finishing on
a high! In fact, I think both of us are getting a little
light-headed as December flies past, Christmas rushes
up — and after Christmas, I know, will surely come the most
memorable New Year's Eve we had ever had.

Like any holiday, the final days seemed to race by. But we
were still tied to a hectic schedule, and couldn't afford to be
complacent. Or careless.

'Don't forget, Arnie, how many skiers hurt themselves on
the last run of the last day!' Poor Lucy — a nervous
thoroughbred always.

'Don't worry, Lucy. But talking of falls — how many is
it now?'

She consulted the Black Diary.

'Yes?'

'I have had only one more fall than you in the whole year
— 160 to 161!'

'That's astonishing,' I said. 'It's so close.'

I meant it. On a good powder day I could easily fall seven times. Other days, not once. In fact, it was Lucy who had gone the longest spell during the trip without falling — almost a month.

In Aspen, a last interview. Jim Williams on Roaring Fork Radio KSPN asked the question they all ask. 'Have you folks decided to get married after this?'

This time we both spoke at once.

'Maybe!'

We headed off for what I knew — both scenically and in terms of snow quality — would be some of the best skiing of the whole trip. Some of my favourite resorts lay ahead: Telluride, Colorado; Taos, New Mexico; and Snowbird, Utah, to name just three. And then, of course, there would be our triumphant return to Jackson Hole, Wyoming.

Utah, where they boast: 'Our powder is so fine you can't make a snowball out of it!' and Sundance — I had a letter from Robert Redford himself burning a hole in my pocket in case our ski trails should cross. I had written to him in London, telling him of our great journey, and received a warm note back, wishing us luck.

For now, we're motoring in style. A maroon Dodge, no less, with picture windows and an engine that purrs as sweetly as a cat. Luxury!

'I wish we could go on like this for ever.' Lucy sank back into the passenger seat, and propped her feet on the dashboard. The strains of 'Enigma II' filled the interior with glorious sound.

*   *   *

At Telluride, a nice touch. They had printed our trip on the lift tickets, for all to see.

'Arnie & Lucy: Around the World in 365 Days.'

And below it: '338 Down, 27 To Go!!'

Next day, the same, only: '339 Down, 26 To Go!!'

Now we could really start to believe it.

Other resorts followed suit, charting our progress for the world to know. Purgatory, for one. And Taos, the star resort of New Mexico, for another.

As we cruised through the crimson desert, the rocks and hard earth like a landlocked sunset, towards Taos, Lucy studied a guide book.

'Oh, this is a bit unfair. Listen to this, Arnie: "Poor old New Mexico. So far from heaven, so close to Texas!"'

'Ouch!' I said.

For Taos, read Little Switzerland. It is quite deliberate. But take away the Stetsons and the cowboy boots, and you could almost be in the Swiss Alps. Put the blame, or credit if you're so minded, on one Ernie Blake, a German-born Swiss, who started up the ski area in 1955 and could squeeze his early clients around one table at the old Hondo Lodge. There are ski trails like Willy Tell, Edelweiss Glade and Winkelried.

Two of the principal hotels revel in the names of St Bernard and The Edelweiss. Swiss flags flutter from poles everywhere. Why, the Chalet Montesano, where we revelled in a luxurious apartment for one gorgeous night, is owned by Victor Froehlich, a ski instructor like his wife Karin and one-time pastry chef from Davos who can also put being a Swiss international junior goalkeeper on his CV.

Strange, wonderful place, Taos. Some of the runs are out of this world, too. Ernie Blake, a passionate anti-Nazi who worked for Allied Intelligence during the war, named some of his favourite trails after German generals who, at various stages of the war, had tried to assassinate Hitler. Names like Stauffenberg, Tresckow and Oster. He added Winston and Spencer's Glade to his list, both runs for advanced skiers.

Lucy nudged me, as I slid the Dodge over hard snow into the lot behind our hotel. 'The sign, Arnie!'

I followed her glance, and blinked. On a post by the entrance: '*Achtung*. Private Parking.'

*   *   *

You don't tend to see many black faces in the mountains, but one place where you do is Red River. The most active group of black skiers in the States are known as The Brotherhood. They regularly get invitations from resorts to encourage this ethnic minority in a sport that some might consider is alien to them.

Some like it hot. Others like it cold. In Red River, Lucy and I came upon a brave sight.

We spotted him as we embarked on the final run of the day before heading for a bath and a sandwich.

Far below we spied a lone black skier, resplendent in a fluorescent yellow ski outfit, struggling to get down the piste. Every time we looked, he was picking himself up. Finally we caught up with him, digging himself out of another deep hole, brushing the snow off his clothes yet again.

'Are you all right?' Lucy would always help a lost soul.

He eyed her with a mixture of gratitude and despair. 'I'll make it, honey,' he said. 'But I ain't gonna mess with these boards no more!'

In a few more days these would be my own sentiments. Not Lucy's, however.

Utah. It had been snowing ever since we left Crested Butte, Colorado, great thick flakes swirling into our windscreen like white leaves before being whipped out of sight into the void. Somehow we had made it through four hundred miles of mist-shrouded highway, the last hundred winding up I-70 through the remote Fishlake National Park with no sign of habitation anywhere, just snow-hung trees, the shimmer of a lake, the bulging silhouette of a mountain.

'Arnie, what's that ahead?'

I had already seen it, a reddish glow coming from flares blazing either side of the road. Revolving blue lights on two Highway patrol cars meant trouble ahead. Accident? Avalanche? A patrol officer strode over, bent almost double against the snowstorm.

'We've had to shut the Interstate. The weather's real bad up there — around twenty cars abandoned in the last hour. You'll have to find somewhere to spend the night.'

We ended up in Richfield, reading the local paper, the *Richfield Reaper*, which was having a field day. 'THE GREATEST SNOW ON EARTH' ran the Page One headline.

Looking through the window of the coffee house at the blizzard raging outside, I could only mutter, 'More like grim reaper!'

The storm abated as swiftly as it had hit us. We dug ourselves out of Richfield, and took the Dodge up six lanes of highway to Sundance. There we knocked on the door of Robert Redford's bungalow-style ranch tucked away amid his 7,000 acres (he once told a friend of mine: 'I can ride all day and still not see a fence'), waved our letter of introduction in the face of an apologetic secretary, and found the man himself was making a movie in Los Angeles. Pity. But thanks for the encouragement anyway, Bob.

Predictably, some of Redford's runs have names straight out of the movies: Outlaw, Stampede, Badlands, Quickdraw, Top Gun. Well, we just *had* to ski those — just for the hell of it!

Redford's nearest ski neighbour, Dick Bass, runs Snowbird. Bass, in his sixties, is the snowman's answer to Rudyard Kipling. Not only does he have the gift of the gab, he also has a gift for rarely stopping. He can quote poetry endlessly and is word-perfect on Chaucer.

He was the oldest climber to have taken on (and conquered) the highest peak in every continent. And that includes Mount Everest. In fact the last time I met him he was thinking of climbing Everest all over again because someone older than himself had done it — and he didn't like that one little bit.

*　　　　*　　　　*

We were almost there, and getting more excited by the day. So how come we were so happy, and then at each other's throats?

I can trace the moment back to the exact second that I put my empty cup down into its saucer, sat back and said: 'Well, no hurry. We can relax for an hour or so.'

But Lucy suddenly flared, the blue touch paper ignited.

'No, no, Arnie. You're crazy. There's no point in being a skier if you don't ski! The sun's out.' She waved a passionate hand at the window. 'The sky is beautiful. The snow is wonderful. We should be out there getting our exercise — '

'Lucy! We've been skiing all morning. You're becoming obsessed!'

Bad choice of word. The problem with telling the uncomfortable truth is that people tend to shy away from it. The green eyes glowed with anger. The anger fixed on me.

Her voice was dangerously quiet.

'Is that what you think?'

And she got up and left.

I saw her next on the slope, huddled defiantly alone in a four-seater quad lift, sitting on one end so that it tilted absurdly as it took her up the mountain. I followed.

And for some silly, egotistical reason, I became determined to lap her. It isn't often that my temper flares, but I was livid.

So you like skiing, do you, Lucy? Well, just get a load of this!

I was at least twenty seats behind her as I rushed to snap on my skis and grab my poles. Half-way up, I saw the familiar lithe red-garbed figure skiing down, at speed. I stared into the middle distance, just in case she looked up. I didn't want her to see me watching her.

By the time I scrambled off the chair at the top, Lucy must have been at the base, starting again. Nevertheless, I gave it all I had. And this time I made up a chair or two, catching sight of a red anorak swinging above me on the main piste, but most certainly not catching her eye.

It took me half the afternoon to gain three hundred yards

on her, with both of us passing and repassing each other, pretending all the while that the other did not exist.

Oddly enough, my anger grew with my resolve.

As the sun splayed its crimson rays into the western sky, the slopes emptying around us into a chill, deserted wilderness, I was still struggling to catch her. It was time for a truce. We skied together, swooping like twin gulls, side by side, over hard-packed snow to the base.

At the bottom, I took her in my arms and silently and unashamedly kissed her, a long and lingering meeting of mouths and minds, oblivious to a giggling party of school kids in baseball caps trotting past, laughing at us. Who cares?

We had found each other again, and that was all that mattered.

'Don't ever do that to me again, Arnie.'

She was out of breath.

'Darling, I promise — '

That night, in the bar, she took my hand and looked across the table at me. Her eyes were the deepest green I had ever seen.

'I do love you, Arnie. We mustn't quarrel like today, ever again.'

'We won't,' I promised.

If only I could have kept it.

*   *   *

'Hey, monkey!'

'You talking to me?' In the bedroom, sprawled across the bed. I was engrossed in working out how we'd spend Christmas.

'Yes, darling, I'm talking to you.'

'Then I'm listening.'

She raised her head from the Black Diary, fixing me with a gaze that was both triumphant and teasing. 'I haven't fallen in four whole weeks. Aren't you proud of me?'

'Enormously proud.'

Lucy was once hopeless off-piste, and she knew it. So how had she improved so remarkably over the year, so that by the end of it she was courageous enough to take on almost any slope, even knowing her limitations? The answer is simple. If you ski every day for hours on end, you are bound to get better.

And she just wouldn't stop, even when the trip was over. I wanted her to stop skiing. The terrible irony is that the day after the accident it would have been the last day's skiing of the winter. I was planning to sit down with her and say: 'What are we going to do with the rest of our lives?'

*   *   *

Neither of us had ever skied on Christmas Day before. On this Christmas Day, bright and early, we skied Snowbird. The resort which boasts that the powder is so fine you can't make a snowball out of it. So — no snowball fight today.

Instead we skied a joyous 20,060 vertical feet, which finally took us over the four million mark! Whooping and hollering like all good Americans do. Sixty-nine Everests!

Each of the high speed cable cars — one red, the other blue — that whisked us up the mountain that memorable day had a massive laurel wreath, as big as a tractor tyre, hung on the front. Seasonal greetings to one and all.

Merry Christmas, Arnie.

Merry Christmas, Lucy!

But there was no turkey.

'Come on, Arnie, we've got to have turkey. And Christmas pudding!'

So I took the maroon Dodge on a tour of Little Cottonwood Canyon, searching for the elusive bird. Live, frozen, stuffed or mounted. Somewhere, there had to be turkey.

'Arnie, Christmas without turkey just isn't Christmas.'

'Lucy, they eat turkey on Thanksgiving. And as for Christmas pudding — we should have had it flown in from

Fortnum and Mason!'

In the end, we settled for duck, sitting by ourselves at a candlelit table for two in the Snowbird Lodge. Duck was the only feathered friend we could find adorning any menu. But at least there were fairy lights draped across the porch, a Christmas tree in the snow outside, and a pianist, although he wasn't exactly playing 'Jingle Bells'.

Happy Christmas, America.

So towards journey's end.

And the New Year.

'We are going to have an incredible last day,' I said in the breakfast room of Copper Mountain Main Lodge, over coffee, scrambled eggs and the local paper.

New Year's Eve.

'Yes, Arnie, let's make it something special. Something that we'll live to remember — '

If only she hadn't said that.

Two days earlier we had arrived back in Colorado in some triumph in our trusty Dodge, driving fast but carefully through the snow-covered passes from Snowbird, Brighton and Solitude, via Steamboat.

We were feeling good, because that Thursday, 29 December, was the day we cracked our ski mileage, with just two days to go. Actual tally: 3,660.4 miles, 10.4 miles a day. Just over our target figure of ten miles a day.

But it had been close.

I checked my Avocet watch. Then hers.

'Darling, we've done it!'

There and then by the big quad lift at the foot of the nursery slopes I grabbed her round the waist and swung her off her feet, skis and all, sending the snow flying.

'Arnie!' Her shriek turned people's heads towards us. But I didn't care.

That day we had actually skied our quota of 10.06 miles to achieve our goal. Ambition realised — or almost. Two more days to go.

I've kept the ticket for that day. No 18986791, it says below the Day Adult, Valued on date Issued Only sticker. And the time of issue: 11.37am. A bit of a give away, that. What a late start! Were we by any chance beginning to ease up a little?

'One day, Arnie, we'll be sitting in a room sifting through old papers and old memories, and we'll come across this ticket.'

In the bar below the slope we poured wine and toasted each other.

'Don't lose it,' she said. 'Here, give it to me!'

We phoned Max Wilkinson at the *FT* in London to break the good news.

'Well done!' He was genuinely thrilled. 'We'll do it as a front for next week. You've got two days to go — don't do anything silly!'

*　　　　　*　　　　　*

Well, we did. Thanks to a crazy, wonderful last day organised by Beth Sharp.

31 December 1994. New Year's Eve. I am wearing Lucy's face. Lucy is wearing mine. We are watching the road unwind towards Keystone, and behind us the entire bus is filled with Arnie and Lucy passengers, laughing, shouting, waving out of the windows at people who think they must suddenly be hallucinating.

It was an inspired idea, both from the viewpoint of publicity and as a day to remember — to ski three Summit County resorts (Breckenridge, Keystone and Copper Mountain) on the final day of our great odyssey.

It meant bussing us around the entire valley, from one resort to the next. And not just us, but the media as well. TV crews materialised out of nowhere, and radio reporters scrambling out of cars with a Uher 4000 or a compact Sony slung over their shoulders.

We would ski the first run at Copper, then board a coach to Breckenridge and finally on to Keystone for the grand finale.

The bus had life-size photographs of us blown up and fixed to either side of the vehicle, and posters declaiming: 'ARNIE AND LUCY SKI THE WORLD!' Inside, someone opened up a cardboard box and produced ... thirty Arnie and Lucy masks!

'My God!' Lucy shrieked, and flung herself against me in mock horror. The masks were utterly surreal. But it made a good picture.

I wore Lucy's of course, and she wore mine. And looking back down the coach was like staring into a weird hall of mirrors.

'Come on, folks, they're waiting for you. Got your skis ready?'

I gulped back the remnants of my coffee. 'Who are? TV or radio — ?'

'They're all out there, too. But it's the Ski Patrol I'm talking about.'

Now this was totally out of the blue, and not on the schedule we had been given the night before. Skiing with the Copper Mountain Ski Patrol is like flying with the Red Arrows.

They wear the same colours, too. Bright red, like the Hawks the Red Arrows pilots fly. We came out, blinking, into dazzling early sunshine and stopped in our tracks as a cheer went up. There must have been forty of them, fit young men and women smiling and nodding, lined up on the hard-packed snow by the American Eagle lift in a guard of honour, with ski poles raised in salute.

'God, this is something,' I muttered. It was a signal honour. 'Our own Praetorian Guard!'

We waved our thanks all round. Then took the fast quad to the top, and assembled there at the head of the main run.

'Okay, Arnie? Lucy? You folks ready for this?' Their leader, Chuck Tolton, could doubtless ski like Franz Klammer.

'As ready as we'll ever be!'

'Let's go, then!'

We went, all of us, swooping and diving like — well, perhaps more like the Red Baron than the Arrows, but it became one of the most spectacular descents of our lives.

Hail Caesar! Our Praetorian Guard stayed round us in a protective phalanx, but never too close to be dangerous or risk collision. We went down that mountain like Genghis Khan in full cry across the Steppes, or El Cid leading a battle charge.

All too soon it was over.

'And I didn't fall once!' Lucy turned a flushed, breathless face to me in triumph, her hair under its bobbed ski hat tangled gold in the Colorado sun as our new friends gathered round us.

'Nor did I,' I responded, trying to bring my own breathing back to somewhere near normal. 'I wouldn't have dared!'

Later, each one of those wonderful patrollers would sign the card they sent in sympathy.

In Breckenridge, the silliness continued. But fun, all the same. On this day, everyone seemed to be on a high.

Again, we had no idea what was coming. A Mountain Man appeared, a bearded hulk in furs. We were handed cloaks, crowns, sceptres. Cameras flashed. Recorders whirred.

'I now pronounce you King and Queen of the Slopes!' Mountain Man proclaimed in a very loud voice and he threw some snow at us with huge gloved hands.

The crowd, mostly British skiers, cheered.

'Arnie, I feel a complete idiot!' Her voice was low. She giggled all the same.

I had to agree. This is like something out of a pantomime — '

'Well, it is the season.'

The King and Queen of the Slopes flapped up the hill for their coronation descent, followed by a multitude of camera-snapping courtiers and subjects. And, somehow, made it back again without tripping over their robes.

Not easy, on skis.

*   *   *

Keystone next and, at long, long last, the end of the trail. A bright yellow tape was spread out like a banner across the slope, with the word FINISH in large capitals engraved on it to beckon us through the final lap.

In the gondola heading up the hill for our very last official run we sit hand in hand, suddenly pensive. Can this really be the end of it? Not deflated, exactly, because the excitement is vibrating in the air like static electricity, humming through the entire mountain. The adrenalin rush our arrival has stimulated is still burning inside us, almost tangible.

'You know what this reminds me of, Lucy?'

'No — ?'

'Last day at school.'

'Yes.' Her voice small and thoughtful. 'I know what you mean, Arnie.'

The enormity of what we have achieved is suddenly hitting us, alone there in our small steel and glass-windowed cage, swaying together over yet another drop, over the ever present, impersonal snowfields that have been with us every single day of the past year.

Are we thinking the same thing? That every time you strap on skis to challenge the mountain, nature may decide that enough is enough, that it's her turn to assert herself?

Skiing has become a popular sport, worldwide. But it is still as dangerous as it ever was, despite the hi-tech equipment, safety bindings and all the wonders that modern science has come up with to protect us. When it comes to crunch time a torn ligament, a sprained ankle or a brokenleg can happen in a split second. And that means any split second.

I watch the slopes, the snow-filled gulleys and the white-cloaked fir trees standing at attention passing below and alongside our fragile gondola, just as I have done for virtually every day of the past year.

I squeeze her hand. 'Lucy! We're almost there — '

Behind us, and far below, four-wheelers, saloons, trailers and coaches crowd the car park. Everyone, it seems, wants to see us finish our improbable journey and fulfil our impossible dream.

The TV cameras help change the atmosphere. Their sheer presence always draws a crowd. But maybe this time, just this once, we had earned it.

A deep breath, and a last look at the range of snow-covered peaks stretching in all directions away from us, gradually dwindling into infinity.

In the distance, the high peaks were beginning to turn crimson, glowing gently. Beautiful, strange, surreal.

'Right, Lucy. Here we go!' Back to reality. 'Together. Stick with me, side by side when we hit the tape! Okay — ?'

'Okay, Arnie.' Excitement and determination in her voice.

Flying Dutchman, a good fast cruising run. Then down to another trail, River Run, easy. We had done runs like this so many times before. So how come this time, she missed the tape?

I saw the cameras zooming in on us as we swept down towards the finishing line, the thin stripe now shimmering gold in late sunlight. I hit it dead centre. Clever monkey, spot on. Lucy, to my left, went skidding past the far pole.

Expletive deleted!

Poor girl, she had to clamber back after sliding to an embarrassed halt.

She climbed back fifteen feet, which took an age. The cameras still turning, all eyes on her. Was she mad! I could see the fury bubbling inside her, but luckily only I knew it. No one else suspected, because she kept a sporting smile fixed like cement on those lovely features.

The sound of champagne corks popping rattled out like a salvo across the valley. We were engulfed in handshakes, back slapping, embraces, kisses till our cheeks were sore.

And in the interviews, some of which went out across the world. One question predominated.

'Hey, are you folks going to get married now?'

'Maybe,' we chorused.

But this time laughing together, holding each other as if we would never let go.

*   *   *

They sent in a helicopter. A month earlier, we had finally made up our minds that there was only one place to celebrate our triumph. Where we had begun. Which meant Jackson Hole.

Just as we were leaving, an American tourist in stockinged feet came rushing across the snow-covered fields and started videoing our departure. He'd seen Beth and Kent Sharp and all our other friends waving Union Jacks at us, and he'd arrived at a logical conclusion.

'That's Lady Di, isn't it?' he shouted above the clatter of the shiny black machine as it blasted its way into the sky.

'No — she's still in Vail. That's actually Lucy Dicker, who's just skied round the world,' Beth shouted back.

Undeterred, the man said, 'Oh, she's pretty famous, too!' And carried on videoing.

The helicopter whisked us out from the snowfield at Keystone, direct to Denver Airport. We watched the waving crowd dwindle, took a last look at Summit County and soared east into the darkening sky.

On the flight to Jackson we talked statistics. Lucy had chalked up the final reckoning in the Black Diary, by now a slightly tattered but still faithful companion that was the only true unexpurgated record of all we had been through. The result, I think, was not unimpressive. Grand Total: we have descended 4,146,890 vertical feet (790 vertical miles), amounting to 144 times down Everest; skied 3,690 miles, all told; driven 33,515 miles, but actually travelled by air, train and car 109,480 miles, more than four times around the globe.

Guinness Book of Records, here we come!

Oh yes. Post-script: Lucy has fallen 180 times. Arnie has fallen a mere 178 times. Close again. Actually, a little too close for my ego. But deep down, how could I not be proud of that girl?

'Look at this, Arnie — ' Jim Felton, PR for Beckenbridge and Keystone, one of my oldest skiing friends in America, had added a postscript to the Diary: 'To Arnie and Lucy. A once-in-a-lifetime ski trip. For once-in-a-lifetime friends. We're proud to be a small part of it.'

But we had made so many once-in-a-lifetime friends. They would all write to me, when the time came. And I hope — no, I know — that I'll see them again, some day. In all, I would get more than three hundred letters from erstwhile strangers writing from across the world.

That's friendship for you.

*   *   *

'Resolutions, Lucy?' Ten minutes to midnight. I leaned across the table to take her hand, avoiding the candle sending wax rivulets trickling down the side of the empty champagne bottle. The glow gave her face a soft golden complexion, and turned her hair into spun honey.

There were eight of us at this very special party at Jackson's Cadillac Grille, most importantly, Bernie Weichsel, one of my dearest friends in the world, and the man who had done so much, as the boss of Ski USA, to encourage my love affair with skiing in the Rockies.

Lucy and I had come straight from the airport, still in our ski clothes. Time was pressing and we couldn't risk missing the moment.

Dakota pheasant for me, stuffed with spinach and wrapped in bacon, topped with a boysenberry — Merlot sauce. For Lucy, herb-crusted lamb, with fennel hearts and potato

Parisienne. And lots of wine. White, as usual, for me. Red for the lady in my life.

Lucy's smooth fingertips responded to mine, stroking them with a lingering tenderness that somehow seemed beyond sensuality itself.

Resolutions. In the candlelight she looked at me, her green eyes deep and searching and serious.

'I resolve, Arnie, to love you with all my heart and with all my being.' And then, flippant for a moment, 'And to keep skiing!'

'And I resolve to cherish and protect you, darling girl, for the rest of your life.'

Cherish and protect.

'What a sentimental monkey you are.' Her voice, suddenly so soft and caressing. Like silk.

The sonorous strokes of midnight from a TV turned up loud in the bar interrupted a moment frozen outside time, resounding through the silence that always comes before a new year.

I leaned across to kiss her on the lips. In that moment of triumph and shared happiness, I had never loved her so much.

Cherish and protect.

I will never forget until my own dying day the poignancy of that moment. Lucy looking ravishing as she innocently greeted the new year. If only we had known what tragedy 1995 would bring, we would have put our lives on hold, pressing the pause button for eternity.

Oh, Lucy.

Chapter 17

Afterwards

She was a rare spirit, with all the ingredients — intelligence, a special, vibrant energy, an irrepressible sense of humour, and most important of all, a warm and loving heart. I cannot think of the last moments of her life without great pain. I wanted so much to know that she did not suffer.
Even now I am deeply fearful that she did — that her eyes and ears witnessed everything. This thought will sadden me until I die. My beloved lying dead, and I still alive but not wanting to be. In the first weeks and months I thought of her almost all the time. I recalled many of the things she had said, humorous and profound: faces and expressions. I could not face the loss of a relationship so precious and so special — the anguish and intensity of the grief and the mind-blowing pain combined to make my life almost insupportable. Such grief — locked in a new dark world of utter anguish, watching the old familiar world blown apart — is unimaginable from the outside. I experienced a powerful cocktail of emotions: fear, disbelief, paralysing shock but above all a longing for her and a penetrating knowledge that this was something from which there was no recovery.

Jane Swire, mother of Flora, killed in the Pan Am
bomb explosion at Lockerbie, 1988
(From an article in the British Medical Journal
reprinted in the Daily Mail)

Friday, 6 April 1995. Springtime in the Alps. The weather is perfect.

Lucy is going to die today.

I look through the windows of our chalet to find the sky outside a glittering cobalt blue, and sunbeams lancing through the pine trees to dazzle skiers on the slopes.

There were eleven of us sharing the two chalets in a scrubbed-pine two-storey building on the slopes of the little-known resort of Vaujany, near Alpe d'Huez in the French Dauphiné. Our genial hosts were Nigel Purkhardt and his delightful wife Annika, who run Ski Peak, a small, friendly ski tour operation.

Nigel, dear man, who was so innocently caught up in the terrible events of that day, would later rename it the Chalet Lucette. After Lucy.

There is a picture of Lucy on the wall. The same picture that is on her grave. Also on the wall is a framed fable by La Fontaine: *La Cigalle et La Fourmi*.

'Lucy's picture looks lovely there,' Nigel told me later. 'Her eyes follow you round the room. It's a very nice feeling.'

It is one of many, many tributes that will ensure that Lucy lives for ever in our memories.

With us too during those warm spring days were our old friends Peter and Felice Hardy and their two children, Max and Barney. We were one huge happy house-party that week. And, apart from Lucy and me, awash with children. That was the whole idea. A cosy, family orientated gathering to enjoy spring and celebrate the end of the ski season. But the children would definitely be staying at home during our outing to La Grave. This is a ski area for adults only. Adults who relish tough but exhilarating skiing.

It was Peter and Felice who had encouraged Lucy and me to join them for one last frolic of the season on the slopes, and we had happily driven up from Lucy's parents' home in Istres in Marcelle's old off-white Fiesta.

We had spent the last days of March with her parents and Lucy had been fretting. After all the exercise in the mountains, she found the lowlands of Provence just too enervating.

'I always feel so lacking in energy, Arnie. And the Mistral — I've hated it since I was a child.'

But I persuaded her to walk a daily lap around the fields near the Richaud family home, joining the brown sheep and white goats as they nibbled their breakfast. We held hands, strolling among the wild flowers and listened to the gentle tinkling of tiny bells as the flocks nosed among buttercups and dandelions. The restful scene was occasionally interrupted by the shrill squawk of a magpie or the laughing cackle of a green woodpecker.

The spring warmth, two days before we are to leave for Vaujany, is interrupted by high drama! On the sunlit patio, I spot a gargantuan battle going on between a pair of ants and an earwig. Two Davids versus Goliath. 'Lucy, just look at this!'

She hastened over. The earwig was being used as a rope in a tug-o'-war, with an ant on each end pulling in opposite directions. It was all huff and puff, without much movement. I detected a slight tremor from the unfortunate Goliath. 'I think it's still alive, Lucy.'

'God, how awful,' she said. And instantly set about a rescue mission, brushing off the ants.

We studied the earwig. 'No sign of life,' the coroner decided sadly.

Lucy, being Lucy, reacted immediately. 'Oh no! I've robbed the ants of their lunch.' And she started searching the stones for the insects to restore them to the lunch table.

So we went to Vaujany. The others in our jovial, carefree group that day were two more Peters, Cornell and Pleydell-Bouverie — and Richard Pettit, clients of Nigel's. In the group that left to ski the fearsome but awe-inspiringly beautiful ski area of La Grave that day, Lucy was the only woman. Felice, who was heavily pregnant, stayed behind. She was not keen on her husband skiing La Grave, either. She had skied there herself, with Peter and me, and knew its reputation.

Apart from Lucy, there were the three Peters, Richard, Nigel and myself. Our guide was Olivier Laborie. The same guide who had pushed me to the limits of my capabilities a year earlier in the very same resort where I was about to have the love of my life snatched away from me for ever.

We were all of us advanced skiers. We needed to be. La

Grave's ski area is in the shadow of the magnificent La Meije, one of the last peaks in the alps to surrender to Alpinists. Even Edward Whymper, the first man to climb the Matterhorn was unable to conquer it. Below the spectacular Meije glacier is an off-piste paradise. But also, a potential hell.

There is no need to look for excitement in La Grave. Just skiing the regular routes is exhilarating enough for most skiers. This is not a ski *resort*. There is no grooming. No ski school.

It is a wild place — a rocky, treacherous wasteland of glaciers, crevasses and potential avalanches. For the advanced skier, one of the most exciting areas in the world.

But you do not attempt to ski La Grave without a guide. We had one of the most adventurous and skilled — Olivier Laborie.

Up to now, we had all of us enjoyed the most blissful four days of sun, skiing and jollity. This looked like being another one.

'Come on, Arnie. It's glorious out there. Let's go skiing!' Lucy turned from the window, her face fresh and eager. She was in a good mood. Unlike yesterday.

Yes, Lucy and I had been arguing again. Only yesterday, when we battered each other with the last angry, hurtful words we would exchange in our lives.

This time, I had wanted to work to conjure up a few hundred words and get them down on paper in order to continue earning a modest crust. There were bills to be paid.

'Please, Lucy, just one day off — we've just skied for a whole bloody year! I *must* do some writing.'

Suddenly she was flaring at me again.

'How can you do that? The season's almost ended. We'll be home again in two days. And — ' she spread her arms for effect, embracing the slopes outside, the sun, the snow, the crisp clean air itself — 'Just look where we are! You can't stay inside!'

I gave up. Later, I made things worse.

As usual, Lucy wanted to buy everyone lunch, or at least leave an extra-generous tip.

'Lucy, you are far too generous? It's a wonderful quality, but we really can't afford it.'

'Stop it, Arnie. Just stop it! Life is for living, or perhaps you hadn't noticed. How can you be so mean?'

Now mean is not a word that comes easily into my vocabulary. Realistic, I would accept. Lucy is carrying on as if she were still General Manager of Touralp, but without a job, a title, or the expense account to go with it. She would have none of it.

So that day we skied, but not together. The others had gone their various ways. We climbed into the four-seat, goldfish-bowl gondola in ominous silence, Lucy sitting opposite — not side by side with me, for once — tight lipped and dangerously quiet.

At the halfway station, as the cage swung into the steel platform and clattered noisily to a halt, she suddenly got off her seat and jumped out. Through the open door, she turned to face me.

'Arnie, one of us has got to do something about this!'

'What — ?'

'One of us has to have the strength.'

For God's sake, was she trying to end our relationship? Here, now, halfway up a mountain? In that awful moment, I thought she was.

'Lucy, don't be ridiculous. I'm sorry. If you want to ski, of course we'll ski. Come back inside, please!'

Well, she did, but only just. Glowering, she stomped back and slumped down, avoiding my gaze. I tried to laugh her out of it, without success.

So okay, it was just a momentary fit of pique. But it wasn't. At the top — tighten boot clips, check pockets to ensure zips are closed. The familiar ritual before a run.

'Let's go!'

I dug my poles into fresh powder and went off first, down on to the glorious off-piste run called the Combe Charbonnier, one of the longest runs in the area. It takes a good hour to ski.

I looked back, expecting Lucy to be tucked in my slipstream

as usual. Instead, I glimpsed her darting figure with its vivid red hair streaming in the wind going the other way, before she was obscured by a clump of trees.

Without me! Instant thought. This is the first time in fifteen months, you wretched, adorable, maverick woman, that we have ever skied separately. But grimly I hold to my own course. Okay, Lucy, do your own thing. See if I care.

Of course I cared.

For the rest of that long afternoon I never saw her again. There were plenty of other trails, and she could have gone anywhere.

Then, when I returned in the late afternoon to the snow-banked car park, there was no sign of her mother's Fiesta which should have been parked there.

Had she really carried out her threat to leave me?

Inside the chalet there was laughter, warmth, steam from the showers, clinking glasses and sounds of frivolity.

And in our room, as I desperately plunged through the door — Lucy in a towel robe emerging from the bathroom with her hair freshly washed and her face child-like, devoid of make-up.

We clung to each other as if we would never let go.

'Lucy! I'm so glad you're here!' Trite, but they were the only words I could muster. Because I really did think that I'd lost her.

'So am I, monkey.'

That night we made love for the last time.

All is well. We are together again.

*   *   *

The name of La Grave is reflected in its ominous terrain. As I have intimated, this is the face of nature at her most menacing and uncompromising. Both for climbers and for those rash skiing souls who dare to face up to the ultimate challenge.

I am talking about seven thousand vertical feet of ungroomed slopes, steep and spectacular pillars of rock, glistening hostile ice, with no marked pistes, flanked by towering ice walls and crevasses that plunge hundreds of feet into chasms and oblivion.

'There are places where you must not fall.' The words of Olivier Laborie, months before, come back to me and a chill touches my spine.

We take the fateful decision. As happens so often in life before tragedy strikes, the hours leading up to it are filled with laughter and carefree enjoyment. Like dancing before a great liner hits an iceberg. Community singing in the coach before a multiple Motorway crash. Or ...

Sometimes it is called being in the wrong place at the wrong time. Lucy was in the wrong place at the wrong time.

*   *   *

It is turning into an idyllic day. The sun is shining. Summer is around the corner, waiting to flood the slopes. We have lunch, all nine of us, at the Choucas, a mountain refuge, laughing and joking over hot vegetable soup and crusty French bread with ripe Brie cheese. Time to ski again. We gulp down the last of our wine, and hasten out to our skis.

'Wait, Arnie!'

Lucy. What now?

'I must have a pee-pee!'

Now, of all times! I stand guard while Lucy scratches and scrambles behind a tree, and the others carry on to the lift. Their laughter fades into the afternoon, as the shadows start to lengthen. Finally, the two of us head for the last run of the day.

'*Choucas*. Do you know what that means, Arnie?'

'It's a bird.' I had seen the winged insignia on the door of the refuge.

'It is a jackdaw, Arnie.' The novice bird-watcher is triumphant after a year of education at the feet of the master.

'Actually,' I declare, rather smugly,'it's an Alpine Chough. And an Alpine Chough is most definitely not a jackdaw. It's just like people in England calling every big black bird a crow.'

We are arguing again, but lightly.

'You might find a jackdaw in the oast houses of Kent, Lucy. But never up here in the mountains.'

'It's a jackdaw, Arnie.'

End of debate. A jackdaw it was.

It is now late afternoon.

The others were waiting, seven of them standing patiently as the sun cooled and dark shadows crept out along the slopes. Jagged rocks cast uneven triangular shapes in the snow above us, and around us.

As the sun went down, it grew perceptively chillier. I glanced at my altimeter watch. Nine thousand feet, and 3.45pm. Time to go home.

Then Olivier said, 'Who would like to ski this *couloir*?' Seven deadly words.

I looked over the edge. Over the rim, the gulch dropped away like a falling curtain of rock and ice. I took in a deep breath of mountain air, and looked around for Lucy. She was comfortably close by, making her way gingerly towards me, one ski sliding six inches in front of the other, then the reverse, over the hard-packed snow that would soon be frozen. I reached out a gloved hand, taking her sleeve.

If you fall in a *couloir*, you may go on falling. Worse, you are liable to hit the exposed rocks on either side. It's as stark and simple as that. So, rule one. You don't fall in a *couloir*. But if you do, rule two: try to stop yourself in thick snow.

Olivier's voice was calm and confident: 'There is an easier way down. You can ski round it.'

Lucy, standing at my elbow, her chin tight with determination. I have to admit that she had been getting stronger by the day. After a year of solid skiing she had this great ambition to ski tougher and tougher runs. But she never did like *couloirs*.

I spoke quietly, so that no-one else could overhear: 'Lucy, it might be better if you went the easy way down.'

Extract from the Good Skiing Guide, 1996, Edited by Peter Hardy and Felice Eyston, two of my oldest skiing friends with whom I had shared many adventures in the Alps and the Rockies.

> *It should have been a relaxing day in the sunshine for a party of mixed-ability skiers. The accident happened at 4pm in the notorious Couloir des Trifides above La Grave. Peter Hardy was aware that two skiers had already been killed in previous days in that same* couloir.
>
> *He said afterwards: Hindsight is easy, but had I known the name of the* couloir *we were skiing, I most certainly would not have gone into it. The rescue helicopter guide later told me that he would have taken a single expert skier down it in the morning only. In the final analysis all of us who go into mountains must accept responsibility for our own safety. We didn't have to ski that* couloir, *the guide gave us a choice, but there is a natural tendency to stay with your friends and put your total trust in the judgement of the accompanying expert. It never occurs to most skiers that this judgement could be flawed.'*

'Well — ?' We were both looking at Lucy, waiting for her to make up her mind.

Rule two on the slopes: don't delay, or you freeze. That also means, freeze mentally.

'Lucy —' I began.

'I'm not sure Arnie. Maybe I'll take the easy way down.'

Her route to safety was only yards away.

'Come on Lucy,' said a voice near me. It was Peter Pleydell-Bouverie. 'If I can do it, you can.'

If I can do it, you can.

Seven more words that sealed Lucy's fate. I know that Peter, a delightful man, regrets bitterly that he said those seven casual words. He was only trying to give her confidence. It was fate, that's all.

*   *   *

Looking back, it is all too easy to see that she should never have attempted it. But as Peter Hardy said, with hindsight, so much always becomes blazingly obvious.

One problem Lucy and I never took into account was the snow itself. In effect, we had been skiing in early summer conditions all day. Fantastic powder. Soft, yielding. But this was different.

The *couloir* we are about to attempt had been sheltered from the sun. The cold is beginning to bite, gnawing at our exposed skin with tiny rapacious teeth, and it is also late afternoon with the temperature dropping by the minute. So how safe is it?

Traditionally, the lore of the slopes is simple. The guide looks after the weakest members of his group. Because I had confidence in Olivier, I abdicated from my usual role of keeping Lucy under my eagle eye.

In the meantime, I've got to get myself down. I stand off to one side, and take stock of what we're about to attempt. I suddenly feel as if I am perched on the rim of a gigantic ice-cream cone, the smooth rock sides below iced over in an ugly blue-grey sheen, the surface snow itself set as hard as concrete. The initial drop must be all of three hundred feet, and steep. Rock walls on either side of the funnel curve down inexorably to a spot where the deepest pocket of snow has gathered at the turn. Once in that funnel, there is only one place to go. Straight down.

Easy for Monsieur Laborie, our friend and mentor of the high peaks, a veteran of these dangerous, marvellous slopes since his schooldays. Easy for him. Less easy for the rest of us.

Near the top is a sharp dogleg, awaiting the unwary skier with a hostile gaze. Then follows a steep gully, almost a thousand feet long.

Where the dogleg snaps abruptly to the right, clumps of rock protrude out of the congealed snow. Jagged teeth, piercing upwards through pale white gums.

I stood quietly and watched the others, debating the best track in my mind.

One, two, three of the others go off into space and disappear out of sight round the dogleg.

Enough deliberating — I'm going in.

'Okay, Olivier?'

'Okay, Arnie. Off you go. Take it easy.'

I turn and give Lucy an encouraging smile. A smile that says: See you at the bottom, darling.

'Good luck, Lucy. Take care!'

Goodbye, Lucy.

I knew the slope was within my capability, we'd skied a few like this before.

Except it was much icier than I had expected. I surge down the slope with the sound of my skis scraping for control, thrown back from the unyielding frozen snow, and my body instinctively adjusting for balance as the walls hurtle past. The surface is rough and bumpy, like skiing over corrugated iron.

The first drop is around three hundred feet, rocks rushing up at me, then a frantic skitter round the bend to the right in the dogleg, with its sharp fangs showing. And suddenly I'm going just a little too fast, not really out of control but using all my strength to slither to an undignified stop to save me from the plunge. Skiing defensively. Not stylish, not pretty. But effective.

'Lucy is not going to like this at all,' I think to myself.

Time to check on her progress. But it's very difficult to stop.

I take a deep breath of mountain air and look around for Lucy.

Above, they look so small. I have descended a lot further than I realised in that helter-skelter run. But I can just make them out round the side of the funnel wall.

Far away, small figures.

My lover and my close friend.

But something's wrong.

They're falling.

Like waiting for Concorde's sonic boom to arrive in your ears, it takes my brain a few seconds to catch up with my eyes.

They're falling, tumbling, hopelessly, against the rock face at the bottom of the dogleg. They bounce off the rocks and the impact steers them down the long steep *couloir* above me.

Even now, I cannot comprehend.

Cannot comprehend that after Lucy's 180 falls during our round-the-world trip, this is the fall that will end it all.

It's all so silent. Surreal. Yet happening at frightening speed.

They are hurtling down towards me like two disjointed marionettes detached from their puppeteer and carelessly flung down the slope.

One moment — normality, laughter, light banter, an argument about a jackdaw, life going on its merry way. The next — chaos, despair, and a darkness over the land and over my soul that may never lift.

But, as every witness or victim of an accident can verify, disasters also happen in slow motion as awareness heightens and time stands still.

Time stopped.

Behind Lucy and Peter, all three of them scrabbling for purchase on the slope, Olivier had lost a ski. He had tried his best to grab at them, but one of his skis had been knocked off and the guide was helpless to stop the terrible sequence of events unfolding in front of us.

I didn't see it, but Olivier hopped on one foot to another ski lost in the initial impact, Peter's ski. He managed to clip it on, and hurled himself down the slope after them.

What I did see was Lucy tumbling towards me. In this nightmarish scenario, branded into my mind for ever, she and Peter slithered into the jagged fangs of rock, and unbelievably went on falling.

Towards me.

I dived to catch Lucy. It wasn't a courageous act, simply instinct born of desperation. I took off in something close to a rugger tackle, skis and all, grabbed Lucy round the waist — and hung on.

Together we fell down that white corridor like two dancers entwined in a grotesque ballet scene.

We kept bouncing. First, two feet into the air. Hit the hard snow, bounced again, higher. I hung on desperately to Lucy.

I felt the smooth fabric of her ski suit clutched in my hands, and the whiplash of her hair against my face as my cheek was pressed tightly against hers. I had Lucy in an iron grip, and I was never going to let her go.

Two rag dolls. Juddering and thudding. Two clowns at a circus. Tumbling for the crowds. Sometimes I was above her, sometimes beneath her. The giddy images flashed through my mind as we fell hundreds of feet, locked in our last embrace.

At that speed and on that incline, there is nothing we can do as we bound ever higher and I try to cushion her against the hard-packed snow.

How long does it take to fall almost a thousand feet? A lifetime?

Finally, as the giant slope flattens out, there is one last huge bounce too many and we are flung apart.

I lie on my face in the snow, unable to move, looking at her. My skis have been torn off, and hers too. A dreadful, lingering stillness descends on the mountain that is more terrifying than any sound.

Lucy lies on her side, staring back at me. Fifteen feet and three years of love, passion, tenderness and a wondrous adventure separate us.

I don't think she can see me. The obscene trickle of blood bubbles from her left ear, staining the snow crimson.

'Lucy — ?' My voice sounds strangled in that cauldron of silence.

Surely she will say something?

'Lucy ... ?' More urgent now.

In the after-shock, waves of nausea. Head clearing. I see something else. A trail of blood in the snow, leading to her.

'Lucy ...'

Frenetic activity on the mountain. Paramedics, with stretchers and blankets. From two helicopters, that had come clattering over the jagged peaks. Now they squat yards away, rotors swinging.

Olivier had summoned them on his mobile radio.

In a daze, one thought fills my head.

Lucy, please don't die.

Blotting out the pain.

Olivier had been there in seconds, kneeling beside Lucy. Then the paramedics brutally pounding on her chest with gloved fists to restart her heart. I can hardly bear to watch.

I'll marry you like a shot, Lucy.

I glimpse her dear, beautiful face, and flinch. It is beginning to puff up, the wonderful healthy tanned skin bruised and swollen.

My God, Lucy — oh my God.

'She is going to live?' I ask the paramedic who is bending over me.

I am bleeding, too. But it's only a scratch compared with Lucy. The friction of our fall together has removed most of the skin from the back of my right arm. The burn has come right through my ski suit and T-shirt.

Peter is further up the hill, huddled in the deep snow. His thigh is shattered, and one knee, too, and his face is badly cut. A year later, he would still be on crutches.

They take him away first, under a grey blanket, to the hospital in Briançon. The second helicopter takes Lucy in the opposite direction, down towards Grenoble. I would have gone with her, but with the stretcher and the paramedics there is no room.

So I kneel in the snow, watching them go. Watching my Lucy disappear into the late afternoon, where the sun's crimson rays are streaking across the sky, racing into infinity.

I never saw her again.

People around me. Voices low, in mutual shock. A hand on my shoulder.

I was taken off the mountain by another helicopter. As we took off and I looked back at the Couloir of Death and Lucy's blood staining the snow. It was the cruellest sight I had ever seen.

*　　　　*　　　　*

The long drive to the hospital in Grenoble. Pale stone walls, impersonal, efficient. In the lobby, Nigel and I hasten through the doors — and there is a figure on a trolley being rushed towards the operating theatre. I run, catch up, and peer down to look at her face, expecting Lucy. It looks like her from behind.

But another face stares up at me. And over by the desk Nigel is asking someone in French (because he speaks it better than I do), and people are shaking their heads, and I know it is the end.

She had probably been in a coma on the slope, and died in the air ambulance.

Back in the chalet, Nigel's wife Annika, the sweetest of women, makes me endless cups of tea as I pace up and down, not knowing what to do with myself. Twenty cups, probably, if I'd counted. Felice returns in tears from visiting her husband Peter in hospital. His injuries are severe. She is beside herself. Then she turns to me and says, between sobs: 'How's Lucy?'

'She's dead.'

Felice, heavily pregnant, finds the news unbearable. Her husband's body shattered. Her dear friend Lucy dead. Me, inconsolable.

That night I climb into the bed which Lucy and I had shared only 24 hours earlier. It smells of her.

Her clothes are everywhere. In neat piles. Or hanging up. Her toilet things are in the bathroom. Mostly Clarins things: toning lotion, gentle foaming cleanser, night cream, and two almost empty bottles of double serum. That triangular silver bottle of Liz Claiborne Eau de Parfum spray.

She'd put the top back on the toothpaste. Everything is just as we had left it that morning. Our love nest, with a view across the valley to the mountains. Lucy will never share this bed with me again. Or any other. But her spirit is there. I can feel, her, all around me, as I snuggle up in the sheets the two of us had snuggled into the previous night.

In my mind, I'm snuggling up to her.

Mercifully I fall into a deep sleep.

In the morning, Lucy is still dead.

*   *   *

Next day, Nigel drove me the two hours from the chalet to Grenoble again to collect her belongings. Her gold chain. Two rings, neither of which fitted me. But what had happened to her watch?

The watch which we had used for three hundred and sixty-five days to help us correlate our statistics. Where was it?

Back on the Couloir des Trifides, for sure.

As far as I know, it is still there, probably buried in the thick snow by those lethal rocks, a tiny yet poignantly significant symbol of her death.

One question troubles me.

Why aren't I crying?

Chapter 18

Now

If I could bring Lucy back for one hour,
and it meant my dying at the end of that hour,
I would do it without another thought.
All I want to do is tell her I love her. And say goodbye.
Two things I couldn't do when she died so suddenly.

Arnie Wilson June 1995

The tears came later. Inconsolable, uncontrollable, surging in hot waves. Every day, for a hundred days.

The awful thing about grief is that you don't get a single day off from it.

She didn't leave a will. Technically everything belonged to her family, which is the way it should be. Including the flat at Sinclair Road, London W14.

The funeral. At the family mausoleum in her home town of Istres.

Nigel Purkhardt had travelled all the way down from Vaujany. To have something in French thrust in his hand to read at the ceremony. Lucy's parents are not religious, and I couldn't bear the thought of total silence while Lucy's coffin was laid to rest.

Lucy's coffin. What a ghastly thought. Lucy, my beautiful Lucy, with her golden curls, inside that box. Lifeless. It was such a shock when it appeared. I'd forgotten they had coffins at funerals. Samantha, my daughter had picked some wild flowers from the fields where Lucy and I had walked each morning, and placed them tenderly on the coffin before it was slid into the family vault.

Lucy's grave is in the town's lakeside cemetery, where she once gave me a guided tour, 'introducing' me to departed members of her family, pictured on their tombstones as is the custom in France. The picture on Lucy's grave is one I took by the shores of another lake. A much bigger one, near Osorno in Chile. I had caught her unawares, smiling a huge, unrehearsed smile, just after we had stopped our truck to pick some mimosa.

Nigel, hardly knowing what he was reading, launched himself into Lucy's party piece. *La Cigalle et La Fourmi*. Scores of family friends and acquaintances stood round the grave, wondering, no doubt, why an Englishman was reading a La Fontaine fable at the Richauds' daughter's grave. The Grasshopper and the Ant. I hugged Nigel round the waist while he read it. I think he needed my support as much as I needed his.

Afterwards, mourners gathered for tea in the garden at the Richaud family home. The garden where I had led Lucy by the hand for our early morning walks before settling down to work. The patio where, only days ago, we had watched the battle with the ants and the earwig.

There was so much of our luggage to haul home to England that even leaving half of it behind with Lulu and Marcelle meant there wasn't enough room in Samantha's orange Volkswagen golf for me. I decide to travel back separately by train.

But first I had to say goodbye — or at least *au revoir* — to Lucy. What a terrible thought. After spending almost every second of 1994 with her, the idea of finally being separated, in such tragic circumstances, seemed appalling.

Lucy's sturdy and cheerful aunt, Josette had let me climb onto a chair with some secateurs to reach a red rose above the patio of the simple farmhouse she shared with her husband André just a five minute walk from Lucy's parents' home. With enormous sadness, Lulu and Marcelle accompanied me to

Lucy's grave, where I left my rose and unselfconsciously kissed the cold marble stone. On it was the picture I had taken of Lucy in Chile. My favourite. Next to the picture were the engraved the words: *A notre fille, Lucette Madeleine Richaud 1953 –1995*.

Leaving Lucy there seemed to create more despair than I had felt at her funeral. Somehow knowing she was lying here, less than a mile from the bedroom where I was staying at her parents' home — *our bedroom* — had been slightly comforting. Now I was going to have to travel almost a thousand miles from her side. This was the real, cruel parting.

Lulu and Marcelle drove me to Miramas for the 11.35 train. We chatted, sadly, for a while, on the platform. I didn't want to leave them. They were, after all, about as close to Lucy as I could get. *If only they could make me another one like her!* Then I drifted backwards out of their lives: my train seat faced the 'wrong' way.

Suddenly I felt very much alone — and, for the first time for well over a year — responsible for my own actions. Lucy, my beautiful 'control freak' had been pulling my strings since the trip started. Like the Prince of Wales, I had not carried money in my pocket for more than fifteen months. I had hardly glimpsed my own passport, and had certainly never had to worry about such things as rail or air tickets. At least I only had one bag to look after for now. How terribly strange it felt after lugging thirteen around the world. Or was it fourteen. I never could remember.

A huge wave of sadness engulfed me. This was so cruelly different from how we had planned it. It was almost 500 days since Lucy and I had left England with such excitement and high hopes. And now I was coming home without her. I felt I had abandoned her in the graveyard in Istres. I had this strangely compelling feeling that somehow I should have brought her home with me, her lifeless form cradled gently in my arms.

It was a profound shock to be back in England on a wet and almost dark Kentish evening.

Later, when I settled into an armchair in Samantha's flat in North London, her sister Melissa's six-year-old son Bevan (my grandson) said he had a spell to bring Lucy back to life. And Samantha said a 'peace lily' that she had given up for dead during the time she had come to France to rescue me had recovered after she watered it.

'If only I could bring Lucy back to life by watering *her*,' I said.

The Memorial Service, on a beautiful summer's day in June, was held in an enchanting country church at Barham, not far from Canterbury in Kent. I'd spent many of my schooldays in this cathedral city, and one of my close friends, Alan Duke — my daughter Samantha's godfather — was the village rector. I asked him if he would conduct the service.

Another dear friend, Chris Tizzard, who had often skied with Lucy and me, had helped me plan the whole day when I had stayed with him and his delightful wife Liz during the agonising few days before the service. Until then I had spent three months with my daughter Samantha and her fiancé Mark at their flat in North London, where she helped me cope with the anguish and the grief.

The church was packed. Lucy and I were lucky enough to share many friends. Among them Peter Hardy, a poignant sight, holding on to his crutches at the end of a pew just in front of me, with his wife Felice. Their baby would be born a fortnight later. They would call her Isabella Lucy. Now I am one of her god-parents.

I asked Chris Tizzard to include our favourite extract from Enigma II, the organist Trevor Webb played Pachelbel's famous *Canon and Fugue* (which I was rather hoping to save for my own funeral!) and many of Lucy's and my friends, including Beth and Kent Sharp, who had flown from Colorado, gave readings.

I sat in a pew near the back, gripping the hands of my eldest daughters, Samantha and Melissa, watching this spectacular tribute to Lucy unfolding. My other daughters, Amber and Lara, sat nearby. Fortunately, all four of my daughters, who were extremely fond of Lucy, had joined us for a re-union two months earlier — at Amiens, in northern France where we spent a very happy and very wet weekend together. Otherwise they would never have seen her again.

The service I had been dreading began. I tried not to cry, but I was not entirely successful.

I didn't particularly want any hymns, but I thought one Christmas Carol would be rather appropriate, even though it was early June. I chose *In The Bleak Mid Winter*.

Nigel Purkhardt gave a repeat performance of Lucy's party piece, *La Cigalle et La Fourmi*, this time helped along by an explanation in English!

Lucy's best friend Sandra Dunne had flown all the way from Australia to deliver the main eulogy.

> '*Lucy was so beautiful and special. Her tragic death ripped at the heart of those close to her. For Arnie, the pain was intensified by the cruelty of the mountains they both loved so much. But the mountains are ever-powerful, and even the most accomplished skier knows the risks.*
>
> *She was madly in love with Arnie — the love of her life.*
>
> *Lucy shared with me her plans to ski around the world with him. Knowing Lucy's determination I didn't doubt that it would happen. Lucy was radiant with happiness. Arnie had a passion for skiing, Lucy had a passion for Arnie and the combination was exciting and challenging.*

And then, this telling and surprisingly honest thought. '*Lucy also had a hot temper, reserved, in the main for those she loved most.*'

That moving statement explained a good deal.

I wore the slim gold chain that Lucy herself had worn throughout our year together, and had been round her throat when she died. And I managed to slip on one of her rings, from her middle finger to my little one, where it fitted after a brief struggle. A cluster of deep, dark rubies held by two tiny hands in the centre. In my pocket, although no one knew it, was a lock of Lucy's hair. A single golden auburn curl from her treasury of curls. After she died, I had asked a nurse in the hospital to cut it off for me, and waited in the lobby while she kindly obliged.

Chris Tizzard and Alan Duke had suggested there should be a book available at the back of the church for people to write any thoughts about Lucy.

My thoughts, written in a large red and gold volume with a stunning painting of an Indian squaw on the front were these:

> *'Au revoir, Lucy my sweetheart. You were a compassionate and charismatic woman who loved life to the full. You looked after me with such devotion. Losing you is like losing a lover, mother, sister and daughter in one tragic moment. You will never know how much I love you until, God willing, we'll meet again. From your Arnie, who cherishes your memory. June 6, 1995.*

It was such a moving service, conducted so dynamically by Alan Duke (though he'd never met Lucy) that his wife Mary told me later that the poor man had taken to his bed afterwards, utterly drained both physically and emotionally. Alan knew how much I'd dreaded this day. Knew how desperately important it was to me that it went well for Lucy's sake. He did not let me down. If Lucy were there, in some shape or form — and I honestly believe she was — she must have been very much moved by her own memorial service. And in spite of all her insecurity, perhaps believed at long last that she was much loved by many.

I had received three hundred letters from across the world, from virtually every ski resort we had visited.

Every one of them mourning her loss.

Peter Pleydell-Bouverie, the man who unwittingly encouraged Lucy to ski the Couloir des Trifides, and who had been standing next to me when Lucy and Peter fell, wrote:

> *'I still find it difficult to fathom how such a beautiful and joyous day could end up so irredeemably marred by such a brutal and tragic event I am sure that you, like myself find it hard to shut out the awful stark images of that afternoon. Much of my spirit remains in La Grave.'*

Max Wilkinson, the avuncular but inspirational editor of the *Weekend FT*, who had become a good friend to us both,wrote:

> *'We all know and accept the risks of the mountains. The risks are part of their beauty and grandeur. And the sport is at least in part a sense of overcoming fear by skill and judgement. Lucy shared that courageous spirit. Nothing can really be a consolation for her loss, except perhaps that there is a kind of nobility in death from a freely accepted task, doing what she loved best. I thought Lucy was a remarkable woman, with such an individual blend of qualities: charm, generosity and wit. These do not often go with the courage and clarity of vision which led her to give up her job and follow you round the world. I know that she was tremendously important to the success of your expedition Your time with her was all too short, but at least you made the very best of it in a special and unusual way.'*

Even my daughter Lara wrote a moving tribute called 'Now There Is Lucy'. It begins:

> *Now there is Lucy*
> *The sky has no need of diamonds*
> *For the world is lit up*

By her alone
Her beauty is sewn
Like rare and precious jewels
Refreshing the dusty Universe

One way or another, Lucy is not going to be forgotten in a hurry.

There is a silver trophy in her memory now — the Lucy Dicker Cup, to be raced for each year by the Down Hill Only club. And a brand new ski bob bought with the help of Mike Browne, our equipment sponsor, for use by members of Backup, the charity for paraplegic and quadraplegic skiers. Richard Branson presented a special award in Lucy's memory too. Thanks to Chris Tizzard and Joanna Yellowlees-Bound, Les Arcs, the French ski resort so close to Lucy's heart, now has an annual Lucy Dicker award for Britain's most innovative ski tour operator. And of course there's the Chalet Lucette, high in the Dauphiné mountains at Vaujany ... with Lucy's picture on the wall, gazing out of the window across the mountains she loved so much.

There is even a heli-skiing run named after her high in the Himalayas, in Himachal Pradesh where we had skied in May during our record-breaking year.

*　　　*　　　*

Now I am the guardian of all the things that are going to hurt me. Photographs — literally hundreds of them. Jewellery. Twelve hour-long videos of our odyssey across the mountains of the globe. I couldn't face keeping the ski suit she died in, but I couldn't bear to throw her underwear away — I sewed it up in a cushion and gave it to one of my daughters. Sometimes I think to myself: if it is possible to die of a broken heart, why aren't I dead? My heart couldn't have been any more broken than it was.

In the early months I sometimes did think of ending it all — not because of the despair, although that was plentiful, but with the frantic notion that if Lucy was out there somewhere, I must find her. It would surely be a far more exciting journey than even my train ride through the night in the depths of an Italian winter to hold her in my arms for the first time three years earlier.

It's part of my make-up that I can almost believe the impossible can be possible. But I couldn't inflict all that grief on my four wonderful daughters. Besides, what would Lucy think of me? I even went to a medium. You are twin souls, she said. Linked by love. There is no question that you will see her again.

Needless to say, wherever this 'message' was coming from, I found it very emotional. Life after death? Who knows. I always believed in it, and I do now, more strongly than ever before.

When you arrive in the next world, wherever that is, they say you enter a region of darkness, gloom and great uncertainty. But each person who reaches that strange world, that other arena of consciousness, pulls themselves further along the road away from the confusing smog of the lower order, into sunlight. And they find this other world where life exists very much as it did on earth, complete with universities, places where they have books, put on plays, where their bodies are very light, electrical rather than physical. Where they can move at will anywhere they want just by wanting to. Where time has no meaning.

Well, as I said, who knows?

My great comfort is that when anguish sometimes starts to get the upper hand, I can comfort myself that one day — perhaps not too far ahead — I might be able to follow you, Lucy, however much agony I have to endure until I find you again. *But if you're not out there, I'll never know.*

Sometimes the only comfort I have is that in a sea of negatives, the clock is ticking... I can never accept that I will never find Lucy again, however long it takes.

Final thought, and dare I say it? I'm not sure which of us has suffered most. Lucy, whose life was cut off at forty-one? Or me, doomed to carry on without her? Is that unbelievably selfish — or just honest?

Now I don't dread the nights so much. Rooms change. Ceilings and walls vary. A room, after all, is just a space waiting to be filled. I am aware that wherever I go in the world, there is scarcely a single place that I have not been to with Lucy. Her spirit will be there to haunt me in every hotel, every resort, every ski trail. We have done it all together, and there is no escape even if I wanted it.

I never could bring myself to move back into No 82. Someone else lives there now.

Now I flit like a gypsy from one part of London to another: my bed-sitter in Highgate; my daughter Sam's flat in Parliament Hill Fields. I even stay with Nigel Lloyd and his wife Janice sometimes — the man, if you remember, who first brought Lucy and me together. A bed here or a sofa there, is all I need.

Tonight it is the ground floor flat, with the clean fresh air of Hampstead Heath filtering through the half-open French window. I lie on my back on the small bed, staring up at the ceiling. Light from the street lamp outside seeps through a gap in the curtains, bathing the room blood orange, patterned with shadows dancing attendance from the trees outside.

I push the bad thoughts away. I'm quite expert at it now. Let them lurk there, unwanted visitors waiting for the door to my mind to open for them.

Instead I focus on Lucy as I want to remember her. In a deliberate, conscious act of remembrance. The face I loved and will always love is smiling, auburn hair poking like soft golden straw from under the bright pink ski hat. Her sea-green eyes fill my universe, and I float towards them like a castaway drifting towards a far horizon, searching for her soul, as her irises become moist pools growing ever larger, engulfing me... Until, gently and drowsily, I am immersed in their green depths and finally surrender as I find at last the abyss of blessed, guilt-free sleep.

Then, out of the darkness and the fading orange glow, a whisper like gossamer silk.

Soft.

Loving.

'Silly monkey!'

Oh Lucy, *where are you*?

Chapter 19

Tomorrow

A few weeks after Lucy's accident — when I was still overwhelmed with a profound despair that would last a year or more — my daughter Lara sent me a card which optimistically forecast that one day I would be happy again. Needless to say, at the time, I felt this was impossible. Three years later — thanks largely to Vivianne, a delightful and very loving Swedish girl who has had the daunting and sometimes painful task of 'inheriting' me and my demons ('replacing' Lucy is not really the appropriate sentiment) and of course my beloved daughters — I am almost my old cheerful self. I am in good and loving hands. And now, like many people who have lost loved ones, I have, finally, started to be able to enjoy remembering the good times with Lucy while managing, most of the time, to shut out the horrors of the day she died. My many close friends, including Nigel Lloyd and his wife Janice – who themselves suffered the agonising loss of their only son a few years ago — have been incredibly supportive. Peter Hardy and I, who shared the awful trauma of that April day in 1995 – have become, if anything, closer than ever. Life is good again, although it will never be the same.

Arnie Wilson,
Haywards Heath, West Sussex,
December 1998.

Acknowledgements

During the very difficult months which followed Lucy's accident — when I found it too painful to move back into the flat which I shared so happily with her before our adventure — I was very fortunate to have the love and support of my daughters, Samantha, Melissa, Lara and Amber. I would like to thank Samantha and her husband Mark for allowing me to share their home for almost three months following my return to England. I also owe a huge debt of gratitude to Jeffrey and Suzanne Rayner who invited me down to their beautiful home in the Surrey countryside for a weekend which turned into a four-month stay. I would also like to thank Sue Ockwell, Nigel and Janice Lloyd and Chris and Liz Tizzard for all their kindness and hospitality, Fran Newitt for keeping the show on the road so brilliantly in 1994, to Anne York-Lay for transcribing many hours of tape, and the Richaud family — Lucy's parents, Marcelle and Lucien, and her brother Maurice and his wife Pascale — for their great kindness since the tragic events of April 6, 1995. My sincere thanks too to Alan Duke, Rector of Barham, Kent for conducting such a moving memorial service for Lucy.

During our round the world odyssey, we were helped by a thousand people or more. The people listed overleaf are just 365 of them — one for each day of 1994. I would especially like to thank the following 52 people — one for each week of 1994: Beth and Kent Sharp, Kari Gemmel, Brian Smith, Lucy

Kay, Kelley Davidson, Max Wilkinson, Peter Whitehead, Bernie Weichsel, Jim Felton, Kristen Kopplin, Gina Kroft, John and Robin Norton, John Resor, Ali Gayward, Claire McKay, Nick Earle, John and Jenny Fairbrass, Robert and Killy Stanton, Patricia Morse, Mike Browne, Martine Radville, Colleen and Jean-Marie Olianti, Nigel and Annika Purkhardt, Heine Kempel, Jesse and Polly Rothstein, Evan Russell, Renée Clover, Pat Peeples, Chris Stagg, Georges Sampeur, John Shea, Mike and Jennifer Shimkonis, Skat Petersen, Sandie Barker, Scott Lee, Andy Chapman, Duncan Smith, Johnny and Dorothy Stevens, Victor Raymond, Dr Greg Walker, Mark Weakland, and Patrick and Jean Zimmer.

I also want to thank Dr Elizabeth Selles, my local GP following my return from France, for her patience, compassion and professionalism: her contribution towards my recovery when I was at my lowest ebb was deeply comforting and cannot be overstated.

Terry Abeen
Paul Abrahams
Jimmy Ackerson
Bill Adams
David Adamson
Max Aitken
Rosemary Aitken
Chris Allaire
Mike Allen
Colin Allum
Zenon Alvarez
Jody Anderson
Christiane
  Antony
Francisco Arias
Garry Askew
Penny Askew
Annette Baker
Blair Baldwin
Jean Paul Balmut
Monica Bandows
Marianne Baring
Sandie Barker
Dick Bass
Harry Baxter
Mike Beckley
Dean Bell
Gilly Bell
Christian Berger
Sandie Berry
Yuan Bertocchi
Bushan Lal Bhat
Don Bilodeau
Peter Boerholt
Olwyn Black
Walter
  Blackerstaffe
Kitty Boone
Gilbert Bremmi
June Brinkman
Steve Brown
Tammy Brown
Brian Buchholz

Anne Burri
Bobbie Burkley
Iain Burns
Kari Buterbauda
Rory Byrne
Dave Carlson
Jono Carmichael
Bryan Carter
Andy Chapman
Paul Chase-
  Gardener
Janet Chisholm
Joan Christensen
George
  Chumbley
Kate Clarke
Minty Clinch
Andrew
  Corpening
Loni Costello
Richard Cootes
Wayne Curness
Kiki Cutter
Will Dawkins
Ali de Lisle
John Denham
Jim de
  Graffenreid
Claudio Diaz
Orlando Diaz
Uell
  Dinginbacher
Tom Dinicola
Sara Donahue
Dick Dorworth
Randy Doyle
Andrew Dunn
Sandra Dunne
Mike Duggan
Gary Dutmers
Manfred Ebner
Richard Edwards
Frances Elder

Carl Emberson
Ingrid Emerton
Charly Enzinger
Bruce Erdmann
Scottie Ewing
Rainer Falbesoner
Betsy Farney
Carmen Fender
Steve Fielding
Juan Jose
  Floranelli
Peter Foote
Shirley Foote
Scott Fortner
Ueli Frel
Riccarda Frey
Arno Fricke
Karin Fröhlich
Victor Frölich
Hans Fuchs
Marco Grass
Edwin Ganahl
Werner Ganahl
Andres Garcia
Brent Gardner-
  Smith
Hector Garrido
Dan Garves
Debbie Gaynor
Ali Gayward
Gerry Geisler
Carol Gibb
Robin Gibb
Claude Giguon
Giles Gittings
Stan Goodell
Hugo Gotsch
John Gourley
John Gow
Jim Green
Kenny Griswold
François Gros
Nick Gunter

Curt Hanlen
Rod Hanna
Alex Healy
Marina Healy
Wendy Helsgrud
Dennis Herbel
Mike Hess
Leo Hodan
Hans Hofer
Patti Hofer
Michael Hoy
Bill Hungate
Joe Inovskis
Dave Irwin
Emil Isele
Jane Jacquemod
Regine Jay-Grillot
Wendy Jacquet
Sandie Jeffcoat
Philip Jenkins
Barbara Jennings
Jane Johnson
Gary Jones
Jack Jones
Lisa Jones
Holly Junak
Mark Junak
Heinrich
  Kalbelmatten
John Kapusty
Khris Keesling
Geoff Kelly
Tom Kelly
Connie Kemmerer
Jay Kemmerer
Leigh Kennedy
Peter Kenworthy
Shige Kitahara
Ken Klecker
Matt Kleppe
Kevin Koon
Franz Krickl
Hans Kroll

ADDITIONAL ACKNOWLEDGEMENTS

Bob Kunkel	Megan Merker	Jean-Pierre	Tolly Tolhurst
Eduardo Kuhn	Patrick Messeiller	Raemdonck	Ronald Turner
Shelly Kuratli	Boyd Mitchell	Alan Reed	Dan Underwood
Leo Lacroix	Taylor Middleton	Gordon Reeves	Eric Vanderkruk
Charlie Lanche	John Millington	Heidi Reisz	Nigel Venning
Hubert Larcher	Amin Momen	Doug Renalds	Mia Viaar
Tim Larive	Jason Monteleone	Klaus Rexer	Doug Wales
Anita Larsen	John Mooney	Suzanne	Tony Waddell
Giorgio Latty	Ted Motschman	Robinson	Heinrich Wagner
Mona Le Duc	Susan Motschman	Elisa Ross	Gary Wardrope
Sandi Lee	Bob Munro	Mark Rowe	Klaus Wartner
Scott Lee	Mark Nakada	Phyllis Riskey	Anita Webber
Marie-Françoise	Louise Neilson	David Roberts	Karry Weissman
Lenon	Mike Neilson	Peter Roden	John Wells
Hernan Lewin	Urs Niederer	Paul Romagna	Pam Wells
Bill Lewkowitz	Graeme Nimmo	Dennis Rose	Mike Woods
Willy Lingg	Kanichi Noguchi	Luis Rubio	Julia Woolley
Charlie Locke	Kyoko Noguchi	Killeen Russell	Ruth Woolley
'Cricket' Rogg	Hector Novoa	Guru Sachder	Felix Wurmli-
Lodmell	Jim O'Doir	Ponteir Sackrey	Kagi
Jim Loyd	Maureen O'Dowd	Heinrich Sandrell	Margrit Wurmli-
Ginna Lynch	Gemma Ohlson	Olivier Sante	Kagi
Nicky Lyon-Maris	Eigo Onuma	Joanna Savage	Doug Yeager
Dave Maizey	Craig Ovenden	Carol Schmidt	Anne York-Lay
Peter Malkin	Jane Ovenden	Will Seccombe	Tim Young
Margaret Malkin	Jim Padgett	Sheru	
Marcella Manuel	Sandy Padgett	Yasuhiko Shida	
Neil Manuel	Siegfried	Peter Shroll	
Gerry Manser	Patscheider	Alex Sinclair	
Christian Marie	Dennis Penney	Ken Sinclair	
Fernand Masino	Robert Perriam	Izzy Slutzky	
Daniel Max	Amade Perrig	Orville Slutzky	
Herbert Mayer	Santiago Perrotta	Ladd Snowsell	
Ira MacAuley	Margit Pfund	Dennis Smith	
Marcelo Macaya	Karl Plattner	Louise Stieger	
Paul McCollister	Geoff Portman	Roland Stieger	
Hamish	Christine Preble	Shawn Stinson	
McCombie	Arden Prehn	Chance Sullivan	
Gary McCoy	Eric Proudy	Tom Stillo	
Randy McCoy	John Puppolo	Dion Taylor	
Robert McEleney	David Purcell	Arthur Tschepp	
Carl McKew	Martine Radville	Cesar Tereocan	
Gilly Mackwood	Gusti Raich	Roberto Thostrup	

RESORTS SKIED BY ARNIE WILSON AND LUCY DICKER IN 1994

JANUARY
Jackson Hole, Wyoming
Pebble Creek, Idaho
Pomerelle
Sun Valley
Soldier Mountain
Bogus Basin
Brundage
Mount Bachelor, Oregon
Mount Ashland
Heavenly,California/Nevada
Squaw Valley
Mount Shasta
Mount Hood Meadows,
  Oregon
Timberline
Bluewood,Washington
Stevens Pass
Cyprus Bowl, British
  Columbia
Blackcomb
Whistler
Silver Star
Big White
Apex Resort
Red Mountain
Kimberley
Panorama
Lake Louise, Alberta
TOTAL FOR JANUARY: 26

FEBRUARY
Nakiska
Fortress Mountain
Fairmont Hot Springs
The Big Mountain, Montana
Big Sky
Bridger Bowl
Red Lodge Mountain
Keystone , Colorado
Copper Mountain
Breckenridge
Arapahoe Basin
Ski Cooper
Mount Lacrosse,Wisconsin
Devil's Head
Cascade Mountain
Villa Olivia, Illinois
Four Lakes Village
Alpine Valley
Paoli Peaks, Indiana
Ski World
Ski Butler, Kentucky
Ober Gatlinburg, Tennessee
Cloudmont, Alabama
TOTAL FOR FEBRUARY: 23

MARCH
(Cloudmont)
Cataloochee, North Carolina
Ski Beech
Sugar Mountain
New Winterplace,West
  Virginia
Snowshoe
Massanutten, Virginia
Wisp, Maryland
Ski Liberty, Pennsylvania
Belleayre, New York
Ski Windham
Hunter Mountain
Cortina Valley
Kitzbuhel, Austria
Pass Thurn
Jochberg
Soll
Brixen
Sheffau

Westendorf
Mayrhofen
Finkenberg
Alpbach
Axamer Lizum
Obergurgl
Hochgurgl
Selva, Italy
Marmolada
Canazei
Corvara
Plan De Gralba
Arabba
Colfosco
San Cassiano
Lavilla
Cortina
Garmisch-Partenkirchen,
  Germany
St Anton, Austria
Stuben
St Christoph
Lech
Zurs
Brand
Gaschurn
Gallenkirch
Gortipohl
Partenen
Schruns
Gargellen
TOTAL FOR MARCH: 48

APRIL
Ischgl, Austria
Samnaun, Switzerland
Nauders, Austria
Pontresina, Switzerland
Davos
Klosters
Flims
Laax
Andermatt
Grindelwald
Wengen
Sannenmoser
St Stephan
Villars
Rochers De Naye
Jaman
Leysin
Verbier
La Tzoumaz
Sivier
Veysonnaz
Thion
Zermatt
Champery
Les Crozets
Avoriaz, France
Montriond
Morzine
Chatel
Courchevel
Meribel
La Tania
Les Menuires
St Martin-De-Belleville
Val Thorens
La Plagne
Champagny
Les Coches
Alpe d'Huez
Vaujany
La Grave
Oz
Villard-Reculas
Les 2 Alpes

La Rosiere
Val d'Isère
Tignes
TOTAL FOR APRIL: 47

MAY
Val d'Isère, France
Tignes
Argentiere
Rohtang Pass, Manali, India
Tokyo Ski Dome, Japan
Tsudanuma
Goryu Toomi
Gassan
Mammoth
  Mountain,California
Stubai Glacier, Austria
Solden
TOTAL FOR MAY: 10

JUNE
Pitztal Glacier, Austria
Kaunertal Glacier
Courmayeur, Italy
(Chamonix, France)
Les Diablerets, Switzerland
  (Verbier)
Saas Fee
Hintertux, Austria
(Mammoth Mountain,
  California)
Portillo, Chile
Termas De Chillan
Las Araucarias (Volcan
  Llaima)
Volcan Lonquimay
TOTAL FOR JUNE: 10

JULY
(Las Araucarias, Chile)
Villarrica-Pucon
Antillanca
Cerro Bayo, Argentina
Gran Catedral (San Carlos
  De Bariloche)
(Las Araucarias, Chile)
La Parva
El Colorado
TOTAL FOR JULY: 6

AUGUST
Valle Nevado, Chile
(El Colorado)
(La Parva)
(Portillo)
Penitentes, Argentina
Vallecitos
Las Lenas
Chapelco
(Las Araucarias, Chile)
Chapa Verde
Whakapapa, New Zealand
Turoa
Mount Baw Baw, Australia
Lake Mountain
Mount Buller
Mount Buffalo
TOTAL FOR AUGUST: 12

SEPTEMBER
Mount Hotham, Australia
Falls Creek
Thredbo
Perisher
Smiggin Holes
Mount Blue Cow
Guthega
Charlotte Pass

Mount Hutt, New Zealand
Treble Cone
Cardrona
Coronet Peak
Awakino
Wanaka (Harris Mountains
  Heliskiing)
The Remarkables
Ohau
Mount Cook (Tasman
  Glacier)
TOTAL FOR SEPTEMBER: 17

OCTOBER
Fox Peak, New Zealand
Mount Dobson
Mount Cheeseman
Porter Heights
Craigieburn Valley
Broken River
Rainbow Valley
Mount Lyford
Temple Basin
Mount Hutt
(Whakapapa)
(Mammoth Mountain,
  California)
June Mountain
TOTAL FOR OCTOBER: 10

NOVEMBER
(Mammoth Mountain,
  California)
(Copper Mountain,
  Colorado)
(Keystone)
(Breckenridge)
Arapahoe Basin
Loveland
Eldora
Winter Park
Vail
Beaver Creek
Arrowhead
Aspen
Aspen Highlands
Snowmass
Buttermilk
TOTAL FOR NOVEMBER: 10

DECEMBER
Telluride, (Colorado)
Purgatory
Taos, New Mexico
Santa Fe
Red River
Wolf Creek, Colorado
Crested Butte
Snowbasin,Utah
(Jackson Hole, Wyoming)
Grand Targhee
Snow King
Park City, Utah
Sundance
Deer Valley
Wolf Mountain
Snowbird
Alta
Brighton
Solitude
Steamboat, Colorado
(Copper Mountain)
(Breckenridge)
(Keystone)

TOTAL FOR DECEMBER: 20

(GRAND TOTAL: 240)

This haunting portrait of Lucy was taken shortly before she developed her passion for skiing and is a favourite of both Arnie's and her parents, who kept it on their mantlepiece throughout her epic journey around the world.